The First Half

The First Half
Memoirs of Geoffrey Gore

Edited and annotated

by Patrick Wilson Gore, MA (Oxon), ndc

iUniverse, Inc.
New York Lincoln Shanghai

The First Half
Memoirs of Geoffrey Gore

iUniverse books may be ordered through booksellers or by contacting:

iUniverse
2021 Pine Lake Road, Suite 100
Lincoln, NE 68512
www.iuniverse.com
1-800-Authors (1-800-288-4677)

Because of the dynamic nature of the Internet, any Web addresses or links contained in this book may have changed since publication and may no longer be valid.

The views expressed in this work are solely those of the author and do not necessarily reflect the views of the publisher, and the publisher hereby disclaims any responsibility for them.

ISBN: 978-0-595-46666-5 (pbk)
ISBN: 978-0-595-90961-2 (ebk)

Printed in the United States of America

Contents

INTRODUCTION

Geoffrey William Wyndham Gore was born and brought up in a south Cheshire schoolhouse in the early years of the twentieth century.

His childhood was overshadowed by the tension in his parents' marriage. His father, William Gore, widowed with four children, had married again; Constance Mary Newman was twenty years his junior. She lost her first child Dodie to diphtheria and became over-protective of her surviving son Geoffrey, and made him her partner in thirty years of conflict with her husband.

Both parents possessed considerable strength of character. William, born in 1853, remained very much a man of the nineteenth century. Constance was already married when Queen Victoria died, but she was entirely at home in the twentieth. Her experiences as a Red Cross VAD nurse during the First World War set the seal on her emancipation.

Nor was all the tension in her life the result of her marriage. Constance was one of eight Newman children and relationships among them were often turbulent and bitter.

The first forty of Geoffrey Gore's eighty years ended with the Second World War. When he came to write this memoir for his descendants, who include a great-granddaughter named Constance, he chose to close it at that point.

P.W.G.

THE NEWMAN FAMILY

Levi Newman[1], my grandfather, was a contrast to his ever-smiling little wife. He looked pleasant enough but rarely smiled except for a brief moment on meeting a friend. There was no doubt of his likeness to John Henry Newman[2], but on a larger scale. When I knew him he had a paunch and a deep, throaty voice.

I first remember him at Hartford, living in the cottage next to the schoolhouse[3]. He would sit in the old rocking chair by the window and take me on his knee and whisker me. He had some pretty stiff bristles and caused me much anguish.

"Leave him alone, Grandpa. Can't you see you are hurting the child?" Grandma would say, and then come up close and put her face into mine. "He likes teasing," she would add.

Then he would take me out, clutching his hand, to watch him feed the hens. One day he took me to his place of work and showed me the little playhouse up the tree for the children.

Brunners[4] lived there at one time. I don't know if the same family was there in Levi's day. The house was situated at the corner of School Lane and the short street which turns up west of the church to Chester Road[5].

Grandpa didn't have much to say for himself, so I learned little from him. Grandma told me that his brother Ivor[6] died on the troopship on the way home from the Crimea and was, no doubt, buried at sea. He had told them in his letters how cold they were and how dead Russians lay about in their lovely fur coats which were taboo to the British who would be shot if they wore one[7].

Grandpa had a dog called Kipper, a rather overgrown Airedale. He bit me once. He was lying asleep on the rug and I was crawling round him. I suppose it was my fault, but Grandpa raged at him and scared me as much as the dog. Many years later I had the sad sight of the old man taking the now decrepit dog on his last journey down to the vet's.

Grandpa liked dogs. He had a big picture of *Dignity and Impudence*[8] on the kitchen wall in a pine frame which, no doubt, he had made himself. The house smelt of dog. I always associated this smell with my grandparents' house but never questioned the cause. The house smelled cleaner when Kipper was gone.

1

My grandfather wore a cloth cap and, in inclement weather, leather gaiters which were handed down to me in due course.

As far as I know, Levi's father[9] spent his whole life at Adlestrop, where there was a communal bakery. People baked their dough in it. They must have had some agreement among themselves about the schedule. The dough was put in the oven; the door sealed with clay, and a big fire of wood made underneath.

Along the wall of the Newman house in Adlestrop there was a line of tubs all connected by short tubes. Pig wash was put in the first and gradually worked its way down to the last whence it was drawn off—oh, what a phuong! I've seen the same thing done at Calveley. Some grain derivative was added to the finished product and it was then tipped into the pig trough.

In the big kitchen was a post, to the top of which a rope was tied. To this, a child learning to walk was attached. It could move round the pole without fear of falling. The rope must have been attached to a slip ring at the top.

My Grandpa made plenty of furniture at Whitegate with the help of his daughter Connie. He taught her how to solder and she taught me. I still have the old soldering iron he gave her. Mother was the one child interested in this. She made me a garden table for *al fresco* meals when I was very small. It stood in our pantry for years.

During the Whitegate period[10], Grandpa fell ill and Grandma packed him off to recuperate at Beaumaris, Anglesey, where he stayed at the Castle Hotel. I never pass that place without thinking of him. I should think getting away from eight kids would do anybody good.

Many years later, toward his end, he was confined to bed. I sat with him at his bedside during his last days. I can see his wrinkled face now with those strangely blue eyes, fine hair and Roman nose. I remember he sat up once, and looked out the window at the telegraph wires.

"Look, Geoffrey, at those worms crawling along these wires," he said. Of course I agreed that I could see the worms. I think that was the last time I saw him, as he died shortly afterward.

Grandpa had bronchitis. I know now how he must have struggled for breath[11]. They had nothing then but a bronchitis kettle charged with Friars Balsam. One put one's head under a towel close to the long tin spout of the boiling kettle and breathed in the obnoxious aroma. It did little good. Grandpa was very heavy and breathing was exceptionally difficult for him.

The quickest way to kill anyone is to keep them in bed.

Auntie Rosie[12] bought him a new suit shortly before he died, and I inherited it, with his pipe and his knife, which I still have. The suit had two pairs of trousers and was, of course, practically new. Of course, it would go round me twice so it was taken to a local tailor in a back street on Castle. He measured me and made the necessary alterations.

When Mums went to pay the tailor, whose name was Ball, he asked her if she could employ him as a teacher at her school.

"What can you teach, Mr. Ball?" she asked him.

"Oh, philosophy," he replied.

Mother didn't think her wee folk wanted any philosophy.

◆   ◆   ◆

Now I suppose I'll have to sell Grandpa's old rocking chair, that he used throughout his life. The oak box in the hall was made at the smithy-cum-wheelwright's shop at Adlestrop. His father had it made for Levi, and he packed his stuff in it and came to Cheshire during the 1860s. That box, too, will have to go. I'd like to stick to the old wall clock in the hall.

◆   ◆   ◆

Levi had experience with horses and it was with these that he was first engaged.

During the Whitegate period, my grandfather knew an old German who had come to Winsford and started in the rock salt industry. His name was Falk[13]. The name still exists in the salt trade but this German was the founder of the family line. He was a strange old chap. Someone met him one day after a severe illness and said that they had heard he was dead: "I heerd you be dead, Mr. Falk."

"Dem dat said dat vished me dere," was his reply.

Falk's mine was above the bridge at Winsford, where subsidence was a problem, as it was in all the Cheshire salt towns. By design or neglect of duty, the old doddies on the town council allowed the bridge to sink until Falk's barges could not get under.

The laden barges of salt used to head down the river for Liverpool, but returning unladen and standing well out of the water, they could not get under Winsford Bridge. Matters deteriorated until there was a complete stoppage.

Falk pleaded, and did all he could to get the council to do something, but they hedged and hedged, worrying about interrupting road traffic, until Falk got desperate and wouldn't listen any more to the procrastination of the town council.

He planned everything carefully. One night he filled two of his barges with bricks until they had only an inch or two of freeboard above the water line, and towed them side-by-side under the bridge where they were a tight fit, then he packed the limited space above the barges with baulks of timber.

Loads of cinders from the salt works were tipped beside the road on each side of the bridge, which had brick walls and a wooden bed.

When there was no more traffic to cross the bridge that night, the bricks were quickly unloaded by gangs of laborers and, of course, the barges rose out of the water, and pushed up the bridge, creaking and groaning.

Brickies got to work and, with the bricks that had just been unloaded, filled up the gap opened at the top of the walls as a result of the raising of the bridge deck. The baulks were knocked out after all the men had climbed back into the barges to weigh them down again, and the bridge sank down onto its new base. Then the barges were towed away.

By morning men were shovelling forward the cinders to make ramps to the now raised bridge. When the first traffic of the day came along, the bridge was ready to accept it.

Falk and his fellow businessmen could get on with their trading once more.

Grandpa thought this was a great feat and Mr. Falk stood high in his estimation. He used to give a deep Gloucester chuckle when he told this tale about *Old Falk*.

Later, there was a strike of salt miners and wallers. To break it, Falk sent off to Poland and brought a small army of Polish miners over. He built them hovels of clinker along the Whitegate road and when Mother, as a girl, went shopping in Winsford, the closest town, she had to pass these places.

These poor folk kept tubs of rotting cabbages outside their doors and Mother told me that she had to hold her nose as she passed. I think Clifford Lunt, a friend of mine from Chester College, was a descendant of one of these families.

Well this is some background to the times in which Grandpa lived. I used to go for walks with him and it was on these walks that he told me most of his tales.

He lived on Darwin Street, Castle, which tapered off into a lane which led away down to Pimblott's Shipyard[14]. The lane was lined with elms, and here Kipper, Grandpa's old Airedale, used to pretend he was a hunter second to none. He was a very unfriendly dog. He completely ignored me except for the time he bit me. But I was very small then and should have known better than startle a sleeping dog.

◆   ◆   ◆

How Levi Newman met Annie Wainwright[15] I don't know. She was from a well-off family but was in the way at home when her widowed father remarried. Annie was deprived of her family heirlooms by this stepmother[16].

She was placed under Bishop Temple[17], I think, at Hawarden, not far from home at Lache Hall[18], and eventually became a teacher. She first taught at Sandbach and later became headmistress at Whitegate, where she must have been married, for all her children were born there, and spent their early years. My rocking chair is the one she nursed all her children in while the old clock in the hall ticked the hours away.

Levi worked either in the stables or gardens of some big house in the district. He and Annie were married in Chester Cathedral[19] where there is a memorial to earlier generations of Wainwrights.

Annie Wainwright said she was related to Joshua Reynolds[20], a connection of which she was very proud. There was a lot of artistic talent in the family. Rosie could draw a picture using both hands at the same time. Charlie did several illuminated rolls of honour during the First World War.

My Grandma was below average height. I remember her as having a very wrinkled rather yellowish face but with kindly, mischievous, bright, intelligent eyes. She was very loving and kind but never lost her dignity or her strange, schoolmarmish aloofness.

She took an active interest in things around, especially in a bit of gossip. Anything she had not got clear she was off to the encyclopedias, of which she had a small set, and she kept her "cockspecker" (a folding magnifying glass) on top of the bookcase.

I never saw her or Grandpa cross and she was addressed as "Ma", and Grandpa as "Dad" by their children. She was a very religious woman, and by that I don't mean a church-door creeper, but in her relations with others. It's strange how she hatched so many bad eggs.

One day, when we lived at The Kennels, a jay came into view.

"Shoot it," said my bloodthirsty Mums. "We'll take the wings to Grandma."

I raced for the .22 and the jay fell dead. Mums cut off the wings. Grandma put them in her hat. They looked natural in the hedgerow of flowers which surrounded it.

Speaking of dress, I remember Grandma walking from Whitegate to Chester[21] in a new blue blouse and, when she had completed her journey, the blouse was white. The dyes were like travel in those days, "not very fast".

Once, during the First World War, we went to Needwood, near Burton-upon-Trent, where Grandpa was gardener at Needwood House. Philip Miller was the head groom and his wife, my Aunt Lizzie, had lived so long in the stables that she whinnied like a horse when she laughed.

I fished in the lakes with the Miller lads. I remember we took the train to Tutbury, but I don't remember much else.

Rosie was teaching in Northwich at the time and made the long journey at the weekend to see her parents.

While haymaking, a fellow had a pikel[22] rammed in him and Mother was called as the only available, on the spot, source of medical aid. Sure and wasn't she a VAD-BRCS[23]? The man lived in spite of her efforts.

I never knew my grandparents to have a holiday but I do remember Mother telling me of when Grandma took them all for a holiday, when they were kids, to Meliden[24]. I think it was, on the Welsh Coast.

When Grandma first came to Whitegate, before her marriage, she lodged at a farm near the Beeches. This was after leaving Sandbach. I think her reverend tutor at Hawarden knew Canon Armistead at Sandbach and that is how she got a teaching appointment there[25].

Her children went to Whitegate School, where Grandma taught. One day the headmaster had young George up in front of him for some offence and was putting the breeze up him by threatening to smite him verily.

Young Connie bounced out of her desk and took George by the arm. "You're not going to hit him," she said, and led him back to his desk.

The headmaster told Grandma afterward, "I daren't have touched him to save my life. You should have seen the fire in that girl's eyes."

Lord Delamere and his wife lived at Vale Royal. Augusta, Lady Delamere[26] was patron of Whitegate School and brought a lot of sewing to be done by the children. Grandma had to handle the job. It was this Lady Delamere who decided on having a May Queen festival. All candidates were paraded before her and one Constance Mary Newman was chosen as first May Queen of Over.

Mums had been to the old wishing stone and wished, and the English equivalent of leprechauns must have whispered in Her Ladyship's ear.

When we were at Queensgate[27], my Grandma was nearing her end, and her mind was going. I went across to 15 Darwin Street and was in the front room with Auntie Polly[28]. We were sitting on the settee and Grandma came in smiling. "Ee, I do hope you will both be happy," and spread her arms out to us.

She had gone back to George and Polly's wedding day. I felt embarrassed, but Polly kept a poker face and played up to her.

Grandma also had a bad habit of waiting until Levi was having forty winks after dinner and then slipping out—always up Hartford way. Poor Rosie had to come out of school and chase her.

She tried a maid (perhaps a key would have been easier) but the maid broke open Levi's big oak box, in which Rosie locked her money and valuables. So she had to go.

Then Con Newman[29] came and she was no good, and finally Dorothy Alcock[30] came.

The Alcocks were related to the Yeomans of The Beach[31], and their daughter, another Dorothy, used to visit nearly every morning, but was too snooty to say two words and would never put a foot over the step. She was squiff-eyed. Her father was a fairly big noise at Brunner, Mond.

I fitted a light over Grandma's bed when she became bedfast. It consisted of a foot of plywood with a switch at the bottom and a lamp-holder above it. It was bolted on to the bed rail, having another piece of plywood at the back of the rail. Dr. Terry was very interested in it. There was nothing like that on the market in those days.

Well, Grandma died and the whole family, except the Alcocks, who were abroad, came to the funeral.

On the morning of the funeral loads of big boxes containing wreaths arrived at the house until the hall was full and we had to pile them into the middle room. These boxes would be collected later and reused.

I remember looking at them and wondering how much sorrow they had witnessed.

There was such a crowd round the grave, all in mourning, that I was squeezed out. At King Frederic of Norway's funeral[32] the priest said: "Never is a family so close as at the graveside or the cot." It's certainly true.

Of course at the family funerals, Uncle Bill, as boss of the undertakers' trade union, took a leading role, trying out innovations that the primitive provincials didn't know.

During Rosie's period of teaching at Darwin Street, Johnnie Weston, owner of The Heysoms[33], was making sheep's eyes at her. He wasn't very bold, this middle-aged bachelor, but I think he was a kindly, genuine suitor. Rosie told him she had dedicated her life to looking after her aged parents and so he gave up the chase. Neither married, and it was strange that Rosie should come and live at The Heysoms after all.

When Mother married[34], my grandparents were living at Davenham, on Church Street, with Millers nearby. Something psychic and weird happened at the wedding. Most people seemed reluctant to talk about it, but Uncle George told me that some evil power seemed to be present in the house. George slashed at it with a roller blind. My mother was found unconscious on the bed. Some attributed the incident to my Father's deceased first wife[35].

George told me the story and he was very forthright about it. I wished I had asked him more, but there was a crowd present.

While at Davenham, Grandpa caused a stir by digging up a rhododendron of immense size and dragging it through the street so that it touched the property on each side. He transplanted it and it survived the ordeal.

Later, after a spell at Needwood, they moved to Darwin Street, Castle.

Grandma was saddened by the fact that in Huxley Street—a street off Darwin Street on the opposite side to her home at Number 15—every family living on the street had had someone killed in the First World War[36]. This was due to the old system of county regiments. It had a bad effect on the civil population and the system was changed in consequence. Of course the same thing happened at Blore Heath[37] in Staffordshire, when the famous corps of Cheshire archers, who fought at Crecy[38], were slaughtered[39].

My Grandma had a way of smiling and at the same time pursing her lips and putting her finger up in a signal for silence. On one occasion, Grandpa was asleep in his old rocking chair and she made the signal to me and then told me she was sure Grandpa was related to John Henry Newman. The Victorians were very upset, angry and shocked when he turned Catholic.

Grandpa, I think, knew of the connection and wouldn't reveal what he knew or even have the issue mentioned in his house. He was very angry with this turn-coat and so he never told even Grandma what he knew of the relationship and no one dare approach him.

When I went to London I visited Madame Tussaud's[40] and, after being fooled by the dummy at the door offering me a leaflet, I stepped into a large room with many annexes opening off it. Through the big crowd, I caught sight of my Grandpa, who had been dead a few years then.

I went straight across. It was the Cardinal, in an area full of famous Victorians. John Henry Newman was of slighter build than Levi. He had the same fine hair, the same hooked nose, and the same blue eyes—a peculiar blue, and resembled him about the face. And, of course, the same family name. I have no doubt they were related. Grandma was always bringing it up.

My Aunt Annie's son, Roy Booth[41], reckoned he had traced the connection, but he was an opportunist and, toward the end of his life, a Church of England minister, who saw advancement in being connected to Cardinal Newman.

Of course John Henry had East Anglian connections, while Abraham was from the Oxford-Gloucester border.

The top of the Pembroke table[42] we have was punctured with a mass of small holes before I refinished it. Rosie told me it was from the days they made wreaths. There is also a coil of iron wire, well rusted, lying about the workshop, which was used in this occupation, at Whitegate, I should think.

Grandma told me that the parson's son at Whitegate had *drinking diabetes*[43] and they had to put the inkwells out of his reach because he drank ink.

When the hounds came round Whitegate, the vicar and schoolmaster would rapidly saddle their horses and follow the Hunt. Those were the days.

My Grandma had a funny wit, and was amused by this.

A chap named Done or Dunne used to come round collecting rents, etc. I think he called at Grandma's house several times but there was no one in. He left a note: "Done again".

Annie once asked the doctor if cucumber was good for one, and how it should be prepared.

"Mrs. Newman," he said, "you should peel it, slice it, salt it, pepper it, and leave it soaking all night in vinegar, and then in the morning throw it behind the fire."

I could see Grandma innocently taking in all this and cooing approval until the *dénouement*.

Levi and Annie Wainwright Newman had eight children: Annie Wainwright (1868–1963); William (born 1871); my Mother, Constance Mary (1872–1949); Lizzie (born 1874); Clara Annie (1876–1936); Rose Ellen (1878–1932); George Wainwright (1879–1953); and Charles Edward (1881–1956).

◆   ◆   ◆

When I was a small boy, I thought Auntie Annie the best of aunts. My Mother was very fond of her too. When I had my tonsils out at the age of three on the dining room table she came over. With Dodie dying just previously[44] my Mother, no doubt, was in a cataleptic state and Annie would be a comfort to her.

Some ten years later she came again, like a bird of ill omen, this time to be with my Mother until she went into hospital for her breast removal. Annie had already had hers removed and so she knew all about it.

We were at The Kennels then, and Booths were at Forrest Street in Latchford, southeast of Warrington. Annie's husband, John Pendlebury Booth[45], had built Forrest Street just before the First World War.

I went to stay at Warrington during the war when my aunt was a Red Cross nurse. She hitched up with a Miss Broadbent who was related to the Brunners. This woman was Commandant and at the end of the hostilities she retired and pushed Annie into her job.

This, I think, was the beginning of the social climb which completely changed them. Social climbing needs money.

Annie had one son Roy who was her pride and joy. They called him Roy so that other kids would not corrupt or abbreviate his name. He was straightaway called "Curly" by his mates, because of his conspicuously curly hair.

Booth was on the War Office qualification list which entitled him to repair military barracks in the Warrington area. He got to know the commanding officer in consequence, and it was through him that Roy got his commission. He was with the balloons in the Royal Naval Air Service, as it was then.

At the end of the war ex-officers were admitted *ad lib* to the universities and one can imagine that for these jumped up errand boys, as many of them were, the standard was not very high and nobody failed.

So my cousin got his B.Sc. and went on to get his M.Sc., much to the satisfaction of his parents. Another step up the social ladder.

Roy was engaged to a nice girl but his parents made him drop her. They chose for him a daughter of the big pawnbroker at Bridge Foot[46]. Lotty's father was rolling in wealth and there were only two daughters to share it. Roy had to keep her company one night when her parents went out and so a marriage became very necessary a few months after[47]. After all they had a knight in her family.

Anyhow Lotty was a nice girl but I had nothing but contempt for a fellow who hadn't a mind of his own. I was later honoured by being chosen as godfather to his second child, John. The Booths made a great effort to get me fixed up with the godmother.

John Booth Senior pretended to be very upset about the marriage, but gave the happy couple a terrace house he owned, with one bedroom and few facilities. They were not there long and moved to a house on the building estate at Fairfield Gardens.

Booth, cheeseparing as usual, reduced the height of the houses by one course of bricks to cut the cost. He thought he was very clever in departing from the plan. The final process is of course to fit the gutters and down pipes. Well, folks moved into the houses and found they couldn't open the bedroom windows because the gutters came down too low. What a to-do!

John was like a raging bear. I think he had to split the gutter and put in an extra downpipe which was more expensive than a layer of bricks.

He turned the one-bedroom house I mentioned into his office.

Annie had a big mouth and once she opened it too wide about the wife of one of her husband's workmen and a lawsuit was heading her way. Of course this would not do for social climbers so it was settled somehow. No doubt Annie got a telling off, for one thing Booth could not stand was parting with money.

Mums and Rosie owned The Heysoms jointly and the Booths did all they could to get Rosie to make a will in their favour. This would have put Mums in a dicey position and they would have had me cornered too.

Annie Newman Booth, I think, started life as a teacher.

She had a look of her father about her. She liked to have her hands on the family and kept in touch with all. After her husband's death in 1950, she made two visits to us but each time my wife Margaret told her I was busy. She used to send the chauffeur-handyman to the door first.

They chose the site of their grave a long time before it was needed. I suppose Booth would have liked a mausoleum but didn't like parting with the money.

Roy started with his father during the housing boom just after the First World War and went teaching at night at the Tech. He then went to Barnsley as a full-time teacher and later became an HMI (His Majesty's Inspector of Schools). During the Second World War, he was a Wing Commander in the Air Training Corps.

When he retired he went into the Church of England ministry and was a curate at Nantwich, later getting a living in Devon, where he died at the altar. He had two bishops at his funeral.

He was a Freeman of the City of London. I don't know how he achieved this.

◆   ◆   ◆

William was destined for the teaching profession but had a secret wish to enter the Church. He was a pupil teacher at the old Navigation Schools on Navigation Road, Northwich.

He walked from Whitegate to the River Weaver and along the towpath each day; poor old Long Barney, as the kids called him.

Later, he had a penny farthing bike. He fell off it on Littledales Bank and badly damaged his leg. My Mother had the first safety cycle, as modern cycles were originally called, in the district.

Part of Uncle Bill's duties was to play "school bobby" and round up absentees. He spent a lot of time on Whalley Road, one of the tough spots in Northwich, now pulled down.

Later he went to the Blue Coat School at Liverpool—a residential school for navy orphans. From here he went to the East End of London with a firm of undertakers—the name Urry is in my mind.

Here he married—a bit of a shot-gun wedding, I believe—Matilda "Tilly" Cole, the daughter of one of the London Fire Brigade chiefs. When he died, all the London fire brigades turned out for his funeral.

The family lived in Leyton Park Road when I stayed with them.

They had three daughters—large girls with "holier than thou" attitudes. The family went to church twice every Sunday and Bill and Madge were in the choir.

Madeleine Ellen had a long thin nose and I told her that it went up and down as she sang—I could see it from our seat in the nave.

Underneath the floor of the church was the furnace and below our seats was a big grid. I think the fumes affected me once and I flopped over during the service. I remember I was sent to Coventry by these paragons for daring to do such a thing in church.

One Sunday I nipped out early and bought a packet of cigarettes. I was severely told off by William. Holding a Sunday paper in his hand, he was judge of all men.

Dorothy Gwendoline worked at Chelsea on a comptometer.

The eldest, Connie, was the only Christian among them. She was a good kid but liked a bit of fun with it. She was a costumier and worked at the shop which supplied dresses to Queen Mary[48]. She had to do the fittings on the old bag.

She married later and, I think, had a child but she was never mentioned by the family. She was blamed, I think, for the circumstances of her birth and was regarded as inferior by the paragons.

Madge got her B.A. and became a history teacher.

Gwen[49] was called Dorothy until my sister Dorothy died, and then they dropped the name in order not to distress my Mother. She lived at Ye Olde Shoppe, Crowhurst, Battle, Hastings, until she died a few years ago.

When I went to King's College, I called on Bill at his office in the Strand—he was now secretary of the Undertakers Union. He never invited me to come again so that is the last time I saw him.

He wrote to me once since and I replied, but I don't know any more about them.

Tilly Cole used to buy cheap eggs. I don't think she knew what a fresh egg tasted like. Her eggs stank when you took the top off and the "white" was all colours. I had to screw up my courage to eat them.

She frequently visited an old neighbour who was ill. She was sure of a heavenly reward for her kindness. Eventually the old girl was taken to Whipps Cross Hospital[50]. Tilly made a cake each week—no doubt with the rotten eggs—and visited her every Sunday. I went with her once and was impressed with the size of the place and I remember wondering at how much misery and suffering was compacted into it.

Well, the old lady died and, instead of sorrow, I noted a sense of expectancy in the family. I was surprised, for I really thought they liked the old girl. Tilly went round to her house and was met at the door by a young man who explained that he was a long-lost nephew the Newmans did not know about.

Tilly was nearly in tears when she returned and the whole family started vilifying this fellow who had cut them out of their "rightful" reward. Hypocrites.

Bill used to tell a wonderful tale of a man he had met in town who had a gun which would fire a pin which would kill. Lord, if I heard that tale once, I heard it a thousand times.

His gate latch broke and he bought a metal drill bit to fit his brace and he *drilled a hole through iron*. He couldn't get over his cleverness and his loving daughters thought him wonderful.

When Mother moved from The Heysoms to the much smaller place at 18 The Crescent in 1942, there were many family portraits that couldn't be appropriately placed. Tilly Cole's was one of them and when Lizzie Miller came over, sent by Booth to spy, she saw this photo in the attic and immediately made trouble by telling the London Newmans how disgracefully Tilly's photo had been treated.

She did not say it was among a large pile of other family photos. Relations were strained with our London relatives after this. They told Mother that they wouldn't be coming to Cheshire again.

Mums replied, "Wait till you are asked."

The Newman family was a very loving Christian family. They went to church twice every Sabbath in order to sharpen their claws where men of old once sharpened their arrows.

◆   ◆   ◆

My Mother's cousin from New Zealand[51] planned to visit the family at Whitegate. The family owned a newspaper. Mother and one of her sisters went to the station to meet him. A charming young stranger came down the platform and without more ado the sisters marched him off home. It was some time before both parties realized they had got the wrong man.

I suppose the sisters then had to go off and find the right one.

When my Mother was a young woman she went to the dentist on Castle named Lee. I remember this stooped old bloke, who had no qualifications, as was the case in those days. Well, he broke all my mother's teeth off level with the gum saying that to extract them would spoil the shape of her mouth. She had to have them all extracted some time later—during the war.

Another time, my Mother and her sister were invited to have tea with the curate at Castle Church. Their mother poshed them up and fitted them out with new corsets—vicars and curates were held in high esteem in those days. Well, the two girls set off for Northwich one hot afternoon. They reached the main Chester road and the corsets were too tight. They crawled through the hedge into Littledales Wood and shed the uncomfortable things and buried them in the leaves and then continued on their way.

◆   ◆   ◆

I can't tell you much about Lizzie Newman. She had a nice daughter named Gladys, a little bit older than me. I was very fond of her as a kid.

Lizzie also had four sons: Willie, Reg, George and Ronald.

During the First World War, the first two dived into an aircraft factory at Tutbury near Needwood and avoided military service. One of them made my Grandma a walking stick out of the wood used for propellers for Royal Flying Corps aircraft.

George went to Aston University at Birmingham and got his B.Sc. and married Vi.

Gladys married Tom.

Ron was Bass agent for Devon.

I think Willie or Reg had a shop in Coventry later.

Lizzie's husband, Phil Miller was a dapper little chap very much the horseman[52]. He went in for all kinds of competitions and won quite a lot of things.

His brother had a goldsmith's shop in Llandudno.

The Millers lived in Church Street, Davenham when my grandparents were there. Their kids went to Winnington School[53]. God help them.

I visited them at Needwood when my grandparents moved there. This must have been during the First World War. We went by train, Mums and I, to Tutbury station. I suppose we were met there, but I don't remember.

I remember going into Needwood Forest with George and Ron, where we saw two men carrying a plank. They did some measuring of a brook which ran through the forest and then sawed the end off the plank.

After some struggling, they upended the plank and aimed it to drop on the opposite bank.

It fell short and dropped in the brook. They had cut too much off the end. There was much arguing as to whose fault it was. The incident was so funny it has remained in my mind.

In later years, Lizzie became Annie Booth's spy, and was sent to The Heysoms. George[54] cleared off with my copy of *The Good Companions*[55] which I had just bought, and a good leather-bound dictionary.

At another time, Lizzie got into my roll-top desk and got access to some private papers, the contents of which she divulged to the Booths. No doubt she was well paid.

She came to The Crescent[56] when Mums was ill, and invited the Booths over. I locked myself in my bedroom and refused to see them. She took Mums back with her to Burton-upon-Trent and, as everything was rationed during the Second World War, I believe they had a good whack at Mums' ration cards.

When Mums died in Warrington Hospital in September 1949, the Millers were at Booths'. That was the last time I saw them.

Of course, it was the Booths who upset the family. They failed to get Rosie's estate and so they duped the family into believing that they had all been cheated. A fat lot the others would have got if Booths had had the estate.

When Mums visited Lizzie at Burton, she said that every week she rewashed clean things in order to have a washing line longer than her neighbour's.

Needwood House is two or three miles west of Burton-upon-Trent in Staffordshire.

◆   ◆   ◆

I only saw Clara[57] once when I was very small and have since gathered that she had a high opinion of herself. She and her husband, William Johnson Alcock[58], intended to get on and they were very successful.

Willie Alcock was a chemical engineer and got experience in many parts of the world, including Carrickfergus, Lake Magadi, and Cornwall.

Just before the First World War, he was in charge of Davies's chlorine works at Northwich. There used to be an old chimney near Northwich station with DAVIES painted on it.

With gas warfare in the offing, he was collared by the War Office, and became second in command to Lord Moulton in the Ministry of Munitions.

It was sufficient to address letters to him: "Alcock, War Office, London", such was his importance.

He was offered a knighthood in the spate of knighthoods after the war, but he and his friends decided against joining the ranks of the blackberry and apple jam manufacturers who dominated the list.

After the war he, like many others, was out of a job and had no prospects. That was when he went to the Far East.

There was a shortage of nitrates, and Peru and Magadi were well-exploited and there was no room for a small entrepreneur, so off to India.

Now most Indian villages had been on the same site for hundreds of years and the sanitary arrangements consisted of the nearest bush, after you'd scared the tigers out of it.

So the ground round these villages was rich in nitrates from human excrement and Willie started mining this. He did very well and the family joined him and prospered mightily.

His son George didn't go, and Charlie died in 1922, in Calcutta, from the effects of the war. Another son joined the Indian navy, I think.

The Indians were choosey and had to be humored in business negotiations. One man came to see Willie to place an order, but finding that he was away, refused to deal with his son who was *locum tenens*. He had always dealt with William and no other would do.

Clara sent us a box of tea once.

Willie, over six feet tall, got his early training at Northwich, where he lived with his aunt on the bank above Navigation Road. He was always keen on chemistry and made many experiments. He supplied his aunt with bars of home-made soap.

He came to see us at Calveley on a motor cycle combination, and he gave me my first ride in a motor vehicle down to the Four Lane Ends[59].

Before her marriage, Clara taught at Barnton. The HMI visited her school one day and asked her if she had got her certificate.

"I get it on Saturday," she said.

The HMI blinked over his glasses. He knew this was impossible.

"I'm getting married," she explained, and the HMI got no change out of her.

Her son Charlie joined the army under age and unknown to his parents. A brief bit of square bashing and he was on board ship bound for France.

Clara found out and tore down to the quay. They tried to bar this turkey cock.

"I am going to see my son," she said, and she did.

I don't know if Bill was in the War Office then, I doubt it, or she could have invoked his aid. Anyhow a bloody general tried unsuccessfully to bar her way.

She used to beat her Indian servants in later years. Of course that was the usual thing in those days. After all what were Indian servants for? Mums didn't approve.

When they came to see us at Calveley, they stayed at the Grosvenor Hotel at Chester. Clara invited my parents to visit them there. Mother told me afterward that when Clara saw her wardrobe no more was said about the visit.

Of their children, I knew George, Muriel and Dorothy.

The Alcocks have been around the Northwich area for some time as I found out when I read the handbook of Witton Church:

> "There are various stones in the fabric of the porch carrying words *prepositus Ricardus opis Alkoke capallanus*[60]."

In the archives at Chester, there is a reference to *Ric'us Alkoke Capellanus* concerning land in Northwich and Lostock.

◆   ◆   ◆

Rosie was devoted to her parents and refused marriage in order to stay with them.

When we came to Northwich she was living with them in Darwin Street and teaching at the school lower down the same street, whose headmaster at that time was Levi Lambert.

She was quite content with life. Booth was always playing up to this simple soul who was very fond of 'Jack'. She was quite a good looker, and I think she must have had plenty of chances of marriage.

First her mother died, and then her father in less than a year, and she was left alone.

Mother's school at Queensgate was growing and she was desperate to get larger premises. She tackled the I.C.I., for they owned most of the building land in the area, but to no avail. They just sat on what they had in order to keep out other firms who would poach their labour.

She approached Harold Moss, the solicitor. His cousin, John Weston, had been contemplating leaving the old house—The Heysoms.

A deal was closed. Mums sold her Queensgate house, and Rosie threw her lot in with Mums, selling her house on Darwin Street.

"A nice little house," was Roy Booth's comment on The Heysoms.

"It's falling down," was Dorothy Alcock's. Some plaster was falling off under the oriel window looking out on the lawn.

Anyhow you can tell the jealousy with which the family greeted the purchase.

Some time after moving to The Heysoms, Rosie developed a pain. Its location was hard to find. Appendicitis and gall bladder were both suspected, so Dr. Terry called in a specialist and the result was that Rosie was taken to Terry's nursing home at Davenham and, I think, had her gall bladder out.

But the surgeon wanted his dough before he'd cut, and all Rosie's money was tied up in The Heysoms, except for a few shares she had and, of course, could not sell immediately. So I was sent post haste to dear Jack.

Annie came with me and we found him in his builder's office. When he heard that Rosie wanted a loan of 200, I never saw a man's face change so. He nearly went berserk—frightened, angry, all mixed up.

His wife just stood there and looked at this miserable entrepreneur, then talked him into acceding. He signed the cheque more in sweat than ink. I didn't know why such a big business man, as he pretended to be, was so frightened of parting with a mere 200, even in those days. I didn't tell Rosie of the fuss.

She was operated on in Dr. Terry's nursing home in Church Street, Davenham.

After this, Rosie complained of noises in the night.

Mother blamed me, so I kept very quiet studying till the late hours. I was teaching and making school furniture all day. I made an individual desk for every kid.

But the noises still went on. It wasn't until long after that I came to the conclusion that it was most likely our spooky lady who had been throwing her weight about[61].

Well Charlie joined the Newman-Bar-None outfit at The Heysoms and one November night in 1932, I was sitting with him in his sitting room, the big central room at the top of the house, when Mother came in gasping: "Rosie's ill get a doctor."

She had drunk a bottle of ammonia[62]. Well I couldn't get the bloody car to start and I was in a terrible way.

There was a doctor of sorts up the Beach Road and I took to my heels in that direction.

Well, to backtrack: Rosie didn't show much outwardly, but she must have suffered greatly over her parents' deaths. She showed the first signs of being unsettled when she decided to leave Darwin Street School and join Charlie at Hartford School.

No sooner had she got to Hartford than she pulled the sewing machine to pieces and couldn't put it back together.

Then the Booths pounced and had her at their place for a weekend. She came back very distraught. They had really gone to town trying to get her to make a will in their favour.

"Roy is Rosie's heir," they were bleating around.

This was serious and Rosie knew it, for if John Booth owned half The Heysoms, both Mother and I would be under his thumb. Rosie scribbled out a new will and I typed it and took it down to Harold Moss.

Rosie had to stop teaching and Mums packed her off to Rhyl for a holiday. In retrospect, this seems a very silly thing to have done, although it was done for the best. I took her and brought her back in the Standard 9 I had.

She was alone there, and brooding by the sea only made her worse.

She died after drinking the ammonia. After she was buried, I was coming downstairs and heard a noise in her bedroom. I pushed the door open and there was John Booth on his knees by her chest of drawers feverishly hunting through her things. He put a hand up for silence. I knew what he was after and went downstairs to where Annie was, more or less, keeping Mother away.

It ended up with Annie and me going down to see Harold Moss. When she saw that the will was typed, Annie jumped for joy.

"Oh, it's typed," she said, under the misapprehension that such things were illegal.

"The will is quite in order, Mrs. Booth," Harold said.

♦   ♦   ♦

George[63] was the second youngest and rather delicate as a child. I have written about Mums rescuing him from the headmaster at Whitegate.

He worked in a solicitor's office in Northwich first—the name Chambers comes to mind. Later he went to Manchester.

His mother visited him once and the landlady said, "Ee, Mrs. Newman, he's such a good lad. He reads a page of the Bible each night before he goes to sleep". She didn't know he was practicing his shorthand and the Bible was the only book available.

In 1908 he married Polly Harrison who was a gay young city sparrow, quite unlike the country girls who were her sisters-in-law. It didn't go down well, and she came in for much criticism, especially when she went with Annie and another girl to Blackpool for a holiday and perhaps winked at some lads.

Gerald was their only child.

During the First World War, George was an orderly at Longford Park—a gentleman's house turned into a Red Cross hospital. I played cricket with the swaddies once, when I stayed with Gerald. There was a wall dividing the front drive from the back entrance.

Gerry fell out with me and some other lads, and went through a door in this wall. I called to him but he was sulking and would not answer. The wall would be 150 yards long. I shied a half brick over to make him speak.

It did. It hit him on the head and I had to take a bloody mess home and face the wrath of Polly.

One day as George came off the train at Stretford, where they lived, he saw a man laying into his wife down a side street. Gallant George went to her defence and then they *both* turned on George.

♦   ♦   ♦

Charlie was a pupil teacher at Hartford School. He was not college-trained and later went to teach at Crewe—St. Paul's Church School at Church Coppenhall[64], where the headmaster was a man named Bamford.

He ran a scout troop and worked hard in many ways to make up for his lack of formal education. I think he failed the entrance exam for Chester College. During the First World War when teachers were in short supply and it was easy to get promotion, he applied for the headmaster's post at Hartford and did a lot of cajoling of the vicar, later Canon Pitts. He got the job and worked as an unpaid curate all through his stay at Hartford.

Years later, Pitts was instrumental in getting me my first job at Hucknall.

Charlie bought an old Matchless combination from Pitts and came over to Calveley on it. He took his brother William out in it and frightened the hell out of him roaring around the country lanes.

Bill came back very shaken and it wasn't because the sidecar had no springs. I think it was because bird-nesting was no longer in his line. He never went in the sidecar again.

Charlie had lived on Samuel Street in Crewe. For a time he lodged with the Penningtons and that is how he was landed with their ever-ailing daughter, Gertrude[65]. This family worked in the Coop, except for her brother, Walter. He was a nice chap who worked in the offices of the railway or locomotive works. She had some relations named Kenyon. One was a senior civil servant; another had a factory in Manchester.

Gertrude was at home with Mamma and no doubt she was well pushed by Mamma. She had a lot of hair but it only started on the crown of her head, she folded her hair so that it bulged out over her forehead and was held in place by a black ribbon.

She had trouble with her appendix at Crewe and suffered it for years before she had the operation and thereafter it was a source of conversation in the household.

Gertrude died a natural death at the age of forty-six. She suffered from a groggy heart and made the most of it. Dr. Terry came to visit her regularly when she was confined to bed and she always dressed up for the occasion. I think she loved being ill and having people fussing round her.

Charlie's wife had been a careful little soul and saved her money up in the Co-op. When she died in 1925 and Charlie got hold of it, he blew the lot on drink. I went up to Hartford one night and found him half-starved, half-drunk and very much under the weather.

I brought him back to The Heysoms, where he lived with us. Then he moved with us to The Crescent, and later to Hartford Road, Davenham, with Mums, where he worried her to death, and, no doubt, brought on her Parkinson's disease[66] with worry.

He was after money for drink and searched her rooms every time she went out. He wanted her to make the house over to him but she left it to Margaret. I tolerated him but had little time for him.

On one occasion, he took his brother George to the Bowling Green[67]. He bought George a beer in the bar and then disappeared. George eventually found him sipping whisky in the back room.

George couldn't get over it, for George was the straightest and most decent of the Newman men, and very like his father, Levi.

Going back to Charlie, I believe he belonged to a reserve Army Cyclist Corps[68] unit during the Boer War.

He gave up teaching when he reached the age of 60, and went to work in the I.C.I. offices until the end of the war.

THE GORE FAMILY

William Gore, my Father, was born at Knowsley in Lancashire. He had a sister Mary who was married to Jimmy Holt. She lived at Kirby[69] near Knowsley.

My grandfather[70] was employed at Knowsley Hall in the capacity of a secretary. He was close in age to the 14th Earl of Derby's eldest son, Edward Henry (1826–93), who became the 15th Earl in 1869, and may have been one of the young nobleman's boyhood companions.

John Gore died young and the 14th Earl[71] and his son then took a kindly interest in the orphaned children and especially in young Willie.

Willie did well in school and, apparently showing some potential for teaching, was in due course made a probationer teacher.

As the Stanleys[72] had property and interests in Chester, Willie was sent to Chester College[73], founded by the Church of England in 1839 as the first purpose-built teacher training college in the country. He was there for two years and graduated with a second class certificate.

He was then, at the age of twenty-one, made headmaster of Calveley School, which was just being completed in 1874.

After my grandfather's death, my grandmother married a stonemason named Auckland who came to live at Fiddler's Ferry. He lived on the banks of the Mersey and had a boat.

My Mother told me all this. I never set eyes on my Father's parents.

Mother visited them once. Theirs was a scrubbed-clean kind of house, small; and the floors were covered with painted sailcloth. Grandpa Auckland, as he was termed, became a foreman-stonemason when the Manchester Ship Canal[74] was being built. This canal is entirely lined with stone, so he had a very busy time.

When they were very old, the Aucklands visited Calveley. Afterward Mother was upset and indignant because they had to go to the station on their own. I think it was fairly soon after she and my Father were married, and she was beginning to find out what she had for a spouse. It was before my time, I should think.

Mother was William's second wife[75].

Harry Baker Gore[76] was William's older son by his first wife, Alice, whom he married in 1879.

I think Harry lived with his grandmother when he was at the Boteler Grammar School at Warrington. Trust our old man to land someone else with his responsibilities. At that time the Auckland family lived in, or had some connection with Winwick. All I know of this is that there's a stone pig built high up in the church tower[77].

When my Father was at Knowsley, whenever the Earl came along in his coach, the lads had to stand at the side of the road, and wave their caps, shouting, "On, Stanley, on!" I don't know if this is their motto or not[78].

As a boy, my Father lived next door to the smithy at Knowsley.

He used to earn pocket money trapping sparrows which were a menace in the cornfields. He derived great pleasure in throwing stones and bits of wood in the track of the men scything the corn to blunt their scythes—early revelation of a mind that caused much sorrow in later life.

My Father always retained great affection for south Lancashire. Now and again I was taken to Liverpool and crossed the river in either the *Iris* or the *Daffodil*. These ferry boats were used in the evacuation of Dunkirk[79].

On the Liverpool landing stage, a one-legged diver used to stand on a high platform and dive just as the ferry came in. He would scramble out of the water and be waiting at the exit for his reward. I was always given a penny to throw on his mat.

On one occasion we went across to the fairground at New Brighton. It had coconut shies and once the man asked me to throw at him. I hesitated at first, but when I saw he was serious, I gave him what he asked for, much to the crowd's delight. He didn't know I was pretty good with a stone—in hand, sling or catty[80]. There was a big horizontal wheel there too and this became covered with kids. As the speed increased, we slithered off across the floor, all except the one in the middle.

There was a tower at New Brighton too, but like its Blackpool counterpart it was demolished as unsafe.

Once we went to stay with Jim Holt at Kirby. Living with them was a young orphan about twenty named Jimmy Gore. He was a great fisherman and I badly wanted to go fishing with him but was not allowed.

The thing I remember most about the visit was the parrot. I had never been in a house where there was a parrot. I had seen them in books and perhaps in a zoo. Jim had a rocking chair which was in front of the cage and once my Father and I were alone together. He was rocking gently and each time he went backward Polly raised her head and with wicked eyes looked at her reflection in the shiny bald pate. She evidently didn't like what she saw for she suddenly struck and my Father shot out of the chair yelling.

Polly fetched blood. Good old Polly.

There is a street named *James Holt* now in the Kirkby Industrial Estate.

Jim worked all his life for a shipping firm—was it the Holt Line? When he left after a lifetime's service they did not give him a sausage. Poor Uncle George Newman was treated the same way by the Stock Exchange in Manchester.

I stayed at Knowsley once with Uncle Aaron[81] and his daughter Edith. I forget my aunt's name. On a walk once she showed me a building that had been used for cock-fighting.

Another time we went blackberrying on the Moss[82] and a farmer's wife, very irate, came and harangued us.

Nearby, they were cutting peat. I remember my Father telling me that he had been driving along the road across the Moss in a trap and the hedges on each side shook with the vibration.

I suppose it was in these lonely parts that John Gore[83] used his horse pistols in the execution of his duty as guardian of the peace for the Earl of Derby.

Edith and her husband, John Marston Rawlinson[84]—innkeeper of the Derby Arms at Knowsley, visited us at Northwich, and we stayed with them at the Derby Arms in the early 'fifties. I don't know what happened to them. Margaret put every obstacle in the way of seeing them again; they've got to be Irish or Scotch to be welcome here.

One old chap was employed by the Earl of Derby to paint the railings around Knowsley Park[85]. Year after year he kept on going round the vast circle. He went quite mad.

While staying with Aaron, I often went to help Mr. Owen in the smithy. I was closing one of the big vices once, it had a long bar handle with a knob on each end I swung the handle so that the major part of it was upright and above the vice. It suddenly dropped while my hand was on the vice and it trapped my finger. My hand was painful for the rest of the holiday.

Edith gave me my first camera. It was a 2A Brownie and I was very proud of it. I had it till we came to The Heysoms and then some kids got their fingers in the shutter.

Mr. Owen worked alone but some heavy beating jobs really needed two pairs of hands. I often acted as striker but I was only nine or ten when I was there. He overcame this lack of an assistant by improvising a hammer. Across the roof of the smithy he fixed a springy sapling. At the free end of this a chain came down to a flat, pivoted bar. The other end of the bar carried the hammer head, maybe weighing twelve pounds. He depressed the sapling end by means of a pedal attached to the aforementioned lever and when he released the pressure, the rebound of the sapling brought the hammer down in a fixed spot with more force than one would imagine.

By the smithy ran a brook in which he cooled his hot iron.

Aaron had a big, new-looking workshop. He had a homemade lathe in there, very big, to accommodate the big hubs of the wheels of farm carts. These had to be big for many big mortises had to be cut in them to take the spokes at an angle. This angle had to be consistent and gave the wheel its dished appearance. We made a wheel while I was there and when the felloes were finally in place—these had to be cut by hand out of ash—the whole was taken round to Mr. Owen who put on the rim. He heated this on a big iron disc with plenty of logs. He told me it was much cheaper to do several at a time, but this wheel had broken during harvest and was wanted in a hurry. He measured the circumference of the wheel, did some mental calculating and then cut a piece of strap iron of the right length. Then we spent a considerable time on the anvil beating this in a cold state till it became a circle. The diameter one side had to be greater than the other because of the dished wheel. I thought it was a marvellous bit of work, so perfectly round and absolutely true. All this art is now lost with the advent of rubber tires.

Finally he heated this ring on the frame, and I helped him to quickly hammer it on to the felloes and then, amid clouds of smoke, drench the rim with water to prevent charring. The felloes creaked and groaned as the rim contracted and the joints closed up tightly. The last bit was a rush job and we were glad to have a rest.

While I was at Knowsley during the First World War, American troops were billeted in part of the park. I never saw any of them although we went into the park once or twice.

Members of the royal family stayed at Knowsley quite frequently. As transportation was slow in those days, it was not always easy to return to London after a function in the north-west. The Earl would often offer his hospitality.

On these occasions, my half-brother Owen[86] would be sent from Liverpool by the Post Office to open a royal post office at Knowsley Hall. He knew most of the royal family and their habits. Queen Alexandra[87] was most unpopular with the staff. Once she was not provided with a napkin and wiped spilt soup up with a valuable antique doily. She was always nasty with the servants.

Although Owen came to Knowsley frequently he never fraternized with his "poor" relations, the snob.

During the First World War, the 17th Earl[88] asked him if he wanted a commission when Owen told him he was volunteering for the army. He refused. Second lieutenants in the trenches had a life expectancy of fourteen days at that time. He stayed a sapper[89] and enjoyed life at Salonika. He was in hospital once, but that was through nearly being run-out at cricket. He slithered over the hard-baked ground and tore the flesh off his arm. He sent us post cards from Salonika. I remember one showed the inside of a Greek prison with two men's heads appearing through holes in a box about 5 feet by 2½ by 2½ feet.

Another was a cartoon showing a Tommy flattened out in no man's land with a star-shell bursting overhead and lighting the place up:

Oh, star of eve, whose tender beam,
Falls on my spirit's troubled dream.[90]

On his way to the home-bound troopship at the end of the war, he walked over piles and piles of horse harness and saddles. He did not know why they had been sent to Salonika. He never saw a horse there.

Back to Knowsley. I earned 1s.6d. off Mr. Owen and had never been so rich. I spent 6d. on something and held on to the shilling until I went to church and then I remembered my shilling. I had to give the lot. The Lord loveth a cheerful giver. I don't reckon He thought much of me that week.

One evening, while staying with Harry, my other half-brother and his wife, Cis[91], they took me to visit Cis's mother. I don't remember much about the visit except that a great effort had been made "to keep up with the Joneses". The old girl was dressed like a duchess and beamed down on me in a condescending way. At the corner of the street Harry had given me a close and anxious inspection which involved spitting on handkerchiefs and scrubbing my neck.

The place was spotless and had an abundance of nick-nacks, and all hoity-toity. I don't think they had much to shout about as one daughter had married an impoverished teacher and the other was in the Everton toffee factory. Cis once came to Calveley and brought me a big tin of the toffee, so that is how I know.

Harry's instep had dropped while he was playing golf, with the result that they would not accept him in the army during the war. At the end of the war a blacksmith turned osteopath, named Barker, came into prominence, and Harry went to see him. The walls of the room were covered with calipers discarded by previous visitors. He got Harry's ankle in his agile hands, gave a sudden jerk that sent Harry up in the air and the job was done. He too left his calipers behind him.

He felt he was a new man and wanted to start a new life so they packed up and went to join Cis's brother in a garage business in Canada.

Father had a housekeeper when his first wife died and, with two boys and two girls, he needed four bedrooms. So a new room was added to the corner of the schoolhouse nearest the gate. It was a light-weight construction supported on a wooden pillar. I believe this structure is now giving trouble. There was a verandah furnished with a seat below. We often sat there in the evening.

After my Father lost his first wife, he walked every Sunday from Calveley to Oulton Park[92] to visit my Mother. They courted in the park which is now a motor race track. Later my Mother came to teach at Calveley and, when their wedding was approaching, an old farmer named Ravenscoft came to see her at her lodgings at the Mount to warn her about my Father. He was quite genuinely upset that such a young girl[93] should get involved with him.

My Mother didn't listen, a thing she always regretted. She said she was sorry for William's children. They had no clothes and no one to look after them.

They showed her no gratitude in later years. Once in an argument about their Father, my half-sister Mary[94] told Mums, "Blood's thicker than water."

But Mother liked the two boys.

"Don't marry for pity, lad, whatever you do," she once said to me.

My Father told me of an old chap who used to go round the farms and, after he had left, there was always a pat of butter missing. He carried nothing and had no bulging pockets and the farmers' wives were puzzled at first. And then they noticed that he never removed his top hat when he went into the house.

One had an idea and made up the fire.

"Do come nearer the fire, Mr … I'm sure you're cold."

Nearer and nearer he was pressed to come, and bigger and bigger the fire was made. He produced a big bandana and kept wiping his face vigorously but could not keep pace with the melting butter. It taught him a lesson.

My Father knew Charlie Peace[95] too. He had a little tub[96] and would drive round the lanes round Northwich sizing up each gentleman's house for a means of entry. He visited Whitehall at Hartford when there was a party being held there. He always had a long crooked walking stick with him. He hooked this round a rail of a balcony and pulled himself up. He rifled all the guests' things as they feasted downstairs and got clean away.

Whitehall is now the Northwich Rural District Council meeting house so one can say that Charlie was not the only rogue to go there.

They used to hold dances in the Winsford salt mine. The twinkling lights on the rock salt crystals made a very pretty effect. People were lowered down the mine in big tubs with a man standing in the rigging above them and using his feet to keep the tub on the right course.

Back to Calveley. There was a dance in the school before my Mother was married and she had to make her way home to the Mount, almost as far as the station. One friend volunteered to take her home—it doesn't appear that her husband-to-be was in the offing.

Well, a daft lad heard this offer and he came up: "Can anyone come with you?"

She often laughed about this and repeated it on occasions when it was appropriate.

Several of the locals would go to the pillar box at the top of the lane to see if the postman had anything for them. It was a chance for a gossip too. My Mother needed it after being shut up all day. My Father didn't like this at all and grumbled about her leaving the house.

Mrs. Yearsley, the sister of Mrs. Major who had kept house for my Father, was a good friend of my Mother's and knew what she had to put up with. She was always at the post box at night.

One of the school managers was a farmer named Willett. He was known as "Cider" and was an ardent tea-totaller and a pillar of the Chapel.

Well, at the time of my Mother's marriage, my Father had taken to drink. My Mother blamed some of the local farmers who were not of Willett's persuasion. Every time he visited them, they filled him up with beer. It didn't take Cider long to get on his track and there was fear that he would get the sack. My Father was buying beer by the barrel and nipping out of school at frequent intervals to have a drink.

By the end of the day there was chaos in school and my Father couldn't stand up. It all fell on Mother's shoulders to run the school on these occasions.

One day she'd had enough. She got the maid to help her and they rolled the barrel to the grid and up-ended it. And then she lit into Father in a desperate effort to bring him to his senses. She won the day and he seemed to reform and, during my early years, I never remember him having drink, except from the whisky bottle, which was only brought out for visitors and, as many of the local farmers were "Bible thumpers", it wasn't very often. When he did pour a visitor a drink he always licked the bottle neck, his great tongue making an upward sweep which made me sick, I don't know what the visitors thought.

Mr. Major called at the schoolhouse once and, in the strange humour of that time and place, Harry and Owen were offered a penny if they would run to the gate naked. They accepted and it always gave my Father great pleasure to recount the story. Perhaps he never asked himself why they had to do that to get a penny. I never remember him giving me a farthing.

As the most learned man in the district, or so he thought, he was called on in many ways. Once he was sent for to make a will for a Mr. Corns, who lived in one of the three houses by the sand-hole, and was dying.

He went upstairs with Mrs. Corns, whom I knew, and she sat on the bed while my Father fiddled with his papers. Suddenly the old man wheezed: "Shift thee great arse woman." She had taken more than her share of the bed.

Before Calveley School was built in 1874, the parish council used to hire a small one-room cottage for their meetings, now, no doubt, pulled down. It stood on the right of the road to Wardle almost opposite the sand-hole. (Do the sand martins still come there?)

There was a big fireplace at one end of this single room and a bed at the other. The building had one or two windows that were not made to open, and a board door with latch. Well, on one occasion some of the farmers' sons wanted a bit of fun, so they went and made a big fire in this room ready for the meeting. The worthies duly met and started their business, no doubt commenting on the thoughtful efforts of the ones who made such a good fire.

The lads then crept up and put a bar across the door and lashed the latch handle to it, this prevented the door from opening. They then pushed one of their number on to the thatched roof and handed him a slate. He wormed up to the chimney and put the slate over it. Then, in common parlance, they beat it.

I don't know how the councillors got out or what happened afterward. I believe there was a big row, both in the room and later.

At this same cottage, these lads painted a white cow red during the night, much to the consternation of the Whalley, the old couple who lived there.

I used to go to Whalley to buy a penn'orth of apples. We had a garden full at home but when I could scrape a dime, I sampled his green apples. I suppose it was because other lads, who had no gardens, did it.

My Father used to tell a tale about a local farmer:

Each year Mr. Major sent to Scotland to buy sheep. When he had collected a flock, his shepherd would set off for home, staying the night at inns, as there were inns that catered for such travellers—penning the sheep and leaving his dog in charge.

On one occasion the shepherd stayed at an inn and left the dog in charge as usual, but in the morning, when he got up to set off on the last leg of his journey, he found both sheep and dog missing.

Very worried, he tramped off home to find the people there equally worried, wondering where he was, because the dog had already brought the sheep home without him.

My Father told me that a man going over the level crossing at Calveley station—the only way of crossing the line—had both his legs cut off by a train. He died, but before he was buried, the legs were stitched back on by a tailor who lived in the railway cottages there.

Uncle Willie Alcock's uncle[97] had his legs cut off while crossing the Brunner, Mond service line alongside the Verdin Park, Northwich. The hospital was at hand and his life was saved. When we first came to Northwich he used to sit in a wheelchair placed in a shop doorway somewhere near Worsley's shop in the Bull Ring.

His legs were buried at Witton Church. I don't know whether his wife did not like the idea of being buried with legs so she elected to be buried at Hartford and, of course, he was later buried with her. I reckon at the last trumpet call we may see a pair of legs headed for Hartford.

Irish labourers were always plentiful in Cheshire. At harvest time and potato digging time they were even more plentiful. Year after year they came back to the same farms. I got to know one yearly migrant very well as a small boy. His name was Willie. He came each summer to Mr. Yearsley's farm[98]. He was a great favourite of us all, and then he came no more; he had been gassed on the Western Front.

Well I was going to tell about a tragedy that happened before my time to some Irish labourers over for Majors' potato harvest. They were given a wooden shed to live in and bedded down on straw. There was an iron stove in the middle of the room. The season was very wet and the soaked men hung out their wet clothes to dry and got down in the straw for warmth after making up the fire with wet material that would hardly burn. They were all dead in the morning with carbon monoxide poisoning.

I have heard the tale many times of the man who sat on a branch he was sawing off. Well the original of this story lived at Calveley and was named Bate.

My Father was sent for by Mr. Pennefeather who lived at the Hall[99] to give his son private tuition during the holidays.

A farmer at Wettenhall went into the bull cote and the bull suddenly put its head down and made for him. He dashed to the stern end of the bull, which seemed safer, and hung onto the tail. Round and round they went. The farmer calling for help all the time. At last his legs were beginning to give way.

"John, John," he shouted. "It's the last time round, John."

Evidently John came in time.

Near the Highwayside was a farm owned by a Mr. Whalley. His bull turned on its owner and killed him.

I often saw his daughter riding the lanes on her pony, but the family never seemed to have anything to do with their neighbours.

On one occasion, Majors' cows were being brought into the yard at milking time and the bull, left in the yard, suddenly swept his horn up the side of one cow and ripped it right open.

Majors, at the top of School Lane, sold a bull to Tricketts who had a farm at the other end of the lane. The darned thing would keep going back to Majors.

In the end, they tied a bucket to the bull's tail and drove it off in the direction of Tricketts's.

Unfortunately the maid was taking me for an airing in my pram and saw the bull coming. There wasn't time to get back home as the bull, encouraged in his flight by the clanging bucket, was making rapid and angry progress. The maid headed for the country by way of the hedge and left me to my fate.

My Mother, panic stricken, watched all from a bedroom window, dashing down just in time to rescue her bawling infant from the muddy ditch into which the passing bull had tipped me. What she told Majors was no one's business.

There was one very dirty member of the labouring classes who worked on a local farm. All means failed to get him to clean himself up and it was a penance to have to work near him. So the young fellows took him down to a pit, tied a rope round him, and dragged him through the water. The incident nearly ended in tragedy, but I think it had its effect.

The roads in my early days were made with loose stones and dirt. Before a road was to be repaired loads of each were tipped at the side of the road.

There was no stone crushing machinery at the beginning of the century. A man was employed to break the big stones that had been left by the roadside.

He had a double-ended pick-like hammer, with a six or seven inch head, and day after day he reduced the big stones to small ones suitable for the road. I have one of the hammer heads worn almost down to the hole, that the roadman had discarded and that we had adopted as a coal-hammer.

These stones were then spread on the road by a gang of men with shovels, covered with soil, watered in, and rolled with a steam roller. The water cart sprayed water from a perforated bar at the back. It was great fun when they came to School Lane.

When my Father first went to Calveley in 1874, the big lads threw the old stone-breaker over the hedge.

When the school opened, farmers sent their sons, who had had no schooling. Some of them were eighteen years of age. My Father was only twenty-one.

When Owen was a lad at Calveley School, he was sent into the wood with another lad to cut some holly. The other lad wielding the axe slashed at the tree and buried the axe in Owen's head just at the hair line on his forehead. He always had this white weal.

Harry was at Chester College just about the time I saw the light of day and then spent a year in France. He and Owen were great cyclists and swopped parts with the Stockdale lads—sons of our parson. One bike they had had cane rims. I suppose if the car age had arrived they would have got a car. Harry was always enterprising.

My Father regarded my half-sister Annie[100] as incapable of becoming a teacher—like Owen. Mary was his pet.

So Annie was sent to Worleston Institute to learn cheesemaking. I think the place had only been opened a short time before. I remember going to see King George V and Queen Mary visit there. Their coach passed us in a country lane so we had a good view. I waved a tuppenny flag and cheered.

Subsequently, Annie worked on several farms. One of them, Barnet's, won the Cheshire Cheese Championship regularly. Three cheers for Annie.

How she met John Key I don't know, but she married him from our house, at Bunbury Church. Mrs. de Knoop sent us a bottle of champagne and my Father made a mess of opening it and, apart from staining the ceiling, wasted most of it.

When John Key came to visit us—I suppose it was for his wedding—he gave me a penny packet of Bedfordshire Champion onion seed. I was very pleased with it. I don't remember receiving anything else from him as a small boy except the cake he bought me on the occasion of my nightmare journey with his sheep, and I suppose I could write that off as sustenance.

He didn't let marriage stand in the way of business and while he was at Calveley he bought a pen of pigs from Roland Yearsley and had them sent home by train.

Key was a Leicestershire farmer's son with no money, but a determination to get on, by fair means or foul.

The latter did not bother him. Annie told me that he once killed a man, and not to get him cross. His father's potato field was bounded by the canal and boaties came at night, tied up their barges along the edge of the field and dug up potatoes. Night after night the field was plundered and, at last, John caught one red-handed, bashed him on the head with his shovel and threw the unconscious fellow in the canal.

CALVELEY SCHOOL

My Father introduced me once to a man named Hitchen who, he said, had built Calveley School. The actual school was built first; the schoolhouse was added later. While the house was being built, my Father lodged with Mr. Lupton's grandfather, Mr. Hewitt. He was the village carpenter and undertaker.

He was a nice old man, well-bearded. He cut the legs shorter on "Dodie's stool" so that she could climb on it more easily. He made many things for the schoolhouse, and fitted cupboards and a jam shelf in my bedroom, which became infested with wood-boring beetles who kept me awake at night with their chewing.

We had coal fires, paraffin lamps, and drew hot water from a boiler with tap at the side of the fire. Water originally came from a well in the yard. There were two filters filled with graded stones and finally sand.

The Vernwy reservoir was completed in 1890 and this water was piped to Liverpool. By law, water must be supplied to any district through which the aqueduct passed and so Calveley was provided with piped water some time in the last decade of the century. Access to the pipeline for maintenance purposes is assured by iron gates in the fences of the properties through which it passes. The line passes under the Nantwich-Tarporley road near Four Lane Ends.

Our sewage was disposed of by a man coming at night. He was supplied with a big barrel on iron wheels which he kept behind an implement shed opposite the school. Here he tipped the sewage.

The school windows were originally glazed with diamond panes, but rust played havoc with the frames. The school could not be kept warm so, about 1914, the diamonds were removed and sheet glass was inserted in new frames. We children loved collecting the putty droppings and making dolls out of them.

Before my time, the children brought a penny a week to pay for the week's education.

The school inspector called once a year and that was on Chester Cup Day because it was the only day a train was available, so my parents knew when to expect him and Mother got food ready for him because she had to feed him.

The inspectorate made no allowance for mentally retarded children. All were compelled to attend school, and were to be taught. It all went down on the report which formed the basis for the teachers' salaries. Such was the intelligence of the inspectorate.

The children sat on five-seater desks with iron supports, and as they nearly all wore wooden clogs with iron frames attached to the soles and heels you can imagine the noise. These clogs were good for "slarring" (sliding) in and the playground was a treacherous place when there was ice about.

I was born the same year that the Boy Scouts were founded, 1905[101]. Perhaps the latter was the better idea. My earliest home was a schoolhouse situated in a lonely part of the Cheshire plain.

This had been the estate of Sir Hugh Calveley[102] who owned land all the way to Church Minshull where the River Weaver formed a barrier. No doubt it was sparsely populated in those days. Here Sir Hugh entertained the Black Prince.

Less and less land was dedicated exclusively to hunting as the centuries passed, and the acreage was divided up into farms, all owned by the squire to whom the farmers owed allegiance.

In my day, Calveley Hall was occupied by Major Jersey de Knoop and his family. Small clumps of trees were dotted about the park so that view from the Hall's windows was not marred by sight of distant buildings.

The front lawns were fenced off with a ha-ha[103].

The fence around Mr. Lupton's house down the hill was also hidden by a bank following the hedge line. This terminated in a clump of trees.

The field opposite the front of the Hall was owned by Mrs. Jinks who had the farm down below the Hall. I believe Mrs. de Knoop made many overtures to buy this field as, no doubt, the fence line was an eyesore. But this was some of Jinks' best grazing land and naturally she would not sell.

The head gardener at the Hall was named Hitch. He was the brother of the Surrey fast bowler, who bowled at me once when he was visiting. I never saw the ball and had difficulty in finding the wickets. I only stood up to the one bowl.

Just outside the back door of the Hall was a big iron cage the size of a room. Here hung game from hooks in the roof. It was the fashion to hang game till it dropped, before cooking it.

In the Hall grounds, there is a chapel of ease to Bunbury Church. I was in the choir there as a boy.

The vicar, the Rev. Edgar Stockdale, was responsible for Calveley and Wettenhall Churches. He managed it by having a morning service at one and an evening service at the other. He had no transport to get to Wettenhall and legged it down the Long Lane. This straight stretch of narrow country lane may have been the boundary of the Calveley estate.

The chapel of ease was built on the outer perimeter of the conglomeration of buildings that surrounded the Hall, which was built in Tudor times. It was the second Hall. The original was of wood and the two stood together at one time for, on old maps, reference to these buildings is in the plural.

The long plain building of the chapel has diamond-shaped panes of green glass. Mrs. de Knoop had the place reconditioned. I don't know when it was built; it seemed of recent origin[104]. The eastern window carried a coloured picture of Christ.

I remember when I was very small and had to be lugged to church because we had no baby-sitter, I fidgeted and my mother, to keep me from causing a disturbance, drew this picture of Jesus in the back of her prayer book. I still have this book which bears her maiden name and also that of her grandson I see.

The de Knoops occupied the first four seats on the left side of the aisle. They had big kneelers and carpet on the seats. The staff of the Hall filled most of the remaining seats on that side.

The church was redecorated on one occasion and the pews were revarnished. Of course, copal varnish soon loses its drying powers if kept a while. I think it was a contract job; a case of the lowest tender getting the job. Well this varnish did not dry properly and after the sermon when it was time to stand there were sound of ominous ripping in the nave ... an awful noise of tearing cloth as the people tried to detach themselves from the newly varnished seats. Some stuck to the seats and had to be levered up. The seats were later scraped and revarnished by another man.

There was a stone fountain near the entrance door. The inner doors were altered within my memory and thick padded leather doors formed an inner barrier to the elements.

The organ was electric and when this was off-colour a choirboy was recruited to do the job manually. I was never fortunate enough to be chosen, but then I hadn't a good record at church as you will see. The choir ladies squeezed into the space each side of the organist and choirmaster, one Sammy Moore, who was the canal agent at Barbridge.

There was always a demand for choirboys and at an early age I was recruited. I remember my first day in the choir. Being the smallest boy, I had to walk at the back of the boys by myself, and immediately in front of the men, as we progressed slowly up the aisle toward the chancel. At the end of the service the reverse took place.

As the Bible says, the last shall be first and I had to lead this reverent assembly. Not for me the slow dignified walk. I stepped out briskly and reached the vestry door by the time the others were descending the chancel steps. Finding no one behind me, I hurried back and joined the gang once more, to everyone's amusement.

We were paid for each time we attended church, on a quarterly basis—choir practice on Thursday evenings, and once on Sundays. We received our pay in three penny joeys. Now I wonder where all those came from.

When we left choir practice to go home we would sing all the way up the drive and Sammy Moore would say to us: "Now if you would only sing like that in church."

All expenses of the church were borne by the de Knoops.

The end of the First World War saw the final breakup of the estate. When Major de Knoop was killed, his wife was forced to sell.

Many tenant farmers were given the option of buying their own farms. Farmers had to make a bolt for the banks to borrow money with which to pay for their farms. Farming had been in a poor way for years and to raise 10,000 or so overnight was not easy.

We were all very worried about it. However, I think the banks came to their aid and no farmer was dispossessed. I don't know how this affected them but I should say it was hard graft until the bank loans were paid off and then the farmers could invest in their own property and make improvements.

When Midwood, the new owner of Calveley Hall, arrived, someone asked him what he was going to do about the church.

"Oh," he said, "close the damn place."

Midwood's son was named Ralph, pronounced *Rafe*.

After buying the Hall, Midwood took his son on a tour of inspection and when they came to the church, they resented this as it meant that their privacy would be violated by churchgoers.

"What do we do, Ralph?" his father asked.

"Oh, to hell with the church," was the reply.

But Nemesis was waiting in the wings, and when this young upstart was pontificating to some girlfriend and leaning on his stick, the latter broke and penetrated his carcass.

◆   ◆   ◆

The fields are studded with marl[105] pits dug during the previous century when it was thought beneficial to marl the land. Much of Calveley, as its name implies, is low lying. On wet land, cows can destroy more fodder with their feet than they can eat.

There was a pit in Ravenscroft's field where we went bathing. When first we went, it was an overflow from a neighbouring pit but the connecting link got well trodden down and it became a permanent pit. Someone told my Mother I was bathing there with other lads and she put a stop to that.

The River Weaver flowed past Worleston and Church Minshull, three or four miles from Calveley. Where the fields had no fall, they were left with a corrugated surface, the drains being in the synclines.

Much of this old drainage work has been destroyed by ploughing and harrowing, as farmers were given a grant during the Second World War for every acre they converted from meadow to cultivated land. This encouraged them to plough up pastureland and so this old method of drainage has largely disappeared. And now, with modern machinery, drainage is no problem.

Every year when I was a boy, as soon as harvest was finished, the hedge-cutting and ditching started. Then you had to look out for thorns in your bicycle tires.

The men wore *yorkers*—their corduroy trousers hitched up and tied with binder twine below the knee. They had no wellingtons and, when ditching, used boards about a foot wide and five feet long with a hole near one end through which a vertical stick was fixed. The men started on a ditch at its lower end, dug it out for five feet and then dropped their board in with the handle at the rear. They now had something to stand on and the water ran away behind them down the newly restored ditch. The sloppy stuff they plastered on the cop, the more solid spadefuls went on the land.

They would search for the end of the pipes which crossed the fields and clean the ends out. Sometimes trouble arose when a farmer cleaned his ditches out and a less enterprising fellow at a lower level wouldn't get his cleaned out. There is a law pertaining to drainage but no farmer would like to do that to a neighbour—that is resort to law.

The farms at Calveley were dairy farms. Turnips, mangels and kale were sown for winter feed. One rarely saw corn.

The cattle were mostly Shorthorns. I remember one farm at Worleston had Frisians and they had a Jersey herd at the Hall.

When they dug the trench for the Vernwy-to-Liverpool aqueduct, they dug through a great bed of cow bones buried during one of the rinderpest[106] outbreaks of the 1800s.

There were some sheep, and around every farm there was always a flock of hens, ducks and geese. These generated pin money for the farmer's wife who took fowl and eggs to market. They used to sit on forms in the market hall with their produce all round them. Most of them had their regular customers.

Butter and cheese were made on most farms. I used to help my sister Annie put the butter up: a pound of butter to a pound of salt (very dear salt). This was well mixed and then compressed into a mold which left a pattern on the pat.

The cheeses were usually forty pounders and much as they are today.

◆   ◆   ◆

There was not much need for law and order in Calveley during the first quarter of the twentieth century.

The local representative of the law was stationed at Alpraham in a house near the turn-off for Bunbury. He was six foot four, and daft.

Shortly after his arrival he called on us. P.C. Gregory strode down the path as my Father was weeding.

"Mr. William Gore," he said.

"Yes," said my Father and went on weeding.

"You haven't got a dog licence?"

"No," said my Father.

"Serious crime, Mr. Gore. Must report it."

Out came a little book and with much licking of the pencil stub the copper eventually got all the incriminating evidence down. He was about to put the book away, then he thought he must give the criminal one last chance.

"Have you anything to say why you haven't got a licence?"

"Yes," said my Father and went on weeding. "I haven't got a dog."

Another instance of what we had to put up with concerned Mrs. Jinks. She was a widow and had two nephews and a niece living with her. Now Mrs. Jinks was good to everybody. No one ever took a collecting can there without getting a contribution and there were a terrible lot of collecting cans going about during the First World War.

One kindness she did was to let Gregory the Cop go shooting for rabbits on her farm on Saturday mornings.

One evening, the policeman caught young Vincent, her nephew and one of the orphans whom Mrs. Jinks was bringing up, riding a bike down School Lane without a light, and nailed him.

Vincent had to appear in court at Nantwich and was fined five shillings.

The Saturday after this first offence, Gregory showed up at Mrs. Jinks farm, took his gun off his bike, and was off across the fields.

"Where are you going?" he heard a voice behind him ask.

He turned. "Oh, good morning, Mrs. Jinks. Just going for a rabbit."

"No, you're not. You are not going for a rabbit now or any other time, so get off my land and stay off."

It was always trivial offences that fell to Gregory's lot because he was not intelligent enough to tackle anything bigger. Perhaps that is why a small country district like Calveley was lumbered with this imbecile.

He wasn't very popular, to say the least of it, lying in ditches and hiding round corners to catch people, as though we hadn't enough trouble at the time.

He had twin sons who always had a ready ear for any tale they could carry back to daddy. They were in the choir, as was their father, and we boys made sure that they were stuffed with plenty of material. We had their daddy lying in a ditch many a night on a concocted yarn.

My friend Johnnie Duncan and I, while waiting with the other boys for the church to be opened one choir practice night, discussed plans in the hearing of the cop's sons for raiding Mrs. Jinks's orchard.

We supported this statement by moving off in the direction of the orchard when the others followed the vicar into the church.

We waited ten minutes and then crept up the aisle.

"Turn 'em out," bellowed this fool of a cop referring to our pockets, and interrupted the choir practice to come out of his stall and frisk us for apples. Everyone looked on as if we were criminals. I never forgot that and Johnnie and I resolved to get our own back.

It was war time and, to save energy, the lights in the nave were put out and just the lights round the organ kept on. It was also the practice for the choirmaster to give the boys a run through first and then to concentrate on the men.

Well, after the boys were finished with, I edged to the end of the stall and then lowered myself to the floor keeping a keen look out for stray eyes. I had Stocky behind me, and Sammy, at the organ, had a mirror in front of him, so it was not easy to move. However, I crossed the short gap between stalls and chancel steps and then crept down the aisle.

Outside, I found the cop's bike. As he was very tall, his bike had two cross bars one a few inches below the other, so identification was easy. It took but a few seconds to turn the water on to his carbide in his acetylene lamp, and then I hurried back without being missed. When we were finally liberated there was a strong smell of acetylene outside.

We wondered if the cop would ride his bike without a lamp.

When we got to the Hall gates I pretended to turn off for home, but crept back and unloosened one of the ornamental chains at each side of the gates. I stretched this across the gate and waited.

Soon I was able to make out the cop. He was riding his bike without a light. I had two stones ready and flung them down the drive in his direction as hard as I could. I was so angry with him, I aimed to kill.

There was the usual bellow and he put on speed but not for long. I had just reached the claphatch across the road when there was a crash and more bellowing.

I legged it for home down the inside of the hedge and emerged near Hewitt Luptons, the joiners. He was a big tell-tale and also in the choir, so I dare not pass his house but climbed the fence and got into the wood at the back and thence home.

My anger had cooled and for the next few days I was very frightened at what I had done.

I recovered my confidence within a short time and as there was a sweet shop at the back of the Davenport Arms at the station, I decided one night to pay it a visit. There I met Bowie Davies who was also a choirboy.

He talked of the frisking I had had and laughed about the expression on the cop's face when he found nothing.

He had been accused of taking a watch from a harvester's pocket the previous summer when the coat had been hung on a gate, so we decided on joint action but didn't know in what direction it would take.

We went along the Chester road to Alpraham to the cop's house. It was a semi-detached with a single gate.

Someone had daubed Ravenscroft's gate with cow muck and this gave me an idea. We went into the field opposite and in the darkness groped about for a cow flop. We daubed the gate top and latch liberally with the stuff. We wanted him to come out in the dark, for daylight would reveal the mess.

We found a stone each and carefully took aim. At least one stone struck the front door. There was the usual bellow of rage as he rushed out to his gate. We raced for dear life through Alpraham. We turned off at the garage and climbed the fence to continue our journey across the fields because we knew he would chase us.

It wasn't long before we identified his tall figure riding along the main road. We raced across the corner of the field to the road which led to Calveley Hall. There was a turn off this leading to the smithy.

We hid inside the fence here, panting. There was no sign of the cop.

Bowie wanted to go, but I didn't want him caught or he would be forced to give me away. I reasoned that if the cop, travelling fast on his bike did not find us on the road to the station, he would know that we hadn't gone that way and would come back along the road where we were. It was evident that the cop had me in mind, for very shortly he came out of the lane to the smithy.

He stopped to talk to a smallholder who lived up there. This man drove his cows along a footpath which people used going to the station and it was deep because of the mud.

Father, as member of the Board of Guardians was called on often with complaints, and so he was at loggerheads with this man, so I didn't want him to see us.

We went further up the fence when the cop had gone and hurried across a field at the back of the houses in Smithy Lane and emerged at the footpath to the station. Here Bowie had but a short journey home, and I would emerge at the style at the other end by Luptons' and once more made my way into the wood at the back and so home.

A Mr. Eaton lived next door to the cop. One choir practice night, shortly after this episode, Johnnie and I came on Mr. Eaton talking to the assembled choirboys and telling them to watch their step as someone had daubed Gregory's gate with muck and Gregory was on the war path. I felt an uncanny silence as I approached. It may only have been imagination.

I couldn't keep out of trouble. When the sidesmen with their collecting purses arrived in the vestry with their hoard, they used to tip the purses up on the table and many hands would prevent the coins rolling off the limited area. I had changed and was waiting by the door. As soon as the purse was tipped up I switched off the light and ran.

There was the usual bellow of rage and the big fellow came after me. He was only a few yards behind. The low, wrought iron gates are mounted between brick pillars over a foot square, and as a result the gates will not fold right back. We had often played with these gates and if you gave them a good swing open they hit the pillar and rebounded. This is what I did on this occasion. David must have felt like me when he saw his foe fall. The cop went headlong over the gate. I was really scared and bolted for home through the Hall grounds. Then I crept back and saw Greg on his feet limping back. Well I hadn't killed him—yet.

Another encounter I had with the cop: I was bringing a big circular foster-mother[107] from the station, and the only way I could carry it on my bike was to get inside it, tying the lamp and all the bits and pieces on my carrier. My lamp perfunctorily shone through the foster-mother door and I could see through the observation door in the conical upper structure.

In this way I was making my way home from the station and had reached the bend in the road at the Hall gates when I was suddenly petrified on catching a brief glimpse of Gregory approaching in the other direction. The foster-mother was resting on my head and on turning my head the thing started rotating and I could only steer by watching the ground below me.

I heard a crash and caught sight of a bike wheel on its side and spinning. I think Greg must have been more scared than I was, perhaps thinking some new type of enemy tank had arrived.

I attended choir practice the week following the switching off of the light, and stood with the other boys while the vicar unlocked the door. He caught sight of me and gave me a lecture. The other lads were all behind him grinning at me.

"You, the schoolmaster's son, should be an example. The only example you are is that of ringleader, etcetera."

This was a very lonely district, with a railway station two miles away and buses unheard of. It was the ex-army vehicles and war gratuities combined that started the bus age. Men with no job and a bit of capital, put it into a PCV and the bus age had begun. The tires were first solid rubber and the roads were potholed. There was no tar macadam, just crushed stone held together with soil. Once this surface broke, the hole rapidly widened. Later the solid tire was replaced with a cushion tire—this was a solid tire pierced with cylindrical holes from side to side, the holes being an inch or an inch and a half in diameter.

This was an improvement but pneumatic tires were not produced for buses at that time although cycles and cars had them.

The car tires were studded with steel headed studs, about six rows of them packed tightly together. This was because the natural rubber, not being durable, was no match for the bad roads and the production of hard wearing rubber was unknown.

We had the London and North Western Railway station at Calveley, but getting self or goods to the station could be a problem. There was no local carrier, one had to trespass on the goodwill of a neighbouring farmer very often.

There were plenty of footpaths then—they were needed. We often went to the railway bridge at Wardle to watch the Irish Mail[108] go through and make crossed swords by putting pins on the line. The maid used to take me to this bridge to watch the slow procession of ancient cars coming back from Chester Cup races along the Highwayside.

We had strict instructions from both parents not to go one step past the bridge which was 200 yards away.

This would be from 1910 onward. Before the First World War cars were not too popular with country folk. Too many had been thrown out of their trap when the wild eyed horse suddenly was confronted by one of these noisy, stinking vehicles.

Still we had a good view of the slow-moving caterpillar of cars.

The canal in those days was very busy. I know because I went fishing there and I frequently had to pull out my line to allow a boat to go through.

Very often some child, ill shod, would lead the barge horse over the stony path. How they all lived in those tiny cabins puzzled me. I remember a rather stout old lady named Salmon dying in the cabin of one of the boats. They couldn't get her out. Mr. Lupton had to go to cut the side of the cabin out in order to bury her.

After milking on a Saturday, it was the custom of many farmers and their wives to go to Nantwich. The trap would be well polished, the candle lamps of brass and all the harness buckles would be polished, the leathers would be well rubbed with neat's-foot oil. Sometimes four would go in the trap, sitting back to back.

Sometimes I was taken, with the rug pulled well up. It was great fun. There was something magic in the clip clop of the horse, the weird shadows thrown on the road by the candles and the horsey smell.

When large numbers of people wanted to go anywhere, such as Beeston Castle Fête, a brake would be used. This was a big open vehicle with several rows of seats, and pulled by two pole horses. There was usually more fun on the journey than at the event itself. Very often this was the only outing that these people got from one year to the next.

Today everyone has access to a doctor. It was not so in my childhood. The only time a doctor came to many people was to issue a death certificate. The doctors serving Calveley were from Nantwich, Bunbury or Tarporley. The Bunbury doctors are still in the same premises, although in 1940 a bomb[109] almost wiped Bunbury village off the map.

A line of shops and houses hugged a narrow lane which ran right round Bunbury churchyard. The end house nearest the surgery was the home of the registrar of births, marriages and deaths.

This doctor from Bunbury took my tonsils out when I was three. The operation was done at home on the dining room table. My mother was given the "tackle" to boil in the washing boiler.

Annie Booth came over to be with my mother who, I'm sure, was very apprehensive. Aunt Annie brought me a ball with a picture of the current Derby winner[110] on it. I forget the horse which won in 1909 but Aunt Annie always dated the occasion by quoting that it was the year that so-and-so won the Derby.

The nurse put me on her knee while I was given the anaesthetic but it wasn't me that went to sleep—not me, I might miss something. The poor old nurse took a header and my aunt snatched me and took over.

Eventually I was put to sleep and the job was done. However the surgery was a bit too severe and I kept having nose bleeds and once the doctor had to come to me from Nantwich—we changed to the Nantwich doctor—and he had an awful job to stop it. I think it only stopped because I ran out of blood.

I remember a girl at Bunbury was taken to Chester for an appendix operation. Only a few years before King Edward VII had made history in this respect[111] and now the wonders of surgery reached us. We kept our fingers crossed, and all was well.

In getting a doctor, we were handicapped by the lack of communication.

We could telegraph from Alpraham post office and there was a phone at the Hall. The alternative was to cycle over to the doctor to get him. I remember mother getting the flu. She didn't make much fuss about it, but one night when I was asleep, she came to my bed and woke me.

"I feel so ill," she moaned. "You must get me a doctor."

I was out of bed like a shot, trembling, for the flu epidemic was at its height, and somehow got dressed. "Tell him my temperature is 103."

I never questioned why she didn't send my Father, but chose to send a young boy five miles for a doctor. I must have had the acetylene ready charged for I got away quickly.

The lamp was the All-Bright type, or at least it was bright for those days. It had no grip on the lamp bracket, I think the tightener was broken and the damn thing jumped off several times on the way to Dab[112].

I raced off to Nantwich. I got to Welsh Row and down the dark passage to the doctor's surgery.

There was no one there. The surgery was closed the doctors were being pulled out of the place by the flu epidemic. I wandered back into Welsh Row. Not a soul. I didn't know what to do. I must have been ten or eleven.

Then I remembered a doctor—the medical officer of health that my Father knew as a member of the Board of Guardians. I went out to search for him. I wandered on trying to find someone to ask but there was not a soul about, the place was dead.

Then I found an old bloke sheltering in a doorway who stuttered terribly. I remember he did a lot of arm waving but I couldn't make out what he said. Desperate, I went back to the surgery and found the lights were on. A doctor had just come in, dead tired.

A tall young fellow answered my knock. I bleated out my woeful tale. "What did you take the temperature with"? he almost snarled. "A cow thermometer?"

"No. A cl—cl—clinical," I remember stammering.

I remember this scene so well. He didn't speak. He took my name and made up a bottle; it was quinine in those days.

"Tell your mother to take this as prescribed and I'll come and see her tomorrow." Poor devil was half asleep.

I raced home. I got back, but how I hugged that bottle. I rode one-handed most of the way back lest the bottle shoot out of my pocket. Mother was anxiously waiting for me and I reckon she took her medicine straight away.

I went back to bed.

Father still slept.

Mother was much better in the morning.

◆   ◆   ◆

We regularly went to church on Sundays. My Father in top hat and frock coat and carrying his walking stick. He never went anywhere without his walking stick.

His visits to the Board of Guardians were made dressed in knickerbockers—proper attire for cycling at that time. He was a standing joke and caused me much embarrassment. I think it drove me into self-effacement, a thing I could never recover from.

At the top of the lane we would meet others, all in Sabbath attire. As I was in the choir, I soon met up with other choirboys and so, like the Canterbury Pilgrims, we all wended our way to the Shrine.

Mrs. Barker and family came from the farm on the main road, by the cattle pound, and, as it was a long way, they came in a little tub. I don't know what they did with the vehicle while they were in church.

We choirboys used to go to sleep during the sermon. Stockdale was usually a bit of a bore. I remember one sermon however. He started on the "twelve year theory" and traced it on through all the horrible events to 1914. I remember him saying and what will happen in another twelve years, what great catastrophe shall we have. He was right too.

◆   ◆   ◆

With no transport, I was very much bogged down as a youngster. I knew nothing of the world outside. We went on summer holidays to Wales for a fortnight, and occasionally to Chester or, on great occasions, to Liverpool, but these visits could be counted on one hand. Still, life was very pleasant and everybody about knew me and would stop for a chat if you could call it that.

Jack "Tap", a workman on Major's farm, always pretended to want my jersey, whenever I met him. I would see him coming down the lane and go to meet him. He was a great pal of mine. Tapley his name was. It is said he filled his boots with straw and covered his socks with grease. There were no rubber wellington boots in those days.

The post town was Tarporley, as it still is. Another of my pals was the postman, Herbert Gregory, who lived at Tarporley and came out on his red bike twice a day, except Sundays, when he came once. The first post box at the top of the lane was an iron box marked V.R.[113] Later, the brick pillar was built and a box inserted.

Before leaving the top of the lane, the postman would blow his horn to give people a last chance to bring out their mail. When I was a small boy, he often put me on his front carrier and on leaving the lane he would pull out his little horn and blow away. I would be clinging on for dear life as he now only had one hand on the bars.

I was given a Yorkshire terrier—this was after the policeman episode—and when we went on holiday we left the dog chained up and Greg fed him each day.

Herbert carried parcels as well as mail. He eked out his pittance by working in some gentleman's garden at Tarporley and brought Father plants for his garden. He would always get you some cabbage plants and the like, if you asked him.

I remember one day when I was playing in the lane, Mr. Frank Ravenscroft came along in his shandry on his way to Beeston Auction. He lifted me over the rails and took me for a ride up the lane, he was a very kind man with four little girls of his own. I found standing in the springless vehicle rather hard and there was no seat.

A calf was lying on the floor tied up in a sack with just its head protruding. Frank pulled me to him and placed me in front of him with instructions to lean back against him. In this way we went up School Lane.

Cattle and pigs of all kinds were carried in these shandries which were two wheeled vehicles usually made of ash. The upper part of varnished wood rails was deep enough for a cow to stand, and its back would be level with the top of the rails.

Another vehicle which came down the lane once a week was Gerald Arrowsmith's trap. His mother kept a small grocer's shop at Barbridge on the bank of the cut[114]. He brought paraffin oil for our lamps and the usual groceries. He had a brother, Sid, who launched out as a butcher. They were both products of Calveley School. I sometimes visited the shop when I was bigger, to buy fishing lines and sometimes sweets if I could raise a penny, which wasn't very often, and sometimes for bread.

Once I went for a loaf and it was newly-baked and smelled delicious. It was a mile and a half journey and by the time I got home, I had eaten most of it.

This reminds me of a somewhat similar case. Majors, like most farmers, made cheese. Two milkings per day enabled them to produce one forty pound cheese each day. When these were pressed and left the dairy, they put them in a loose box near the gate ready for transportation to the factor.

Now at the top of the lane lived a ne'er-do-well family, the Gibsons. The father was a man of small stature and small mind, and his wage packet would be of like size. The five kids were always ready for a meal and Mother often gave them a jam butty whenever the situation presented itself.

Well the two boys, small like their father, found this Aladdin's cave. While one kept watch, the other went in, and between them they hollowed out a cheese from the back. When it was time to move the batch of cheeses the men came upon this light one. After that the door was locked.

Some time after this we lost all our Aylesbury ducks. They disappeared one night and Gingles, my dog, lived only ten yards away, so we knew it was done by someone she knew, or she would have raised hell.

The police were brought into it, and they went round Gibsons looking for feathers but they had no success. We never knew who had done it.

Next day Mrs. Gibson came down crying and denying they had had anything to do with it. Of course, we hadn't mentioned any names.

Jimmy Davies and Sam his brother lived in the row of cottages at the top of School Lane. They had Wilkinson's old house, the end one of the first row as you come from the Hall. It was a smallholding and had a wide gate for carts.

George Davies, their father, was a son of the old lady next door. He worked at Majors' and in addition to his wages, he received a calf each year. As well as the croft behind their house, they had a croft down School Lane by the Rookery.

In the outbuilding behind their house, by the small haystack, was a baker's oven, a brick tunnel about a yard long, closed by an iron door, and standing two feet above ground level. There was a fire grate below. It was never used in my day.

Below the croft at the back was what we called the Park Lane, a wide grass track connecting the park with School Lane, made primarily for the Hunt. George grazed his cow there and so saved his meager grass. The lane has now gone, although it was a right of way. We went to church that way, over the style.

Twice a day, Jimmy's mother and other lasses from the cottages donned their embroidered bonnets which swept down over their necks, and went to Majors to help with the milking on this 250 acre farm. As I mentioned earlier Jimmy's grandmother lived next door and two of her sons went to the South African War.

When I was old enough I used to take a bundle of washing up to Mrs. Davies "at the top of the road" every Monday morning. And I remember outside her back door were two long, almost coffin-shaped boxes painted green with white wording. They bore many strange devices of which I could make little sense, but I could make out the name Davies among all these Coys, Divs, Regs and numbers without which no army could exist.

Yes, her two sons had been out to South Africa. I suppose these were their kit boxes. They were all good lads, especially to their mother. They were slow of step and had minds of their own. I should think they were steady workers but not the sort you pushed.

During the First World War, Majors' land girl[115] lodged at Granny Davies'. She once gave me a hectic ride. It was one of her jobs to get milk to the station and sometimes I went with her. I remember one frosty morning I was scared to death; she was a real daredevil.

It was well-known that if you drove a horse fast it would not fall on a slippery road. She went down the Highwayside on this particular morning and flogged the horse all the way. For most of the way, I think the horse had only three feet supporting it, the fourth slipping, although it had studs in its shoes. It was a terrifying ride for the couple of miles. The horse was nearly down on its backside several times and we were flung forward, but the lass only laughed her head off. I never went with her again.

The next house was occupied by Charlie Griffiths, at one time under-chauffeur at the Hall. When Hebditch left, given the shortage of manpower during the war years, he was promoted and became the only chauffeur.

Later Tant, the bailiff at the Hall, retired and bought a smallholding at Wettenhall. Charlie moved into his house near the Hall gates and this suited all concerned, as he was nearer his work.

Duncan then came to take Tant's place, and so I met my best pal, John Duncan. For several years we were never very far apart, but when the Hall was sold, Mrs. de Knoop's staff had to find new jobs. Hitch, the head gardener went to the Wirral, and Mr. Duncan became bailiff for Major Cotton at Spurstow.

The Gibson family came into Charlie's old house. Mrs. Gibson and Granny Davies were the two who took the salute when my Father passed.

Bob Orange, a sub-normal young fellow, came to lodge at Gibson's. There were two bedrooms and the family consisted of mother and father, two teenaged daughters, two school-age daughters, and two small sons—the cheese stealers. The result was that Jinny, the eldest girl, enlarged the family each year.

When the German prisoners came to the schoolhouse, she got herself talked about by hanging around the gate, but the Jerries didn't seem to have the animal instincts of the Yanks in the next war, and she was stood up.

Jimmy Davies was diagnosed as having tuberculosis by the school doctor. I am not surprised as his home was a dark, unventilated place. The doctor advised a glass of stout every night. I saw Jimmy once when I was passing—he would have been about fifty then, but I heard later that both he and Sam were dead.

When Sam came into mother's infant class, she asked her pupils if each of them could come out and recite a piece of poetry. Sam startled everyone by starting off: *"Two piss ... two piss ..."*

My mother was about to stop him thinking that something indecent was going to emerge, but Sam went on:

> *Two pistols on my knee,*
> *A so ... a so ... a soldier I would be.*

Sigh of relief.

Raymond Hitch, the son of the head gardener at the Hall, was a pal of mine. We went to Crewe together, but there is something in the northern blood which does not take kindly to southerners so Ray and I were never more than "good friends".

One amusing incident I remember about Ray. The government sent out an appeal to all schools to collect conkers[116], just as they sent out an appeal to collect blackberries for the army issue Blackberry and Apple Jam so *loved* by the Tommies.

My Father was explaining in class that these conkers were wanted for padding inside shells.

Ray suddenly shot his hand up excitedly. "Yes, Sir," he said. "If you put them in the fire they pop orf." Everyone laughed and Ray withdrew into his shell.

Tom Lupton, heir apparent to the carpenter's shop, builders' yard and not-so-profitable undertaking business, was my first friend. His mother had been Tricy Hewitt. Her father is mentioned elsewhere and I only knew him for a few of my early years. But I spent many happy times with Tom.

We made sand castles of the sand in the builders' yard.

We went to Nantwich in the tub, with Nancy in the shafts.

We had parties.

We watched the men sawing up tree trunks in the saw pit in the field. What a rotten job the bottom-sawyer had. He would come up covered in sawdust and sweat. His eyes red and painful. Some trees were worse than others in the discomfort they caused.

We were great friends, Tom and I, until I went to Crewe and then I had Ray Hitch as a school friend, and later John Duncan outrivalled both.

Kids don't like pals who are too tied to their parents and I am afraid Tom could do nothing or go anywhere without his parent's blessing.

My Father was strict but he had little interest in me and could not care less what I did as long as I made myself available when he wanted me to help him. One such thing stands out in my memory. I had scarlet fever during the war. My mother brought it home after being in contact with victims of an outbreak at Barbridge.

The house was well disinfected with sulfur candles afterward but, during the illness, I was relieved at not seeing my Father at all. My Mother had to stay away from school and she slept with me.

The yellow van came to take away my infected bedding when I was better, and I was allowed out. Straight away, my Father got me to wheel the barrow for him. He was renovating the drive. After so long in bed I could hardly stand up, but I had to wheel this barrow and I remember the difficulty I had in trying to raise it from the ground. I am afraid I made slow progress.

I could never understand my Father, I don't think a psychiatrist would make much headway.

I also had the flu not long after and so missed most of the school year. Unfortunately, I went back to school the day the terminal examinations started and the seating for the exam had already been allotted. I had no desk and I remember approaching a teacher called Atkinson, nicknamed Cheenah. He bit my head off for not having a desk.

I didn't seem wanted by anyone in those days. My Mother was my only prop and I suppose we were very close to each other. I hated school and with this double absence I got terribly behind just at the critical time in school life.

Mother went to Northwich where she met an old flame. His son had just become a boy artificer in the Royal Navy. She came home enthusiastic about it. Would I like to be one? I would like anything to get away from my Father. We wrote up to inquire about enlisting, but I was a year too old. We were notified, however, that the Royal Air Force was taking boys of my age.

I applied and was given details of the entrance exam which I took at my old school, Crewe Secondary, although I had just left. I took the exam with another boy from the school, also a schoolmaster's son.

My Father, seeing a chance of getting rid of me, had put me in touch with Skerry's College in Liverpool, where Owen studied to get into the Post Office.

Anyway, when the exam results were published, I was in seventh place in the British Isles. I think my old headmaster was taken aback when the results passed through his hands. He offered me restrained congratulations. One could not expect much more from a Scot.

Well I passed the medical too, and I was all set to go. Then we heard the boys were being sent out to India to train on the Afghan border[117], so Mums put a stop to that.

Well I'm sorry the RAF was robbed of a second Bader but my life seems to have been steered by situations beyond my control.

At that point, the private school business cut across any further plans, and we came to Northwich. We thought the I.C.I. would welcome me with open arms—how wrong we were.

I went to the Northwich Technical College after Father had unsuccessfully, and without a word to me, tried to get me into Sir John Deane's Grammar School. I was too old.

I never won any big prizes at school but Miss Preece, our geography mistress at Crewe, walked into the class one day and passed around a picture of the Lake District. It showed a lake with the river at one end of it. There were thirty-six of us in the class and we found it had already gone round the girls' class without result.

Miss Preece asked us to say which way the river was flowing and how we knew. She came to me. I saw a delta at the mouth of the river and said so. It could only flow one way to make a delta. She was very curt and passed over me.

At the end she smiled. "Gore, come here."

I walked out, not knowing what to expect. She gave me the promised sixpence. I had won my one and only prize. Perhaps this was the beginning of the "11-plus"[118] type of question.

I was a great favourite of Dobbie. Mr. Dobson was our Yorkshire woodwork master. When food was scarce during the war, Mother sent him a box of eggs. He sent for me and told me he was not in the habit of accepting things from pupils but nevertheless he was very glad of the eggs and arranged to buy eggs from Mother. I went to his house and his wife made a great fuss of me. They were not university class, as the other teachers were, but plain country folks and I liked them very much.

The only trouble was that in class he called me "Geoffrey", while the other boys were addressed by their surnames. When he called "Geoffrey" in his broad Yorkshire accent, it echoed round the room.

I learned all the woodworking joints in his class and simple soldering and tinsmithing. With that elementary training I went on, with the help of books, to turn out many things.

Dear old Dobbie, his lesson was the one bright spot in the week. Later when I reached a higher class this subject was cut out and various branches of mathematics replaced it.

I remember in 1916, the year I went to Crewe (or was it the second year—1917?) we had five or six teachers of mathematics. First one would be called up and then another. I was just starting algebra and I was awfully confused and my parents could not help me.

When I was out of quarantine and recuperating from either flu or scarlet fever, I remember I was left at home to my own devices. I eventually turned my attention to some schoolwork and fished out my Hall and Stevens algebra. I remember I turned to simultaneous equations—things I had not mastered. I worked through the example in the text and then I worked an example without reference to the text and I got the correct answer, much to my amazement (there were answers in the back of the book). I was bucked and started on other examples and soon I was romping away.

From then I went ahead in other directions but had a terrible lot of leeway to make up with having been away so long.

One day at school we were surprised to see an airship going over. So big, so silent. It was an impressive sight. One lad in the class had his camera and photographed it.

I had seen my first aeroplane in 1913. It was one evening when we were going for a walk along the footpath to Cholmondeston. We often went that way and brought back wood for the fire. I didn't like collecting firewood on these outings. It was such an impediment to my foraging about in rabbit holes and ditches. Sometimes I found a discarded snake skin, sometimes the snake itself—which would send me scuttling.

When the meadow grass was getting near cutting length, Major's field seemed to be full of the cries of corncrakes. They have all gone now. People I have talked to have told me that they have not heard the cry for years. Some attribute it to the war years when grassland had to be ploughed up.

There were few boys in Calveley. Most of the farms were well stocked with girls. I often went to play with the Boffey girls at Wettenhall. We had some happy times there, playing hide and seek, fishing, and roaming the fields.

Mary died young, Winnie died with her first baby, and only Hettie and Nellie remain. Nellie was my girlfriend in the infant class. Their sister Emma had been Dodie's great friend and they both died of diphtheria within a fortnight of each other at Christmas, 1908. They are both on the photograph where mother had me in her arms alongside her infant class. Emma is a fat-faced little girl.

When Dodie died, her last words were: "Listen to the bells, Emmie. Listen to the bells."

Another family of girls that I played with were the Ravenscrofts from Elm Farm. We had some fun there too, but their mother was very stiff and starchy and very Primitive Methodist, with long connections with the Chapel ministry.

We went once to the chapel when her brother, an African missionary, was over. He gave me some gnu's horns. He had brought Frank Ravenscroft some tobacco leaves.

I was once shown the girls' bedroom which had been newly decorated. A patch of wall near each bed had been left undecorated to be covered with the artistic work of the kids.

This reminds me of something. Dodie and I were measured against the wall in the front room of the schoolhouse—a ruler placed on our head and a mark made on the wall, with the date alongside. This was done each time the room was decorated which must have been pretty frequently.

Once, when playing with the Ravenscroft girls, I lost track of them and ran across the lawn at the front of the house to find them. I had never been there before.

I found them all right. They had one of those long earth closets with a seat to fit any age. All five were ensconced on this throne with the doors open.

I didn't know which way to look. I was so embarrassed.

Frank fed his cows on locust beans and we liked to go and eat these. The girls had no brother and whenever I went to play with them, we usually ended up by having a wedding. I remember we went across to a spinney near the farm and here, at the side, was a small brook and a marsh. Some of the finest marsh marigolds grew here and, in season, these were gathered to decorate the bride.

There was a fox earth in this spinney which Mr. Farrell, the stopper-upper of the Hunt, blocked up late at night on the eve of a local meet. There was a small bridge over the brook with a hunter's hatch for the convenience of the Hunt in passing from one farm to the next.

Another farm where I used to play just had one daughter, Mary. This was Sam Williams' farm at the top of School Lane opposite the cottages. There was a big farm pit surrounded by bushes and when we were small we used to dig channels at the edge of this pond and make castles.

When farmers killed a pig, this was gutted and the carcass cut in two down the spine. It was then placed in a big wooden tub or turnel with walls about a foot high and containing brine. The carcass was soaked in this and frequently rubbed in salt.

Mary was sitting on the edge of this one day after the carcass had been removed and she fell backward into the brine. Spitting and crying she was lugged off upstairs to get changed.

Someone knocked Sam's bull's eye out with a stone. He blamed Jimmy Davies, for what reason I don't know. Jimmy was very indignant and sought revenge.

Now Sam's house was whitewashed on the outside and, like most farm houses, had a cheese chute. This consisted of a stone table behind which was a hole in the wall like a window opening but, in this case, with no glass; just two doors which closed over the opening. A cart would back up to the opening when the doors were opened and the cheeses stacked on the table would then be rolled out on to the cart. In the case of Williams' house there were two windows on one wall and a cheese chute of similar size.

One dark night when I went up to play with Jimmy he outlined his plan. I think he had been waiting for my (im)moral support. He planned to go in the dark and bash some bricks against this cheese chute door and frighten the hell out of Sam.

Well, what can you say to a friend in need?

We found some half-bricks, Sammy Davies, Jimmy and myself. We went across the field opposite the cottages and into Sam Williams' orchard which was beside the house. Jimmy led, and in the darkness we could make out a black patch on the otherwise white wall. It was war time and even the tiniest gleam of light could get one into trouble with the Defence of the Realm Act.

We clutched our bricks and, at a word from Jimmy, we flung the bricks at the black patch.

There was not the expected thud of the bricks on wood, however, but the crash of glass. Jimmy had picked a closely blacked-out window instead of the chute.

I wouldn't have done this to Sam.

We fled; we ran and ran for all our worth. We reached the railway line in what Roger Bannister[119] would think good time.

We rapidly climbed through the fence and sat panting on the bank of the cutting. No one had followed us. We crept along the railway in Indian file and on reaching Wardle Bridge, we cautiously stepped onto the road. We went down the lane to Bumble Bee Bank, over a hedge and eventually got into Major's field. I had only to go down this field to reach the schoolhouse. Jimmy had to cross School Lane into Park Lane and he and Sam could get home the back way.

I had to pass Sam Williams' house the next day. I was very apprehensive but saw no one. Coming home on the bike, I put on speed as I did not want to be seen talking to Jimmy. All three of us were very scared for a week or two. We played it cool and cut a low profile as they say today. Once more we escaped trouble and nothing came of the incident.

In Williams' yard, within call of the back door, was a hut about six feet by four. A door occupied one end; at the other end was an iron stove. A seat ran along each wall and hanging above it were old smelly coats of all descriptions. This was the workmen's hut and similar places would be found on most farms.

Sam died of flu during the war.

In my younger days, while at Calveley School, I had other friends, friends who told me stirring tales of far off lands such as Ellesmere Port and Birmingham and sometimes of London. These were the boat children from Barbridge.

The boat children had a bad time. They came to school when they had to—when they stayed at a place for a few days they were expected to go to school. Suddenly the school yard would be filled with new faces and the teachers would sigh, knowing full well what was ahead of them. Perhaps they would get them on as far as reading a primer, then the children would disappear as quickly as they came.

Many lived in the row of houses at Barbridge, perhaps too many for the barge. On the whole, the boat children were very nice and well disciplined, if a bit smelly. Very polite and loyal. I remember one youngster, Tommy Wilkins, that mother was fond of. When he didn't turn up at school one day she made enquiries. He was ill and had been taken to the hospital.

"What's the matter with him?" mother asked his friends anxiously. "Something wrong with his flashlight," she was told. Mother restrained further enquiries.

Many of these kids had to walk at the horse's head along the rough towpath beside the Shropshire Union Canal.

One little girl, named Howard, was a source of interest because her father or grandfather had a peg-leg. I have seen pictures of old salts with these, but Mr. Howard was the only person I ever saw with one. He unscrewed it when he got into bed. This was real Long John Silver stuff. The boat kids captured my imagination in those very early days.

A rag and bone merchant named Peter Brown lived in Barbridge. I was often threatened when I was naughty that I would be given to him and I kept a wary eye open when he was about. He sometimes got a schoolboy to go round the farms with him, collecting old iron on his flat cart with a pony that was usually far too big and so gave the cart a huge tilt.

When passing the school, the child would be hidden under the pile of rags on the cart. I knew, but I never let on.

Another pal was the caretaker's son, Billy or "Kiddy" Davies. No relation to Jim and Sam. They were farm labourers' children—Billy, Hugh, Mary and others. They lived at Bumble Bee Bank by Wardle Bridge.

Billy and I had a dare. He stood on the small corbel on the outer face of the Wardle Bridge and let a train pass a matter of inches below him. I had to do it to keep my end up. Neither of us did it again. I was nearly blown off the narrow ledge by the blast from the funnel as it passed a few inches below me. My bare knees were scorched, much to my mother's consternation.

Billy came each night with his mother to sweep the school. Before sweeping they had to water the floors with a watering can containing Jeyes Fluid. They took a spoonful of this out of a five gallon drum and diluted it in the watering can. This damped down the dust before the floor was swept. In winter, Mrs. Davies also had to come down at midday to stoke up the boiler.

The Jeyes Fluid drum was kept in the caretaker's room which also contained neat bundles of sticks bound with wire. They were delivered at intervals by two inmates of Nantwich workhouse where the sticks were produced from old railway sleepers. The two men had to push their hand truck all the way from Nantwich[120].

Father never gave them a bite or a drink and, of course, Mother daren't when he was about. The caretaker's store had a unique smell of Jeyes Fluid and creosote. It was peculiar to this room.

When I was at Calveley, there were two brothers Bourne, and their sister Gladys, at school. They were farmers' children from Stoke near Barbridge. They came with an alarming tale one day about Annie Boughey(?) of the Yewtree Farm, further along the Nantwich-Chester road, having smallpox.

She and her mother had been (I believe) to Liverpool and bought some furs. I think parrots from the east had been in contact with them and spread the germ.

Each morning the Bourne children brought a report of Annie, until she died. She was nursed at home. They made a coffin from an oak on the farm and took it on a farm cart to Acton Church where she was buried.

It wasn't long before Frankie(?) Bourne became ill. He got weaker and weaker in a prolonged illness. The doctor recommended brandy as a stimulant but his father was a staunch Methodist. He was forbidden to have it. Well, he died.

The maid took me to Sunday school when I was very young, and later I went on my own. We were given a little sticker about an inch square, showing some scriptural scene or person, and this we stuck on a card. When the card was full, we got a prize. Miss Stockdale took the class and sometimes she gave us old copies of the *Boys' Own Paper*. I think this was the finest magazine for boys ever published. It was full of public school stories, and I suppose this would not suit our socialist society today.

We saw few other people. The lad who fetched Williams' cow up would announce his presence with a "Coowooop" and I very often joined him.

The tramps, when they had had a wash and a rest at the Nantwich workhouse, would sometimes make a tour around the country lanes via Wettenhall, and they would give us a call. Mother always found them something when Father wasn't about.

I had some bantams given to me as a child. They lived with the hens.

My Father, about 1913, suddenly decided he would keep hens. We had never had any before, so off we went to Bunbury or maybe Peckforton. I rode on a little saddle on my Father's crossbar and away we went to see Harry Witter. I don't know why this name has stuck in my mind, perhaps it was because soon after this visit we heard that Harry had committed suicide.

My Mother always conveyed this kind of information to me in such a way as to arouse pity. This was very Victorian. Other peoples' troubles affected her, and also me, in a truly traumatic way.

Well we got the hens home. There were six of them, fine White Wyandottes. These grew into big heavy birds both good at laying and also for the table. This breed has lost its pre-eminence because nowadays breeders only want egg-laying machines and not table bird so that the White Leghorn has outrivalled them.

Father would sometimes kill an old hen for a meal. I remember him once decapitating a hen and, headless, it ran round him daubing his best trousers with blood.

Just a hundred yards from the school was the nearest pit. At one side an old willow tree overhung the water. Its trunk almost floated on the water and on this perch we would fish for sticklebacks. We got a reed from the edge of the pit, kicked up a sod or turned over a dried cowflop, and there wriggling out of daylight were several little red worms. One of these we tied to the end of the reed or rush and dangled it in the water where soon a swarm of tiny fish would vie for a bite at the worm. As soon as one had gorged part of the worm we would pull up and toss the fish onto the bank. We put them in a jam jar and very soon we had half a dozen.

Sometimes we fished in the canal and would bring our catch back and throw them into this pit. More often than not we would see the little dead fish floating on the surface the next day. I think the change of water must have been responsible.

Once I caught an elver[121] in the canal. It was twilight and I was about to pack up. The elver landed on the bank and wrapped itself round bunches of grass and reeds. It bit me as I struggled to free it. Anyhow, I got it home and Mother fried it for me.

When my half-brother Harry came home, which was not as frequently as Mary and Owen did, he always started some useful project. We built a henhouse from scrap wood and I remember I had to go to Lupton's for some door hinges. He also got Mr. Lupton to sharpen a saw.

The only trouble with the henhouse which in most ways resembled a bought one and stood eight feet high, was that owing to shortage of suitable timber he put the floor boards in parallel to the door so that it was hard for me to scrape out the droppings with a hoe when standing at the door. The floor boards were of unequal thickness and this made the hoe stick. Still, kids are lazy devils and I didn't like this chore.

Another thing Harry made was a pigeon cote for me. At the top of the gable on the house wall was framework consisting of a horizontal rail and a vertical rail springing from the center of the latter and supporting the joint of the fascia boards covering the eaves. Well Harry filled this framework in and put a floor to it. He left a square entrance hole and built a landing board. The pigeons liked this and often I found an egg up there which I had for breakfast.

We were always keen to collect waterhen's eggs. These could be eaten unlike starlings' eggs. Once I saw a nest on reeds in a small pit. There was a gap between the reed bed and the bank made by cows stepping into the water to drink. For some time I pondered how to get to this nest. Sometimes we used a spoon tied to a long pole, but I was without such aid. At last I decided to jump on to the reeds. My feet sank into the mass and to keep myself out of water I started to run as well as I could. The reed bed was afloat and started gyrating. At last I could keep the pace up no longer and lunged for the shore. I reached it without total immersion but I kept away from *pizzy beds* after that.

We were told as kids that Johnnie Green Teeth lived in pits, but I never saw him.

I had a ferret at Calveley and went poaching. I slipped out of the little window at the back of my bedroom at The Kennels, which had been made so the game-keeper could overlook the back of the premises. Then I slid down the house roof and away.

Pommy Tinch was more of a polecat than a ferret[122]. He was very big and used to lie round my neck like a muff. He used to bite my hands to pieces.

When de Knoops sold the Hall and the Duncans went to bailiff for Major Cotton at Spurstow, I used to go there nearly every Saturday with Pommy, and Johnnie and I went rabbiting. It wasn't far away. Johnnie's father lent him a single-barrelled 12-bore.

Once when we were out, a couple of chaps came into the bottom field with sacks and whippets. They undid the first sack and turned out a hare. It ran off in the other direction and the dogs brought it down.

Johnnie's Scotch blood was up; he had never seen anything like this. The next hare ran in our direction. Johnnie raised his gun and shot it under the noses of the dogs. The men were out to make a row, but Johnnie reloaded and confronted them. He gave them two minutes to leave or he'd empty his gun into the dogs. They saw he meant it and cleared off.

I had taught Johnnie to shoot and his father trusted him with me. We crept down to where the rabbits were. In fact, very near to where the above incident took place, and Johnnie aimed his gun at a big rabbit hopping about the entrance to the burrow. He fired and we ran forward. There was not one rabbit but a mass of dead youngsters, he had shot a doe in kindle and killed the lot.

Later a swell guy came to stay with Major Cotton and, whether the latter was tired of him I don't know, but he was sent to Hayfield, and Johnnie took him shooting. He told Johnnie great tales of his adventures big game shooting, but he didn't kid Johnnie. The latter could see in the way that he handled a gun he had never even seen one before.

As they got near home they came to the usual muddy gateway where cattle cut up the land into clods, with water between them. Johnnie put his thumb on his hammers and gently let them down with the triggers. This chap saw his fingers on the triggers, but he did not hold the hammers with his thumb, and let fly into one of these water holes with both barrels. The mud enveloped him and Johnnie took a bedraggled big game hunter home to be cleaned up.

The Miss de Knoops were ardent wild birds' egg collectors. An apple tree in the hen pens had a hole in it and inside was an egg. It was a dunnock's[123] egg but Johnnie and I thought of playing a trick on Miss Betty. We didn't know then how embarrassing this bit of fun would turn out. Well, we took the egg home and with the aid of a water colour paint box we added a few spots of various colours to this plain egg.

Miss de Knoop apparently found it and took it home with glee. We saw that the egg was missing but thought no more about it until, after morning service the next Sunday, Mrs. de Knoop invited us to the Hall and there we were asked if we could identify this egg. Miss Betty couldn't find its like in any of her reference books.

We were both biting our lips but, after close scrutiny, admitted we couldn't identify the egg. I have often thought that Mrs. de Knoop suspected that we had been up to something and turned the tables on us.

I don't suppose bird or animal life in the area has changed much since my day. The only difference is, I think, the disappearance of the corncrake. I wonder if modern insecticides have robbed him of his natural food. The field opposite the school was always a mowing field and the long grass full of corncrakes, but we could never find this Harry Corbett[124] of the meadow.

Sand martins took over the sand pit in spring. Their eggs were always too inaccessible for us to get. I found a kestrel's nest in the park once and, I'm ashamed to say, I stole both eggs.

We were often invaded by foxes. I chased one once and he leaped onto the park wall and looked down at his panting pursuer, not in the least concerned.

Every year the local farmers culled the rooks. Farmers with rifles met at the rookery near the school to reduce the rook population. After the shoot we would find a bundle of the lousy birds on our back step. We had rook pies for days afterward.

Still, if you could get someone else to pluck them and brave the flea bites, they didn't make a bad pie. I don't think I could face it today, but in those days it was a normal dish.

We were often given beest[125] or beestings by the local farmers—this is the rich first milking of cows after they have calved. I used to love it as a child but I am afraid it is taboo now. I was given some at Church Minshull[126] but we threw it away. It was often made into beest pudding, which I was very fond of as a child.

We had a dog named Tyke when I was small. My Father made a great fuss of his drinking water and put a lump of yellow sulfur in it. I don't know what this was supposed to do, but anybody with any sense knows sulfur like that does not dissolve.

He had a lot of these mythical beliefs such as, if you cut yourself in the fork between thumb and first finger you would die of lockjaw. Father also thought paraffin would cure his baldness and every time he filled the oil lamps he rubbed his pate.

We had a hanging oil lamp that his older children bought him as a Christmas present. When he had finished reading his paper at night he would get up and turn the lamp down although I was doing my home lessons and Mother sewing.

My Father kept a diary each day. Not that anything of importance happened, but his daily record was full of what "She" had been doing and I'm afraid this was often far from the truth. Mother had a key to his desk and read his daily efforts. Often her blood was boiling.

Mother bought Father a new fountain pen each birthday. He never bought her anything, except on one occasion, he came home with a push-pull vacuum cleaner across his back. It was a concertina thing mounted on a central tube and had a foot similar to modern vacuum cleaners. You pulled and pushed the concertina, moving it about the room. It gave us a shock when he brought it in.

We feared for his sanity or his temperance. He gave us another shock when he bought me *The Children's Encyclopedia*[127]. It was unbelievable. He never bought us anything before or after. He was a most unpredictable chap.

During the summer holidays my Father would take his bicycle and tour the Continent. Once he got as far as Turkey. From Turkey he brought back two little statuettes, together with a hookah pipe which he tried to smoke, and with which I was allowed to play when my Father found it too much for him. I should say that it held at least two ounces of tobacco at one filling.

I often think with some concern how a man could leave his wife and kids in that lonely house for such long periods. He said it was necessary for the bread-winner to keep up his health. Of course my Mother was a breadwinner too and did her stint in the infants' school as well as her housework.

My Father collected her salary. "I'll keep it for you, my Pet. You'll have it someday." But when that "someday" came and she wanted to buy a house in Northwich, he flew into a temper.

"I've not been keeping you for nothing," he said, or something like that.

She turned to Owen and Mary and borrowed from them. When they went to buy the house, the solicitor asked in whose name it was to be registered. My Father was about to speak but my Mother rushed in with: "My name please." I think there was a note in her voice that quashed opposition. It was a close shave.

My Father had a wonderful cupboard by his chair and on very special occasions I was allowed to bring out some of the treasures here. There was the hookah pipe from Turkey, and a bag of old coins. One had a bullet hole in it.

My Father told me it was a pastime to toss a coin in the air and then shoot at it. I tried it once and lost a valuable penny and many wasted bullets. This bag I mentioned was really an old-fashioned purse. It was shaped like a figure eight with a central hole. Each half of the eight was closed with a sliding ring so that silver could be kept in one half and copper in the other. Only one side at a time could be opened. I think these purses were carried on the belt.

There were old watch keys and a lot of bits and pieces that had the stink of age about them, and I was always glad to wash my hands when the treasures were once more replaced in the cupboard.

In this cupboard my Father kept his seeds. Once I remember when I was very small and my parents were both in school I raided this supply and was going to have a field day planting them. Unfortunately I was interrupted and in my haste to hide the evidence I tipped the lot into a hole and covered them up with soil. It wasn't long before nature had its way and these darn things started to come up. For days I paid anxious, early-morning visits to my cabbage patch to hide the evidence. I wish seeds today would grow like those did.

I remember the coronation of George V and Mary in 1911. After the coronation we were given a party at the Hall. A big tent was set up near the Hall gates by the Squire, Jersey de Knoop, and children were given a coronation mug filled with jersey milk from the Hall's herd. I was quite small and the maid had me in tow for the presentation. But I remember seeing some of my pals, the estate workers, assembled at the door end of the tent, all watching the proceedings with smiling faces; I walked one way, and looked the other, with disastrous results to the milk.

To celebrate this important event, beacons were lighted throughout the land as they had been to warn of the coming of the Spanish Armada. One bonfire was lighted on top of Beeston Castle crag. Coincidentally, George Beeston, at the age of eighty-nine, commanded the *Dreadnaught* in the subsequent battle, and broke the Spanish line[128].

Well, we could not see Beeston from the hollow in which the schoolhouse was built so we walked up to Mr. Lupton's house, where many villagers had assembled to see this historic event. We seemed to wait ages before we saw the flare. Eventually they got the bonfire lighted.

Mr. Lupton showed me the oak plank he had cut my sister's coffin from. Tommy was my best pal in those days. He still carries on the business in Alpraham. Everyone was gathered outside Lupton's gate up which young Tommy was climbing.

He was blowing hard in an attempt to whistle. Suddenly to everyone's amusement and in the hearing of all he said: "Ad your whittle come yet, Jeopardy"?

Everyone laughed and the name stuck. I never lived it down. Mother often called me that, even at The Heysoms. Tommy was a year or two younger than me.

Once a year on August Bank Holiday, a fête was held at Beeston Castle, within the outer bailey. One paid entrance fees at the twin towered gate, and then crept through a door within a door.

This was one of the few pleasures of the county. True we had Chester Races, Tarporley Hunt Steeplechase, and one or two point-to-point race meetings together with Chester Show and Knutsford May Day, but for real entertainment that all could join in, there was no equal to Beeston Castle Fête[129]. Many people got there early in the day, some having walked ten miles or more.

On this occasion, labourers who normally worked from dawn to dusk, were let off after milking to go to Beeston. From six o'clock onward, the farm labourers and their wives appeared in droves.

The big brakes tipped out their loads at the gate, the horses led to a field nearby. The empty brakes awaited the return journey. These brakes were four-wheeled vehicles with a pole, as two horses or more pulled them. They were like a big lorry with boxed-in sides and no protection from the weather. The occupants either sat round the outsides or on transverse seats. There were no springs to these cumbersome vehicles and the occupants experienced a rhythmic jolting.

When the vehicle was being loaded at the main departure point provision was made by means of steps for entry at the back, but when occasional wayfarers were picked *en route* they had to get in as best they could. Most climbed up a wheel and then standing on the rim cocked their leg over the side and were pulled in by friends.

There is a story of two old women waiting for the brake to come, amid a crowd of youths who were hoping to see more than they usually did in those days. One old girl climbed up the wheel and, amid cheers from the watching crowd, cocked her leg up and showed her voluminous petticoats *inter alia*. The second followed and climbed to the rim of the wheel, then half-turned to the waiting rowdies and said: "If tha sees owt thee muther asna got, throw thee 'at at it." Then she was pulled aboard.

One could tell in a moment when the brakes full of farm workers had arrived. The men who followed the plough had a peculiar walk and looked very unnatural in suits they only wore on this one day in the year, apart from an occasional funeral or wedding.

The wives in their voluminous petticoats were a picture of happiness. Their eyes roved rapidly round the scene quickly taking in all that was happening, and yet having time to notice a friend who, perhaps, they only saw once a year on this occasion. It was a very happy scene and what little money they had saved throughout the year flowed freely, the children getting their share. Perhaps father was more generous than mother liked him to be.

They would walk around a bit in order no doubt to get rid of the aches and pains produced by their rough ride on hard seats.

Soon they were watching the greasy-pole. Here a large piece of sirloin was placed on top of a pole, like a young telegraph pole, covered in grease. The meat was for the taking. Some came ready prepared for this event, having old clothes which they donned in some out of the way corner, such as the caves.

The old hands would bide their time and let callow youths wipe off most of the grease in their attempts. When they thought the time was ripe—they daren't wait too long or someone else of like mind might beat them to the prize—they went forward. Many got to within striking distance but when they took one hand off the pole to grab the prize they quickly slid down the pole and shamefacedly and disappointedly returned to their backers.

The best fun for the spectators was the greasy pig. Here the ladies had their chance. An agile, mid-sized pig, covered in grease, was released on the hillside.

Like the men, the women had come prepared, most with a bag apron—those hessian aprons worn by most women workers in those days. Away went the pig, away went the women, away went an army of boys, big and small.

The pig left them far behind in its panic, but dogged does it. Some women dropped out very quickly, the more energetic continued the chase. At last they were closing in on the pig, several grabs were made but the pig escaped each time with vociferous exultation. At last an old hand would see her chance and *flop* she went on top of the animal, her apron encompassing it.

Strong hands and arms enclosed it, and away she went proudly back to the adjudicators.

Perhaps she worked on a farm and her boss would come forward and undertake to ship the pig back home. It would be tied up in a sack with only its head showing. No doubt its legs were tied too because they say if a pig can get its head through anywhere, it soon goes all the way.

A man with a large number of oranges, each threaded on a string and supported by a knot provided entertainment for the children. They chased him and grabbed an orange which would then come off the string over the knot.

There was an ankle judging competition. Farm lorries made a stage and a curtain was hung across the centre. Behind this the ladies paraded one at a time and delicately raised their skirts, a terrible thing in those days. A party of jovial farmers were the judges. I think there was a lot of cheating done; they all knew who the entrants were.

In 1916 the Beeston Castle Fête was in aid of the Red Cross, so Mums was mixed up in it and it rubbed off on her ten-year-old son. I was given a cowboy outfit and took my Daisy air rifle. I had a picture of Kaiser Wilhelm on a board, fastened to the outer curtain wall of the castle, not far from the caves. At three darts for a penny I think I did quite a good trade.

Naylor was there. He built, and lived at Beeston Towers. He had a timber business on the Manchester Ship Canal.

Convalescent soldiers in hospital blues and red ties were in evidence.

Just below the keep of Beeston Castle, a platform had been cut in the rock to make a level platform for cannon. Big iron rings were embedded in the rock to anchor the guns which once guarded the gap through which armies approaching Chester must pass.

Cromwell destroyed the castle and took away the cannon, but the flat apron and the rings found a new use. On fête days big marquees were placed here, the rings providing good anchorage. I only saw the marquees up once. I think it was too difficult to get supplies up there and many people did not like the journey up the difficult path to the top. Later a field across the road was used both as a car park and a sports ground.

My Father was on the committee when this field was brought into use. He was detailed to accompany a young man to erect some fixtures for the sports. The young fellow went up the ladder but when he wanted something handed to him, my Father was holding his *pince nez* and gawping at the crowd. At last the young chap carried on alone. I heard some rather unflattering remarks from the crowd.

The crowd had nothing to look at until the race started and my Father provided them with a suitable alternative. He had no idea he was being made fun of. It's a wonder some of the cat calls didn't penetrate his thick head. I crept away and left him to his fate.

◆   ◆   ◆

The first school caretaker I remember was Mrs. Gregory. She was a very nice person and I spent much time with her; the school was very lonely at night.

Next came Mrs. Vickers whom my Father unkindly christened "the Leghorn", from the chicken-like way she peeped round corners.

Next came Mrs. Davies from Bumble Bee Bank. I never remember a time when this skinny little woman was not pregnant. They were farm labourers with a big family and lived well below the bread line. Their poverty was brought home to me by the following incident.

During the First World War far more men were called up than the country could spare. Women could not do everything. The result was that at harvest time men had to be released from the Forces to help. Two such men were employed on a threshing machine going round the farms and this unfortunate contraption had to rattle its noisy way past school just as the children were leaving for home.

Many boys dived for the tow bar to get a ride. One man emerged from the cab suddenly to clear them off. My pal, Billy Davies, was on the bar. He slipped as he jumped off and went under the wheel of the machine.

My Mother, being a Red Cross nurse, went to his aid and applied a tourniquet to his crushed leg, but help was so long coming that Billy died on the way to the hospital.

I was attending the grammar school at the time and didn't see the accident. Billy was buried at Bunbury. Mr. Tom Lupton, myself, and two others acted as bearers. I was about eleven, and the heavy bier which had to be shouldered by the four of us was quite a load. The grave was at the bottom of the hill at the back of Bunbury Church and the gravel path gave way to grass at the top of this. We managed all right until the slope increased and then we were impelled forward and I think all four of us would have been interred if Mr. Lupton's father, the undertaker, and other men had not rushed forward with restraining hands and slowed us down.

We went back to Bumble Bee Bank after the funeral. Mrs. Davies came to us in the yard. "Well, you've seen the last of him," she said and held out a plate of sandwiches made of dry bread and a piece of bully beef.

I took one bite and I never tasted anything so horrible, starlings' eggs included. We nibbled and talked until she moved away and then, keeping a look out for the other young Davies, we got rid of the sandwiches as soon as possible. Gosh, the meat was terrible.

At the inquest it was revealed poor Billy had had no breakfast at home the day he was killed. A neighbour had given him a piece of bread. He had had no dinner.

Mr. and Mrs. Davies both died in the terrible flu epidemic of 1919. The children were taken into care. No doubt it was for their own good as they were not being fed properly.

Sam Williams, as I noted, and Mrs. Tapley also died of flu. That is four people within half a mile of each other in the stretch from the Highwayside to the Hall gates.

Except for Jersey de Knoop, no soldier from Calveley gave his life, so it goes to show how devastating this epidemic was.

Of course, I had to get it. I'd never miss anything for nowt.

◆   ◆   ◆

When I was young, the school inspector found difficulty in getting to Calveley. The only time he could get was on Chester Cup Day.

So all was prepared for his visit. He had to walk from the station which no doubt did little to sweeten him.

My Mother had to feed him for the day, and on these occasions I had to make myself scarce. I remember once when very small I peeped through the dining room window to see what this ogre looked like while he was dining but his glare did nothing to encourage a closer relationship.

He set sum tests on the board, collected the papers, heard everyone read and gave dictation tests. Then he collected his papers and off he went, much to the satisfaction of all. Weeks later we would get the report.

In those days a bad report from an inspector could affect one's salary, and they took no cognisance of mental inability. Years later at Hucknall[130], I had a complete idiot in my class who could not even speak.

In her infant class my Mother had a boy of farm labouring stock named Whalley. He was always in trouble through bad work.

Well, this lad Whalley was given a jolt or two by Mother to get him on. He countered this by staying at home which made matters worse because the school "bobby" was very keen in those days. So this lad had to come to school under protest.

Then he thought of a new dodge and was supported in this by his parents. He came with his hand heavily bandaged with a dubious looking piece of rag. Now Mother was a newly fledged VAD and keen to show her nursing ability.

"Poor boy," she thought. "He wants a proper clean bandage on that cut which appears to be bleeding." She took him to the wash basin and took off his bandage under much blubbering and crying. She put the exposed "wound" under the tap and was surprised to see seeds of strawberry jam floating in the "blood". There was no injury whatever to the hand.

She helped him back to his desk with a smacked-bottom and for the rest of the day he never put his pencil down.

Sammy Dutton was brought into the room of the school "nurse" one day. His throat was cut. We had heard of people dying with cut throats and we infants waited spellbound for him to die. Mother patched him up and sent him back to his class. We were disillusioned.

There was a staff of four at Calveley School. We had a Miss Wutherspoon from Darnhall Mill. She was very nice, but when she left and got a job nearer home, she became notorious as the woman who shut a child in a cupboard. There was a terrible outcry, although she wouldn't have hurt a fly.

Miss Yearsley joined the staff later. She was Mr. Yearsley's sister, and taught me in Standards I and II. I remember we did metrication with her, all the four rules length. They had some funny ideas on education in those days.

We unkindly called her "Goslin", but she was very nice. She had a habit of stamping her foot when she was cross and wanted us to be quiet. Then she would get a pin and poise it before us dropping it. "Who heard it drop," she would say and every hand would shoot up in a noisy clamour which defeated the object of the exercise.

Bert Murray was another teacher. He cycled each day from Crewe. He later died of tuberculosis. There was a Miss Morrey too, no relation.

The school day would start about ten to nine in a morning. My Father would pull down the rope and start tolling the bell in the belfry on the roof of the school, which not only urged on late comers, but gave the time to much of the parish where very few had timepieces. There was a striking clock on the Hall stable but the school bell was more audible.

A few minutes later, a boy would come in and pick up the flag and hoist it on the mast. The bell would stop tolling and my Father would go out into the lane and listen to the buzzers at Crewe works as a final check on the time. Having verified his gold hunter was correct, he would go and stand on the steps of the front porch and the classes would assemble in lines before him. He conducted a short deep breathing exercise after which, at a command, the front line would move schoolward each pupil saluting the flag.

The school assembled in the big room, a hymn was sung, and the Lord's Prayer recited, then each class would move off.

Registration followed. Absences were marked in red and recorded on a small chart kept in the register and collected once a week by Mr. Cain, the attendance officer.

When I was at Calveley School, prior to 1916, the infants still used slates. A monitor went round each session and with a small mop which she dipped in a jar put a blob of water in the centre of each side. With a little rag supplied by the "firm" we cleaned the slate and let it dry. If you wrote on it when wet it was hard to remove the marks. Sometimes a slate pencil would have a hard bit in it and this would make the pencil "skrike". These pencils were as long as ordinary pencils only much thinner and were of solid slate tapered at one end. When no one was looking and we had made a mistake we spat on the slate holding it close to our mouth for cover and then clean the slate by gripping the edge of our jacket sleeve and wiping the slate. No wonder childish diseases were rampant in those days.

Every school was supplied with a set of shapes, such as spheres, prisms, and cubes, which were most essential for a drawing lesson. The Victorians were terribly keen on this "important" side of the curriculum. I never saw these things used at Calveley but, year by year, they had to be entered in the stock list.

The school was heated by hot water pipes leading from a subterranean boiler. The coke had to be carried fifty yards, then down steep steps to the boiler. Then the clinker had to make the return journey. All this work was done for a pittance. I don't know why women always had this job, I suppose it was cheap labour. I couldn't see a man doing all that hard work today.

The school doctor called annually; there were no school dentists in those days.

There was a monthly visit by a nurse to Calveley School to examine children's hair for fleas. With a bad infestation the child's hair was cut off and her head smeared with yellow ointment.

I once saw a flea on my neighbour—we sat on five seater forms—her name was Marion Ravenscroft. Miss Yearsley our teacher buzzed over to her and pretended she could find nothing—Marion was Frank's daughter and later became Lady Embertson.

Of course, it was very hard for farmers who had their heads against cows during hand milking to be free of these vermin. I had my head combed weekly with a fine toothed comb and I can remember the crack as mother squashed any flea she found. We were a buggy lot in those days. Still we scratched and got on with it.

At Christmas each year the children were invited to the Hall for tea and entertainment. They assembled in classes and marched in twos from school to Hall. Round the church they went and into a gaily-decorated coach house. It was always a wonderful spread with crackers and paper hats. The tea was followed by entertainment—usually a conjuror. Then prizes were given to all, very often a book.

Before tea we stood and sang as grace *The Old Hundredth*:

All people that on earth do dwell ...

Whenever I hear that tune it always takes me back to those parties.

At breaking-up day in summer there were more presents. Very often these were jerseys. It was Mother's job to record the size for each child. The girls had one color and the boys the other—red or blue. Of course, these were donated by Mrs. de Knoop.

At Christmas the choir was taken to the pantomime at Chester with tea at Clemences. This too was paid for by our benefactors from the Hall. One time we were taken on a canal barge along the Shropshire Union to Wrenbury.

We decorated our classroom on Empire Day[131]. At this time of the year there was not much in the way of flowers and leaves so we made a base of moss and went into the woods for ferns. I forget what else we used. We knew what Empire Day was for.

At dinner times in summer the girls went into the field adjoining and made long daisy chains. The boys played "fag cards". This game was played with cigarette cards. The two players stood about six feet from a door or wall and holding a card between first and second finger threw it toward the wall. The idea was to get as close to the wall as possible. If you didn't throw hard enough the card didn't reach the wall. On the other hand if you threw too hard the card bounced back. The winner took all.

The most popular game with the boys I think was inker-tinker. About a dozen boys divided themselves into two teams. Some capitalist who had a penny tossed for order of procedure. One boy bent down grasping a bar of the fence and then a second boy bent and grasped him until the whole six were in a line of bent backs. The other six then ran and jumped onto the backs of the first six. The best jump-ers went first and tried to land on the back of the leading boy in order that there would be room for the rest of the team. The impact of landing was terrific and if the bending boys collapsed then they had to go down a second time. If on the other hand the leaping boys could not all get on or if they fell off then they went down. Sometimes there were as many as three boys on top of each other hanging on by their eyelids. The last boy, when he landed, had to shout, "Nerky one two three." The top team had to hang on until they heard this cry.

We had iron bowlers made at the local smithy. Mr. Welch was adept at giving exactly the right twist to the iron stick by which the bowler was propelled.

Tops were another great favourite. There were three kinds of tops. One was a solid squat type favoured by girls and which did not move very far, and then a long legged type with a flattish cap. The third kind was similar to the second but had a longer leg and would go great distances.

Tippy was another favourite game. It needed all the skill of a baseball player. A stick over an inch in diameter and about six inches long was sharpened at each end.

The tippy was placed in a ring drawn on the ground. The players then took a two foot stick, raised the tippy off the ground by giving it a light tap at one end, and then struck it hard. One had to hit the tippy centrally to make it go any dis-tance and that was the purpose, because the rest of the game resembled rounders with dens or bases.

It was the era of the acetylene cycle lamp. These, of course, contained calcium carbide which one bought at any garage in tins. We liked to get a syrup tin, put in a piece of carbide, spit on it, ram down the lid which had a small hole in it and then put a match to the hole. There was an explosion and the lid flew off.

Conkers was a seasonal game and so was making and playing with pop guns.

The pop gun was made out of a piece of elderberry wood, not too old and not too new. The pith was removed and then a rammer was made. This was a pared stick, reduced for part of its length so that it would go down the hole in the "eller", as we called it. One end of the stick was not reduced and served as a han-dle. The reduced portion which went into the barrel was cut so that it was half an inch shorter than the barrel. This was to prevent a soggy paper plug in the gun from being pushed out. This plug was an air-tight seal and was moistened from time to time.

Into the other end of the barrel we squeezed a wild rose hip. Then the plunger was pushed in at the paper plug end and the hip came flying out with a loud report and some unsuspecting mortal would think he had been stung on the back of the head.

We made whizzers too—little bits of board six inches long and an inch wide, with a hole at one end through which a length of string was put. The wood was then notched on the four edges for the whole length. When this was swung round rapidly it made a weird sound.

Balls were very rarely seen and I never saw a doll brought to school.

Dumb-bells were the only "drill" equipment, but usually we had nothing.

I remember when I was at Calveley School an itinerant film projectionist called and asked if he could give a show. My Father seemed satisfied and the projectionist duly collected his pennies and we all sat expectant to see the film. I had a magic lantern of my own but I had never seen a real film show. I remember the film was sepia coloured and, as the projectionist turned it by hand in a rather jerky manner, we saw a slave chased by dogs. When he was recaptured, this sweating, writhing creature was flogged to death. No comment.

The police came to Calveley School on several occasions. I remember one incident which upset us all. There was a footpath from the school to Cholmondeston, made especially for the kids, just as there was one at the bottom end of School Lane leading across fields to the bottom end of the Long Lane. Well, a lad from Cholmondeston took a girl from Barbridge along this footpath and, according to her story, she was interfered with—the usual torn clothing to prove it.

His mother took him to Nantwich one Saturday morning for the court's punishment to be inflicted. He was birched[132]. I remember that Saturday well, I was eight or nine at the time and had a friend with me. The birching was in our mind the whole day.

School-leaving age in those days was fourteen so this lad must have only been thirteen. There was no evidence but the girl's. As she came from Barbridge, the boaty village, I wouldn't have given her accusation too much credence.

I often went along the path to Cholmondeston with a lad in my class. His name was Frank Jones and he was a labourer's son. The path passed through a hunting hatch between Major's fields. This is a miniature five-barred gate used by the hounds. There was a savage bull in the far field. This was illegal because the footpath crossed it.

Young Jones resented having to go round this field each time he used the footpath and, once when I was with him, he climbed on the gate and, no doubt showing off to me, he belted the bull about the head with a stick. The bull did not like it at all and bellowed. I withdrew but Frank went on belting the animal.

Billy got his head down and charged the gate, he cracked a rail and got his horns entangled in the gate. On raising his head, he lifted the gate off its hinges with Frank on it, and careered madly across the field. I legged it for home—damn Frank.

♦　　　♦　　　♦

One summer while we were at the schoolhouse, George Alcock[133], and Gerald Newman[134] and his mother and father visited us. It was great fun having "brothers". It was always so lonely at the schoolhouse. Other children kept clear, partly because they shunned my Father, and partly because my Father forbade their visits.

We got into all kinds of mischief. I showed George how to make a sling and demonstrated it. George got well to the rear of this, but unfortunately the stone flew out backward and Gerald and I had to support a lame cousin all the way home. Another time we chased Gerald round the school with the old horse pistols. Poor Gerry was really frightened.

We all slept together in one bed.

I don't think Aunty Polly was very keen on our teasing Gerry. She took it out on George. I suppose that, as a guest, she could hardly tell me off.

The kitchen at the schoolhouse is L-shaped. It contained a dresser in the alcove on which we climbed in order to look into the infant room where the managers' meetings were held. We always looked to see if Cider was there.

The rest of the managers were quite normal.

At the side of the dresser was a plate rack consisting of four shelves and two sides which held the shelves. This plain piece of furniture was made by my Father after many weeks of journeying to woodwork classes at Chester. He was, I think, very proud of it.

Opposite the plate shelves was a salt box which hung on the wall. Into it crushed salt from the big block was put. The block was cut with a carving knife; it was very hard. Then the maid would roll the part cut off with the rolling pin.

The nails in the box eventually corroded and it fell to pieces when we were living at The Kennels.

Leading off the schoolhouse kitchen was a room under the stairs which we called "The Bogey Hole". It was L-shaped and in the far recess we stored potatoes, perhaps five hundredweight. Of course these sprouted and it was my job even as a small one to sprit[135] these. I think we had to do them twice.

There was the usual iron range in the kitchen that required frequent blackleading. The blacklead was bought in packets. It was solid and had to be softened with water and put on the grate with a brush. The grate was then polished with another brush. The fender had a bright grid-shaped top and this had to be cleaned with emery paper. The tap on the boiler at the side of the range was of brass and this had to be cleaned.

This boiler had to be filled by pouring water into it at the top.

At our next home, The Kennels, there were two somewhat similar ranges, but the boilers there had a ball tap at the side of the range and the boilers were filled automatically. I thought this great progress.

In the autumn, my Mother would make Christmas puddings and these were put in basins, over which a cloth was tied, and these were hung from nails near the ceiling. Mother also made a bottle or two of cough medicine tasting chiefly of black currant. It was very viscous.

There were a lot of home-made remedies in those days. Apart from the black currant brew that mother made for colds, there were other strange remedies. My Father made an eye wash from plantains.

An old woman who came to help Mother when I was young, said to Mother when I had a cold: "Give him *borats* (borax) and honey."

Mrs. Gibson came down one night. Her daughter Jinny had a bad chest and she wanted some goose-grease to rub her chest with. Father kept a dirty old jar of this stuff in which there was a paint brush with which he daubed my boots. Thick stinking stuff—each year he added new grease from the Christmas goose to the existing contents of the jar. I was awfully ashamed of going to the grammar school with boots covered in this muck.

I had a Norfolk jacket too which I hated. Mother had to buy me the cheapest clothes because of the pitiful allowance my Father gave her. All his money went in investments in gold shares. The postman brought a continuous supply of share offers from stockbrokers who had found a sucker.

All his investments in the Russian oil wells had of course gone. I don't know how much he had in these, but he made it an excuse always to say he had lost all his money there. I suppose it was as good an excuse as any.

When the schoolhouse was built, there was an open brook running along the hedge at the foot of the garden. On this, my Father's four oldest kids used to sail in an old tin bath when he was away at the Board of Guardians meetings at Nantwich.

The bath suffered and when I inherited it, the bottom was held in place chiefly by plasticine.

Father had the brook piped and this spoilt the fun. He put a cage of sticks over the top end to prevent debris being carried into the pipe, because the brook came through a culvert in the park wall which enclosed a small wood. Foxes came through this culvert too and raided our hens, taking them back through the culvert before we could act.

My Father was a good gardener. He had a poor fellow named Owen come once a year and dig the main part of the garden. He was like a skeleton and did tailoring for a living. He was known as Tailor Owen and we employed him from time to time. He walked all the way from Wettenhall with his spade to dig the garden and I think got a shilling for his pains. I'm sure the poor chap had never had a decent meal for years.

We had a load of muck dug into the garden each year and we grew some very good crops. My Father had the main body of the garden tilted so that our vegetable garden was higher on one side than the other.

I asked him why this was. He told me that he had done it so that the garden would face the sun. I have since realized that the slope faced west, which could not have been a great help.

Along the north edge he planted four apple trees; there were others at the far end. He had the trunks whitewashed each year. He had the bigger boys out of school to gather the fruit. The garden hedge was lined with half a dozen damson trees and a Victoria plum—a tree I could climb, to sit in the branches pinching the fruits from around me.

In the garden there were about six apple trees and a Siberian crab. Father sold penn'orths of fruit to the kids at school. Blackbirds were fond of the crabs and he set a rat trap baited with a big crab apple.

The starlings built under the eaves of the school and in the belfry. One Saturday morning I went round with the ladder and collected thirty eggs. I took them to mother to fry for my dinner. She broke them open carefully and duly fried them. I sat down in high glee. One mouthful and I was spitting for dear life. I never tasted anything so horrible.

I have only a vague recollection of my sister Dodie—she called herself this name—as she died in December 1908, just before my third birthday. She had so many friends over the school wall I could not tell "tother from which", as they say. With the school next door I never properly had her isolated; she was always in a mob of little girls, many of whom came home with her from school.

However, after she had gone there was a dearth of little girl visitors to the house. I know after Dodie's death, I became very lonely and no doubt it made me a bit of a lone dog.

I remember my Father taking me out of the back door one dark night. He pointed up to the star-lit sky and saying: "There's Dodie's star—can you see it?" I remember I had some difficulty in finding the star at which he was pointing.

We sometimes walked to Bunbury to put flowers on Dodie's grave. From the station, across Clay's field there was a footpath which hit the road again a few yards short of the church and this is the way we used to go.

Dodie was constantly in our conversation and thoughts in those days. I inherited many of her things. We each had a red cloak used as a dressing gown, and when I grew out of mine, I was given hers.

Her boots were there too—long uppers with hooks on. And her hair ribbons that she soaked each night and wrapped tightly round a jam jar so that in the morning they were flat and crisp. There was a needlework box, which Margaret still uses, and a book, *Peter Pan*, which were to be her Christmas presents. She never got them as she died on 21 December.

It was the day of the Calveley School Christmas party, when Mrs. de Knoop gave the kids an annual treat and a present. My Father had taken the children to the party. My Mother stayed at home with Dodie who had diphtheria.

Dodie died during the party and Mums sent up to Majors for them to get to the Hall and tell Father. Roland went with the message.

It must have been a terrible Christmas for Mother. She said that without her Faith in God, she would never have got through.

Of course it affected my life. Mums fiendishly protected me and this isn't good for a child. If we met anyone when out and they spoke to me, before I could answer she spoke for me, and things like that. I hated it.

People around were all so good to me. My very young days were very happy and the sudden jolt from these surroundings to Crewe Grammar School when I was nine was a devastating blow. I was very unhappy. When my cousin Charlie Alcock[136] joined up at 16, I seriously considered my chances of doing the same, but I was two years younger than him[137].

After my sister died, I slept in my parents' room on a small trundle bed in the corner by my Mother's side, so she could look down at me.

This bed was given to me by my grandfather Levi. It was very precious.

In her girlhood, Mother had decorated a screen that her father had made with Victorian Christmas cards and cutouts—just a two-fold frame, covered with black material. It was placed round the head of my bed because it was under the window and the house was fitted with iron framed windows which admitted more draught than light. This screen gave me endless pleasure as I lay awake looking at the cards. I dare not make the least sound and this helped to keep me quiet.

I knew the history of each card: "This one came from my Mother's cousins in New Zealand, and this one came from a little girl who was killed by one of the first cars, etc."

I wish I had this screen now, it would be worth something; so too would be the metal plate that Harry and Owen covered with stamps—dull, ugly, black and blue stamps. I thought it ugly.

Sometimes as a child I would be moved out of my rather dull north-facing room into the front bedroom which faced south toward the road. This room had a double bed with a canopy. Here I could lie and hear Majors' cows in the field across the road. Very often they were coughing.

Crewe was six miles out to the southeast and I could hear the railway work's buzzers. Sometimes when the wind was in the wrong direction it was difficult, but never impossible, to hear them. Other noises that reached me were the farm dogs barking, and when Majors killed a pig the squealing went on for quite a long time. They stabbed the pig and let it bleed to death believing that this made the bacon whiter.

I could hear the pigeons in the yew trees in the wood which separated us from the park. My own tumbler pigeons, which Mr. Dutton gave me, would coo and rush past the window, surging upward and then come tumbling down to earth again.

When we had visitors I had to leave this room and go back to the smaller north room over the kitchen, which had the jam shelf running its whole length and in which the wood beetles were busy chewing holes.

I could hear the rumble of the trains on the Chester to Crewe line. At one point the rumble would suddenly change. This was very noticeable. My Father said it was because there was change of geological stratum at that point. He could have been right. On foggy mornings I would hear the fog signals going off on the railway.

The postman would blow his little horn as he entered School Lane to warn all that this was his last port of call before returning to Tarporley and that they must get their letters posted.

From the schoolhouse we often saw the hounds. If the meet was at the Hall they started off either by going toward Jinks's farm or by going along the Park Lane whence they would cross the field opposite.

I often followed the hounds and remember once getting lost, I had wandered so far away from my own territory. It was late when I got home, tired out and mucked up to the eyes.

It was decided that I was to be confirmed[138] but this matter did not proceed smoothly. In the first place, the day I was to attend my first catechism class it was realized that I had scarlet fever, so that my confirmation had to be postponed for twelve months. When cured, I had to attend the vicarage once a week until I was word perfect in repeating the catechism.

Another hitch occurred when I got to Bunbury Church for presentation to the Bishop. I had been entered on the list as a girl and there was an argument about my qualification for such an august ceremony.

I was at last allowed to join the procession but walked up the aisle with a wench[139]. Father reckoned Stocky[140] had been at his tricks again. This little Taff[141] didn't like Father and, of course, I gave him plenty to fall out about.

Conditions at the schoolhouse were far from normal. Whether my Father was to be blamed or pitied was the question. His continual harassment of others in the house resulted in their creeping about and avoiding anything which would start a row. Such rows usually ended with my Father making out that he was the all-loving parent. This was his usual get out.

The strain on Mother must have been immense. Nowadays she would have left him but in those days divorce was not easy and the laws were all bent in favour of the man. She did consult her solicitor, Harold Moss, when she came to Northwich but he advised that she had little to gain.

One kept in the background and never dared to speak. Some days the only thing I said to my Father was: "Goodnight, Father," to which he might or might not have replied.

My Father represented the district on the Board of Guardians of the Nantwich Poor Law Union and so we got rid of him every Saturday. Saturday was the day in which a load was lifted from us, when we saw him mount his cycle, with the aid of his back step and three hops, and make his way to his beloved Board of Guardians.

It was then that little friends came creeping up to the house from all directions. There could be no fun when he was about, but on these Saturdays we really let rip. About three o'clock Mother would appear on the scene and set us about the job of tidying up and getting ready for the return of the lord and master. No sooner had he got his cycle clips off than he made a tour of inspection.

The effect this had on me showed early in life. I suppose the signs of strain on Mother's face, and the feeling of insecurity told on my nerves with the result I could not sleep at night and crept from my bed in a state of terror. The doctor jumped to the conclusion that living at the school was a strain and recommended a break, with life on a farm.

My Father went to see a neighbouring farmer named Ravenscroft and for some months, the happiest in my life, I went daily to spend the day with this family consisting of two bachelors and an unmarried sister, Mary, who kept house. James was the leading light. His brother John was not simple by any means but was less suited to lead. John was one of the nicest chaps I ever met. He was a little childish in his ways, I suppose. He went up the back stairs to his room—a location usually reserved for servants in these large farm houses, and had "pobs" for his dinner.

I was always with him. He took me to the stack yard to get some hay for the calves. We took nothing to carry it in and I wondered why, we climbed on the stack and threw a pile of hay down in a heap and then John said, "Follow me."

He sat down and slid over the side of the stack and landed on the pile below. I hesitated. I was scared but had an infinite trust in John. Eventually I did what he did and for a breathless moment felt myself flying through the air.

"Now we must tie this lot up," he said to his wide-eyed companion who could see no sign of a rope. John went to the stack and put his hands into it, then he pulled out a handful of hay at the same time twisting it. He went on pulling and twisting and I was surprised to see quite a long hay rope being formed. When this was long enough he tied up the bundle of hay with it and off we went.

James was a hard man. He told me with much delight how he had taken his old dog to the wood, dug a hole, tied the dog nearby and shot it. He was much amused by the dog not knowing what was going on till too late. I never liked James after this, and he could never get through to me.

He took me to the auction at Beeston and to the mill. It was the first time I had seen the working of a mill and I was very interested.

Butchers came to the farm to buy cattle. One came from Northwich and was told that my Mother came from that district. He and James tried hard to get me to reveal my Mother's maiden name but for some reason I resisted their probing.

Another visitor to the farm was the salt seller. He was an untidy looking specimen with a donkey cart. The poor little beast had to pull him and the load of lump salt laid out on the flat side-less cart. The salt lumps were, of course, those used in butter making. They were about eighteen inches long with a square section of about seven or eight inches. Mary usually took a lump off him. When a newcomer arrived at the farm there was always an inquiry as to who I was.

I sometimes went into the house to Mary. She always had a biscuit for me and a drink of milk. I remember going into a little garden shelter they had and finding a colourful leaflet with *Home Rule* on the outside. I was not interested in the political battles which must have been going on then.

In the house was a gramophone and there was one record I loved to hear. I supposed I connected it to the salt man. It was by Tom Foy[142], I don't know why I remember this name I have never met it since. The record was called *My Donkey and Me*. The opening lines were:

> *My donkey and me, my donkey and me,*
> *Two of us, oh what a pair!*

On the other side was a dialogue about an Irishman being taken to the dentist. His companion, also Irish, read out the name plate: "Mr. So and So, Dentist—Teeth extracted without pain" and, being Irish, he pronounced the last word in the usual Irish way (two syllables).

When the job was over, fully covered by the record, came the settling up. The dentist asked for his shilling but Mick resisted on the grounds that he said on the brass plate that he pulled teeth without "payin".

I thought it very funny and was never tired of hearing the record.

I had to feed the very young calves which in those days were all born at the same time and so there was a loose box full of them. I had to carry two buckets of skim milk larded with meal into the box.

They came rushing at me. I put one bucket in the corner behind me and with a short stick kept the others at bay letting one feed at a time and taking careful note of which calf had fed. But the rush was too much for my spindly legs with the result that I sat down in the bucket behind me.

In the orchard at the side of the house was a walnut tree. It was the first walnut tree I had come across and my liking for walnuts dates from that time.

There are no walnuts quite like freshly-gathered English nuts even if they do stain one's hands and create the impression one has been smoking cigarettes.

I collected the eggs for Mary. The hens lived in the space above the piggeries and there was so little head room no one else could collect the eggs that dropped during the night.

The hens also laid in an old ivy bush or tree which had grown rampant over an old disused earth closet in the garden. I too climbed into this. Many of the eggs I found at first were ancient but I kept track of later eggs.

One day John took me to a building near the house and I saw a sheep was shut up in there. John got the sheep's head under his arm and producing a knife from somewhere slit the sheep's throat. I never turned a hair. My John could do no wrong. I'd be squeamish today.

He skinned the animal and cut its head off. He gouged its eyes out and showed me how the lenses magnified. I am still surprised at how I reacted to all this. I treated it all quite casually and it wasn't till John mentioned, between his spoonfuls of pobs, that I never turned a hair, that I realized that I should have done so.

I helped muck out the shippons[143] and feed the cows and chain them up when they came in for milking. They were strange with me at first and all turned to give me an old-fashioned look when I went to chain them and later take a skip of bran and thirds to each.

There was a bull there too. He was a small Shorthorn, like the rest of the herd, but he was nasty and was kept in the shippon all day.

When cleaning out the shippon in which he was penned, I was warned not to go near him. They showed me a brush with a broken stail[144] which he had kicked when someone had tried to clean near him. I needed no warning to avoid bulls.

I went with the men to gather turnips which were later put in a clamp[145]. We each had a big knife like a *kukri*[146]. The experts pulled a turnip with their left hand cut out its roots with a slash, tossed a turnip over and another slash cut off the leaves, and almost in the same motion the turnip was on its way to the cart alongside. I improved as the day went on but had not the finesse to cut off the leaves and hurl the turnip into the cart all in one go.

The best fun we had was when we got to the bottom of a straw stack. These stacks are built on a bed of sticks and logs to keep the straw off the ground, and here the rats made their home.

Alongside the stack was a cart road from the yard to the fields and on the other side was the big pit across which an elm tree lay stretching across two-thirds of its width. I loved playing on this trunk. Another few yards and it would have made a bridge.

Well, with regard to the stack: all hands were mustered. Some workers removed the last layers of straw and others waited by the stack with sticks. Mrs. de Knoop's gamekeeper had been sent for and he came with his retriever and gun. As soon as the log base was exposed the rats began to bolt. Sticks swept through the air and first one rat lay dead and then another. Those that escaped took to the water with just their heads visible as they swam. The keeper finished these off.

One old chap who had come to see the fun hadn't bothered with *yorkers*. A rat dodging the sticks shot up his trouser leg. One of the other men struck at what he thought was a bulge in the old chap's trouser leg and swiped his calf.

Later in the pub that night, the old chap exposed his calf to all and sundry.

"A *rot* did that," he said showing the weal of the stick. It no doubt earned him a drink or two.

Across the road from the farm was a big sycamore tree called *The Pincushion*. It stood on the edge of a bank and the roots were exposed by the years of burrowing by rabbits. It no longer exists.

Under a flight of stone steps at the farm was a small room with a door, and in this a hen was sitting on a clutch of eggs. When the chicks arrived—I went each day with Mary to see what progress had been made—Mother gave me a small tin of chick feed each morning for them. It was the custom on Cheshire farms for the woman of the house to have the proceeds of the poultry section so this chick-rearing was Mary's province.

One day Wilfred de Knoop, on holiday from Eton, came shooting on the farm with the gamekeeper. I suppose the farm was part of the de Knoop estate.

People with only passing contact with my Father thought him a charming man, always so very considerate in asking about their welfare and offering his condolences when necessary. He was kindness itself—except at home. I don't think he realized this; he had some kind of mental kink.

Well, it was this pose that fooled the doctor and it wasn't long before I was requiring his help again. Perhaps if my most "anxious" Father had not been at the interview with the doctor, we might have gone some place but once more the doctor was bitten by the school bug and so I was withdrawn from school again and this time sent to another farm, the Moat House where a dear old couple, the Simcocks, made me very welcome.

They had a grown-up family. The youngest son, Arthur Simcock, was my mate on this occasion. At the back of the farm buildings he had a *tossing-the-stone* alley. It was an old Cheshire pastime. One held a big boulder, weighing six or seven pounds, on the palm of one hand and then heaved it as far as possible.

Arthur was a keen motorcyclist and had one of the outbuildings filled with spare parts of many bikes. This was in my line too.

There was a brass plate on a stump behind the farm marking the spot where a tree under which John Wesley preached had once stood.

I don't remember any outstanding events while I was at this farm, but I have since thought it strange that a Moat House was necessary less than half a mile from the Hall, that stronghold of knightly power.

Perhaps the Hall was occupied by lesser men when the Moat House was built, but Calveley Hall was ringed with woods and in these woods was an almost continuous line of yew trees. One limb of nearly every tree was carefully sawn off horizontally; one could still see the saw marks.

This must have been the arsenal of the Cheshire archers, hence I cannot accept the idea that the inhabitants of the Hall were not military-minded when the Moat House was built.

As in the case of many such houses, only part of the moat now exists. This is at the front of the house and enhances the lawn.

During the First World War, the Simcocks held a party to raise funds for some good cause. Bessie Ravenscroft and Roland Yearsley were there. I was the only child and that was because we had no baby sitter. I knew nearly everyone there and the men gave me their cigarette cards—going to a party, one always stocked up with a new packet of cigarettes and I had never had such a windfall.

Well Bessie and Roly were in love, but Roly's prospects were in cold storage. He could have no farm until Albert Major, his uncle, was out of the way and Albert, or Urchin as we called him, was still in his fifties, so the love game proceeded very slowly. Even I could see Bessie was in love, she never took her eyes off Roly.

Well Bessie is a widow today, with her son dead—a mucked-up appendix operation. Her daughter married and inherited the old farm.

Back to the party: they played many games, and then they played the game where one person went out of the room and on coming back had to find in what way the room had changed since his or her departure.

Roly went out of the room and someone said: "Geoffrey, you give your cigarette cards to Bessie," who was near me. I handed them over.

Whether Roly guessed, I don't remember, but what I do remember is that in the anguish of love Bessie had torn my cards in two. She apologized and blushed, then everyone laughed, all knowing the strain she was under. I remember we sang, *My Little Grey Home in the West.*

I was at Simcocks all through harvest and did my whack at the horse's head. I had to take the cart between two lines of hay cocks and when the first four cocks were on the cart I had to shout: "Howd-ya!" in true Cheshire style, and lead the cart on to the centre of the next four cocks. The cry was, of course, to warn the stacker on the cart to hold fast while I led the horses forward.

This is how they made hay in Cheshire in those days:

The first men in the field were men with scythes who went round the perimeter and cut the headland[147]. The horses walked outside the mowing machine and so needed this space. For transport along the road, the cutter bar of the mower was raised vertically. On the field it was dropped and its small, outer wheel kept it an inch or two above ground level. The actual blade slid into its case and was hooked onto the drive which caused it to oscillate. After some use the knife was withdrawn and the blade sharpened or replaced. The blade or knife consisted of a backbone with triangular teeth riveted on to it. A steel table with folding legs on to which the blade was clamped for sharpening was taken to the field. The blade projected over the edge of the narrow table and a file was used to sharpen each tooth. Often one man would sharpen a spare blade while the other was being used, so that there was no delay. The field was cut and the hay lay in swaths.

Next came the swath turner or similar machine which tossed the hay into the air to aid drying. If it rained before it was taken in, the hay was often tossed again.

When the hay was dry, along came the horse rake with long curved tines. Every seventy yards or thereabouts the man riding on the machine raised the tines and dumped the accumulated hay into a pile, then moved on to collect another rake-full. When he had finished, there were long lines of hay extending across the field.

Now the pikels came into their own. A pikel has two tines. There are various sizes of them according to their use. Men used them to pile the hay into cocks, bearing in mind that a cart would come down the rows, and so enough room was left for the cart. And the cocks were arranged so that there would be a cock on each side of the cart to avoid unnecessary stopping.

The medium sized pikels were used to load the cart in the early stages but as the load grew higher, some long handled pikels would be available.

The man on the cart was an expert who built up the walls of the load first and trod it firm, afterward filling in the centre. The load had to be built very carefully as the cart had to cross rough ground and often had a mile to go. The load when completed was tied in place with two ropes coiled and kept on hooks at the rear of the cart.

The man on top then slipped down a rope. If the journey to the farm was difficult, a chain horse was added. Usually a farmer used two carts so that no time was wasted.

Sometimes the hay would be stacked in the field and thatched with straw. The straw was spread out on the shaped stack and pegged in place with hooked stakes to which binder twine was attached. Some men were very clever at this; no doubt an art handed down for generations.

Where possible, the hay was taken back to the farm and pitched through openings in the upper wall into the space above the shippons. This is often called the hay loft by the present generation, but when I was a lad it was called the baulks. A baulk is a heavy beam which supported the roof timbers and I suppose on these a floor of sorts was laid and became a storage place. This place was truly the baulks, but the name was retained for the more refined building. The round hole in the walls no doubt had a name but I cannot recall it.

Between the rows of stalls for the cows was a narrow passage called a bing and in the ceiling of this place was a big hole fitted with a ladder. The hay from the baulk was dropped through this hole, and on the lower level, a man with a short-handled pikel tossed it from the bing into the feeding troughs in the bing walls which the cows in the shippons faced.

A short handled pikel was useful for this job as there was not too much room and there was a danger of sticking the tines into a cow.

But often an ordinary pikel was used or one cut short. Any hay left when the baulks were filled was stacked in the stack yard. A space was left between the stacks in case wet hay became heated after stacking and caught fire, which it occasionally did. A wise farmer went round his stacks for some days after stacking and pushed his hand in at various places to feel if they were heating up, in which case the stack was quickly pulled down.

The carts I mentioned had frames fitted to the top of them to extend their carrying capacity. These frames are called *cratches*—strongly made of ash and fitted into metal loops on the cart.

Other terms which have practically died out in Cheshire are:

Group:	a channel in the shippon to receive the cow droppings;
Bothy:	a room, often upstairs in some outbuilding, used as living quarters for a labourer;
Turnel:	a vat made like a barrel with upright staves about a foot high. The whole being oval about five feet long and three feet wide. Here a pig's carcass was scraped with the help of boiling water to remove the hairs and then salt was added and rubbed into the flesh for a period of ten to fourteen days to cure it. We shall never taste bacon like that again.

Farming methods were different too. The farm cart disappeared when the horse went. The carts with their six foot diameter wheels had been used for everything. The farmer also had a lorry, useful for sacks, and a shandry for livestock.

My brother-in-law, John Wilson, did carting the Irish way, of course. A special low cart was used with a tail-board dragging on the ground. There was a windlass under the cart at the front. The cart was backed up to a cock (the Irish cocks were the size of a young stack), the chain was put around the cock about a foot from the ground, and then hooked on to the end of the windlass. This machine was then turned by a handle, and slowly the cock slid on to the cart. One man could do the job above.

It takes an Irishman for "controivin".

What is called "carting" in Cheshire, is called "lugging" in Shropshire.

I must have stayed on at the Moat House until Christmas because I remember being taken to school to watch the children get their presents from the Hall—jerseys, red or blue according to what sex the child was.

Well after the presents, Father gave out the bags of sweets. I sat and watched. Then when he had finished this he looked round and said, "Come out anyone who has not had one."

I was eight at the time and timidly crept out. My Father turned on me and before all the school vented his wrath on me. I was taken by surprise and crept back. He spoilt what had been a very pleasant occasion, to see so many of my friends smiling with happiness.

Not long after I left Simcocks, Ida Simcock was killed. She went out cycling with a friend. They reached the Highwayside at the foot of their road.

A car was coming and the other girl crossed the road. Ida hesitated and then started to cross. The car hit her. The driver was a man named Williamson, from Wardle Hall.

Cars in those days would do sixty and yet had only two wheel brakes. My first car had two wheel brakes and I know they were not very satisfactory. The second-hand sales ads used to have descriptions of the cars followed by the letters t.w.b. or f.w.b. as the case may be.

Horse-drawn passenger vehicles had to be licensed in those days. Simcocks had bought a new trap and they had not had it two days before the cop heard about it and hovered, unknown to them, near their gate until the trap came out. They were caught and had to pay up.

The old woman who worked at Simcocks called the cop a *to-ad*, making two syllables of the word. There was venom in her face too.

Well the farm has changed hands now and all the Simcocks are dispersed. The Ravenscrofts too have gone.

I call the pre-war years the Jingo Years because in my nonage I was wont to warble, together with other immature-voiced lambs, the topical song[148]:

We don't want to fight,
But by jingo if we do,
We've got the ships,
We've got the men,
And got the money too.

I have forgotten the rest of this daring threat. It no doubt gave us great comfort. The song was popular during the South African War, like *Good-bye, Dolly Grey*. It gave comfort when times were bad and, in the end, gave encouragement to a world which was being upset by the Kaiser, who was probing for an opening to disrupt the peace.

We had a tea caddy on the high, kitchen mantelpiece. It was square and bore Queen Victoria's portrait on the lid. On each of its four sides it had a general, namely White, Buller, Kitchener and, my favourite, Roberts[149].

My Mother told me his son had been killed by the Boers. He got the Victoria Cross—the only case where a father and son won this award[150].

Buller, commander-in-chief at the outset, was accused of making a mess of his part in the South African War and I think he was sent home in disgrace.

Mother told me Dodie used to sing another popular song beginning:

Cheer up, Buller my lad,
Don't say die
We all know it wasn't your fault.

I think he had been short of supplies and the politicians responsible made a scapegoat of him. They never change, these politicians[151].

One evening, sometime before 1914, I heard strange shouting coming from over the park wall. I had never heard anything like it before. I listened, and heard galloping horses. I crept through the hedge and made for the park wall. It was some eight feet high but I was an adept at climbing it. I hid on the ivy-covered top, my heart pounding with the effort and also with the sight of what lay before me. My toy soldiers had come to life.

There were about a dozen lancers on horses, charging, wheeling, tent pegging, stopping, all at the command of one rider. I knew his voice, it was Jersey de

Knoop, the Squire. They were in dress uniforms—blue and red—and looked very smart.

This was one more case where the people were ahead of the government in their appreciation of the danger ahead. I was witnessing History—the last remnant of Knight Service, a form of land tenure begun by the Normans.

The farmers on the Calveley estate, some half dozen farms, held their tenure on the understanding that they contributed a son and horse for the local squadron of the Cheshire Yeomanry. Jersey added his household staff to make up the numbers.

Another example of how the South African wars lingered on in people's mind was in the toys given to children. I had a box of Royal Welsh Fusiliers complete with the Nanny mascot and a similar size box of Zulus with spears and shields. I think it must have been Christmas 1908 or 1909—I know it was after Dodie died and I was brought into my parent's room, being weakly and the sole survivor of the family.

Well, on this Christmas morning I awoke early; my eye caught sight of something just above my head. It was an evil-looking thing—a horrible face with flaring hair—looking down at me. My hand touched the hair and I was terrified. I dived for cover under the bedclothes.

I daren't cry out; my Father made such a scene if he was wakened and Mother was always panic-stricken to silence me. I understood. I think children understand more than we give them credit for.

I must have gone to sleep again. I awoke in daylight, the evil thing was still there. A face surrounded by long wafting locks set in motion by the draught from the bedclothes. Well the "thing" was a hussar's red helmet, the face was a perforated silver paper badge covering the front panel and very much resembling the symmetry of a face. The hair was the flaxen plume attached to the wooden knob at the top. There was a sword too.

I suppose my Mother put it there so that I should see it when I awoke on Christmas morning. The trouble was I saw it rather early, before it was properly light.

My night fears were soon over and I was parading the house in my new helmet with a sword at my side. I played with that helmet for a very long time.

It's strange how great fear is more lasting in one's memory than anything else.

I also had a box of wooden bricks with which to make a castle and a wooden cannon which fired marbles, or what you will.

Over my Father's bed head hung a bag that I was forbidden to touch, as an animal in it would bite me. I later found out it contained a pin-fire revolver.

◆   ◆   ◆

Perhaps one of the greatest changes that have taken place in this country is in the social services and pensions. In my youth, old people got something from the state, and the amount was increased by Lloyd George[152]. Many families, rich and poor, had a widowed mother or father living with them. Children looked after their parents in those days. The very "down and out" went to the workhouse.

We had a lot of Irish labourers living on the farms. One I knew well and was very fond of, was called Mick. He had two big corn bins as his home at the Ravenscroft farm. The bothy was divided up into these bins, each about four feet by six feet. One, filled with straw, he slept in and he kept his possessions in another.

I remember one sad day when he had got too old for work and too poor to go home to Ireland. James Ravenscroft put him in the trap and drove him to Nantwich workhouse. I was seven or eight at the time and was very upset. He sat there by the farmer all hunched up and he never looked back. The place was not the same without Mick.

My Father was the representative for Calveley on the old Poor Law Board of Guardians. The workhouse—the Barony[153]—came under their jurisdiction. One day, as a treat for Mother and me, he took us to visit the place.

I was very small at the time but the visit made a great impression on me. The workhouse master, Mr. Mathias[154], dropped whatever he was doing and showed us all over the place. As we crossed the yard I saw a gang of oldish men sawing and chopping sleepers into fire sticks. These were wired into the bundles that the two men with a handcart delivered to all the schools in the Nantwich area, including Calveley.

Some men were sawing up the old railway sleepers on a horse. Others with big axes split these logs into amenable sized pieces and others, sitting down, took over the job of reducing these pieces to sticks, using hatchets.

We then went inside, down a spotless tiled corridor, and at the end I saw a sight that upset me and made me hide behind my parents. A half-open doorway at the end of the corridor suddenly became filled with the grinning faces of women lunatics, mostly mongols, I fancy.

I suppose they saw so few strangers they were having a good look at us. They were all dressed the same. They were very clean, everything in the place was spotless. But the faces of these women still haunt me; they were imbeciles.

In another room, where the more violent were put, we were shown the padded walls and a straightjacket. There were straps on the wall. I was really getting upset by this time.

We left the lunatic wing and entered a ward full of bedfast women—the women's hospital. It had long lines of beds down each side. There was one woman the master pointed out to us, lying on a water-bed, her face was yellow and she was never still, now and again crying out in pain. I believe she had cancer. She stopped her pitiful groaning and half-raised herself on one arm to study us. I remember she looked at me in a most embarrassing way. I was glad to get out of the place.

I saw no children. I suppose they were at school, but we were shown the long wall cupboards in which their blue uniform dresses hung. They reminded me of the cupboards in the vestry at Calveley Church which housed our choir cassocks.

Before we left, the master took us round the large vegetable garden which must have contributed in no small measure to the supply of vegetables for the institution. We went into a small greenhouse and, as far as I can remember, the only things here were cacti. Mr. Mathias gave me a cactus in a pot which I had for many years, but it never grew any bigger.

I suppose we went round the men's quarters, but I don't remember a thing about this. I was most impressed by that poor woman on the water bed, and those mad grinning faces.

I nearly forgot to mention the tramps. Children today would not know anything about these unwashed, hirsute humans that crawled like beetles along our roads with their sticks and bundles.

We often had them at the schoolhouse. If my Father saw them they were sent off in no uncertain manner. My Mother would usually give them a hunk of bread and cheese. Sometimes if they were sent packing, my Mother would give me the bread and cheese and I would slip out through the playground and give it to them in the road.

I never liked this job. Firstly, I was frightened of my Father catching me in the act, and secondly, I was scared of tramps. They had a bad name. These tramps could get a night's sleep and supper at the workhouse, but in return they had to do a stint of work to pay for it.

The tramps were then free to go, and made their way toward the next workhouse. They could put on an act. One might come to the door, whining, a poor, crippled old man, hardly able to drag his feet along. Put a dog after him, and a tramp could compete with anyone in the 220 yards.

I remember once going to Parsonage, my dentist. In the next room, his assistant was dealing with the workhouse children. I could hear the merciless *thud thud* of the foot treadle driving the drill, and the wails of the kids.

It upset me terribly, especially as Parsonage was going to fill my two front teeth. He took the nerve out first by probing in the gum with tweezers. He did one tooth one week, and next Saturday I had to come back for the next one to be done. I got as far as the door and then I had other ideas and my Mother and the nurse chased me down the street. It must have looked funny.

I went to Crewe Grammar School in 1916[155]. From the very start I hated it. I was in poor health, as my recent stay on the farms indicated. It was September when I began that long trudge of two miles or more to the station. When I came to the footpath across the fields I had to feel my way with my foot in the gully at the side of the path in order to keep in the right direction. Later, Mother bought me a bike, but the journey by road was even longer. I had to catch an early train, and there was a mile walk at the other end. In winter, it was still dark when I started, and night coming home.

I followed the road to Leyston and then over a style to the station, crossing fields by muddy footpaths. One foggy morning, I was groping my way along and tumbled over a beast lying on the path. It quickly rose as I toppled over it. I found myself face to face with Ravenscroft's bull.

I ran and ran and lost the path. I came to a fence and rapidly climbed it and tore my stocking. When I got to school, I told the caretaker what had happened and he took me to his wife—their house was in the school yard. She roughly hooked the rip together for me and bathed my injured leg. I didn't realize I was hurt until she found wet blood on the stocking.

Of course it was against the law to put bulls in fields where there was a footpath. This bull was notoriously nasty.

While we are on the subject of bulls I must tell you about the Jersey bull at the Hall. Now this was a real nasty customer, as several had found out, and he was paraded along the lanes with a man on each side of him with a pole and snaffle attached to his nose ring. He was that dangerous.

Well, one firework night[156] I took a box of fireworks I had bought in Crewe on my way home, and walked across the park to Johnnie Duncan's. His father would not allow us to let them off because of the danger to the haystacks. However, he was going out, and when he had gone we went well away from the stacks and let them off at the far extremity of the farm buildings where the empty shippons were, and the piggeries.

We came to the last firework, called a Cannon. These made a hell of a bang and the short stubby cylindrical case would be ripped open. We tried to stand it on the horse mill—the driving pillar with a bevel wheel at the base which drives a horizontal shaft which enters the buildings and drives the mangel cutter. But it wouldn't stand on this, nor on the pigsty wall.

Then I spotted the big finger hole in the bull-cote door. By lifting the latch a little, we were able to anchor the Cannon nicely. We lit it and stepped well back. With so much mauling the wick had got damp and we were about to give up when the thing exploded.

The bull had been interested in this, and had his head down sniffing at it. When it exploded it blew the latch up and I suppose the bull reared and his head hit the door at the critical moment. There he stood in the open doorway, not at all pleased with the events of the evening.

Johnnie was standing by the pig-cotes. I was on the other side of the bull-cote door and could not get to him.

The bull came at me. I turned and fled up one of the planks which are used by the barrow when the shippons are being mucked out. The plank came to an end on the midden and there was still six or more feet of muck beyond. The bull was following me and I was trapped. On he came, this lovely creature, worth hundreds, and which had a shampoo every day.

He was now up to his belly in muck and still coming on. Johnnie ran in the bull-cote and got the pole but could not get at the bull's ring. On he came, now half buried in muck. I looked back to see if there was any way of making a jump from the end of the plank but the fading light made this rather dicey. John poked with the pole and the bull turned his head away from me. I dashed down the plank, leaped over the angry head and joined John who was in a great state. If his father came and saw the bull in this condition we boys would be for it, and if the de Knoops came everyone would be for it.

We desperately struggled to get the snaffle in the bull's nose ring and at last succeeded.

Then we pulled and pulled and the old bull came out of the muck smothered in the stuff.

I held the pole. Johnnie fetched the hose with which the cote was washed out every day and he sprayed the creature on all sides till he was clean. Then we led him back to the cote, released him, threw the pole into the corner and cleared off. Nothing came of the affair, we were never discovered. By that time I was a hundred per cent believer in artificial insemination.

I had no more encounters with bulls that I can think of but I met my doom with an old sow which escaped on Nantwich Road in Crewe. I had a new mack on at the time which buttoned well down below the knees. This pig bolted in my direction and with legs as wide as I could get them I blocked her path. She went right through my legs lifted me in the air and left me sprawling on the pavement much to the amusement of all.

Majors turned their pigs loose in the autumn and they roamed the lanes after nuts and acorns. They used to buy tons of slack coal for the pigs to eat and when I fetched the milk from their farm there were always a few grunching away at this stuff.

Majors had a new workman. I didn't like the looks of him. Later he left, and soon afterward he was hanged for murdering a young girl in the fields Wettenhall way. I think his name was Price.

When I fetched the milk, I often got squirted with milk as I passed the shippons. When a cow had been milked the milker would empty his or her bucket into a big bucket standing outside the shippon door. Half a dozen cats would stand on their hind legs and drink out of these buckets when they were full. When two buckets were filled, someone put on the yokes and carried the two buckets into the dairy.

During the First World War the train service was often irregular, with the train waiting in a siding for more important trains to pass. I remember once at Worleston, the one stop on the journey between Calveley and Crewe, we went into a siding and the New Zealand troops on board got out after a while and wandered into the fields. We did get to school eventually, but I don't think the teacher believed our unlikely excuse for being late.

Coming home once, we had a drunken sailor in our carriage and he was up and down all the time threatening everyone. He sat next to me and when I reached Calveley and wanted to get out, I found he was sitting on my coat tails and he cursed me when I struggled to get free.

Another chap, an Australian, showed me a glass bottle filled with red and white things which he told me were diamonds. We were alone in the carriage. I supposed he fooled people with them. I knew there were no red diamonds, but I agreed with all he said. He had got the patter off very well.

At school the staff changed week by week; that didn't help me master new subjects. Toward the end of the war, some teachers were very poor specimens. Once a Jew came to teach us Science. He came for one day and then disappeared. Perhaps he disliked the place as much as I did. The headmaster, a 6 foot 4 inch tall Scot named McCurtain, went round the school shouting: "Where's that bloody Jew?" He never found him.

You could call me a mixed-up kid, and neither parent could help me. I suppose that as I was weakly, the long journey to school got on top of me. I had wartime flu and scarlet fever in succession—this was when we had moved to The Kennels and I missed practically a whole year. I was glad when the day came when I could leave school.

I was always leaving things in the train I took to school. Owen gave me a Burberry of which I was very proud. I left it in the train and went regularly to the station to see if it had turned up. At last the porter said to me, there's no mac here but there's this coat. He handed me my overcoat which I had never missed.

During my first few months at Crewe I made my way from school to Crewe station[157] on my own. Now the Chester train on which I traveled to Calveley was in two parts. The front portion was an express that went out a few minutes before the slow train behind.

On one occasion, I got in the wrong part and went hurtling through Calveley. I tried to wave to anybody who might be on the platform but all had gone to earth. I had a very long wait on Chester station before I was put on a train back. In the meantime, Mother had been going crackers. She had gone to the school, to the station-master at Crewe, and to Mrs. de Knoop. No one had seen me.

We had fourteen minutes to get out of class and get to the train at night. Sometimes we only just made it. One of our party was a cripple but it was surprising how he could get along by holding on to someone's satchel strap. Mine was always breaking.

On the way we would see the lamplighters lighting the gas street lamps. They rode on a bike, pulled up an instant at the post, and poked their torch stick into the lamp, pulled the tap down and 'bob's your uncle!', they were off to the next post.

In the morning, we sometimes saw the knocker-upper[158]. He was grotesque. A swollen, impassive, red faced man with large hands like hams that hung at his side. He would put his back to the door and swing his hands like pendulums against the door. I don't know what was the matter with him. Someone suggested he had been exposed to red hot metal in the works.

One of the most memorable events in my school life occurred when I was in one of the lower forms. A chap named Hutton, son of a Nantwich schoolmaster and brother to a lad who later became a great friend of mine, won a Distinguished Conduct Medal[159] on the Western Front. As a result we were given a half-day holiday. I suppose if the award had been won by a Scot we should have had the whole day.

Well there was some excitement in the school and, as a result, someone fell foul of McCurtain and he cancelled the holiday—or so he thought. About six of us decided otherwise—damn the headmaster. We went off to the station, for the old Crewe station was a lovely place to play, especially hide and seek.

Tearing about the station, we attracted the notice of Travers, the station master who had been approached when I got lost. Now Travers had a son at school and knew there was no holiday, so he phoned McCurtain, who came to round up the truants.

I had found a lovely place to hide. The Wyman's bookstall was built over the track just behind the buffers, so there was a space under the stall filled with old cardboard boxes, book covers, paper, etc. One could move from one end to the other and spy down two platforms.

They could not find me.

After a while, I started to get bored. No one came into sight to search and I could not understand it. At last I crept out and a woman porter saw me. She tipped me off that the headmaster was after my blood. I peered round a corner she indicated and there was Mac his gown flying, his 6 foot 4 inches towering above four or five small boys.

A porter said: "Here's another of them."

I fled. I felt like Peter at cock-crow. I hid in a toilet till train time and then mixed with other boys and got home. I got Mother to write me a note of absence and took it next day. I heard Mac had yanked the others back to school in a taxi.

Geoff Hutton, the brother of the soldier I mentioned, was playing cricket with us on another occasion. He was fooling about and was fielding mid off. A skied ball came toward him and he pranced toward it pretending to head it. He did not estimate the speed at which a cricket ball moves and really did head it. I thought he was dead.

At the beginning of the war I was given a blue Persian kitten. With pheasant hatcheries in the park, the keepers—they had not been called up then—shot all trespassing cats, and mine disappeared like many others.

Another incident I remember was just after the war. I took a friend of mine to the station at Crewe. His train to Alsager went off before mine, so I saw him off. He later became head of Freckleton school in Lancashire—the one on which an American bomber crashed many years later, killing the kids[160].

As the war was over, the railway company had cleaned all the blue paint off the windows, which had been put there in compliance with the Defence of the Realm Act.

Being short-sighted, Billy hadn't noticed this. He got into his carriage and, thinking the window was down, crashed his head through the window and showered me with glass. He bore the mark of this accident for a long time.

Once during the war, while waiting for my train, I heard the horrible screech of bagpipes and went to investigate. A hospital train[161] had just come in. Parading up and down the platform alongside was a little Scots fellow making a row far beyond his stature.

I was told that he was the as-yet-unknown Harry Lauder[162].

The guts had been ripped out of the coaches and two shelves, one above the other, ran round them. On these the wounded were lying. One or two were on their feet and came down onto the platform. I was given a bundle of letters to post by one of them and I dashed off at full speed as I didn't wish to miss any of this excitement.

The train soon pulled out and I felt a trickle down my face, somehow the wild music, the wounded and their going home, caught me on a soft spot. I crept away from the other lads to wipe my eyes.

When the war was over, women porters disappeared. There were two-and-a-half million men out of work. Motor trucks appeared on Crewe station. These were electric-powered and would carry a load themselves and also tow several other trucks like a small train. The batteries were under the truck floor and the driver stood on two footplates which folded up when out of use. There was a "dead man's" lever which started the truck when it was pulled down. When released, it flew up and switched off the electrics.

A new type of engine was built at Crewe after the war—the first post-war engine from the works. It was called "The Patriot" and it was some time before we discovered it and then we all mobbed round it taking in every detail. I think it was a 4-6-0 superheater.

FIRST WORLD WAR

The First World War played a great part in my life as it did in the lives of many others. The first I knew of the war was when my Mother called upstairs to me one morning in order to get me out of bed. I was never a good getter-upper as a child.

"Get up," she called. "There's a war on".

When I came down for my pobs (bread and milk), she whispered, "Your Father's very worried."

He was a great student of history and politics and was very well-informed on such matters. Farmers, often in devious ways, managed to encounter him when matters of importance were in the air to get his opinion.

They sought his opinion about this matter and, in spite of the cry, "It will be over by Christmas", they didn't like what my Father told them.

By 1913 people were uneasy about the activities of the Kaiser and his efforts at starting trouble in Europe and Africa. People knew that war was probable. All but the politicians saw the danger signs. That astute little Welshman, Lord Roberts, was one of the foremost in pressing the government to get off its backside and rearm as quickly as possible. It was no good. Politicians then had as much pre-science as they have today.

Well, remembering the Crimea, some people acted, and a call went out for Voluntary Aid Detachments. These were formed by the Red Cross and St. John of Jerusalem organizations. Those women who volunteered were trained as nurses. A VAD unit was formed at Bunbury under a Dr. Archer. My Mother, always an enthusiast who threw herself wholeheartedly into any job she was engaged in, joined the British Red Cross Society[163].

The nurses were all amateurs—farmers' daughters, housewives, and so on, who began training. Dr. Archer took these classes, so he knew what the women could do. The women volunteers made their way to Bunbury from all directions. My Mother went there on her cycle and that is how the acetylene lamp came to be purchased. We were all very proud of it.

Later, during the war, when there were Zeppelin raids[164], one had to tie a handkerchief over the lens to subdue the light.

We had an oil lamp with a one inch wick but this was illegal—far too bright. I don't know where that lamp went to.

Well, Mother rode her bike to the Red Cross training sessions. It was given to her by her father, like her sewing machine. She couldn't produce much that had been given to her by her husband except an engagement ring of glass stones—so Mr. Rutter, a Northwich jeweller, told her when we came to live at Northwich.

I think there were two permanent, trained nurses seconded to the Bunbury VAD hospital.

Naylor from Beeston Towers, one of the authors of the book *From John o' Groats to Land's End*[165], became an orderly, and this is how my Mother was given a copy of his book. She was often on duty with him.

Her stint of duty had to be worked in with caring for her four-roomed house and small son, and teaching all day in the village school at Calveley.

Later Mrs. Evelyn de Knoop became interested in this project. We now know why, because when war came she made a small Red Cross hospital at Calveley Hall at her own expense.

She encouraged other women from Calveley to join in the effort. The Miss Stockdales, the vicar's daughters, fell into line. Enough joined to fill her big Daimler which she offered, together with the under-chauffeur, Charlie Griffiths, to take them to the classes.

I remember the first time they went to class in the Daimler, Charlie played a trick on them, rushing down the railway bank toward Bunbury Locks, where there is a hump-back. This hump threw the car full of nurses off their seats all in a huddle.

"Keep your seats ladies," laughed the mischievous Charlie. During the war, Charlie Griffiths, who had become head chauffeur, devoted any spare time he had to turning shell cases. Shells were very near Major de Knoop's heart.

When war came, I was often used as a dummy for the nurses to practice bandaging on. It was most essential that this was done properly, just as it was essential for the army doctors to wear spurs. How could one perform an operation without spurs? Better to be without scalpels. Spurs went out of fashion only when the doctors injured themselves trying to walk downstairs.

And it was essential to have bandages perfect—military precision. They went round a limb and then a complete turn and these twists had to be perfectly in line. The leg bandages had to be put on with the preciseness of puttees and, by jingo, these had to be right or the sergeant major was onto the poor miscreant.

Cavalry regiments, artillery, and the like, put their puttees on upside down. Something to do with riding causing a normally-wound puttee to unwind.

There were of course no cavalry regiments as such. They just retained the names. The only cavalry used in the Western Front were the German Uhlans who only existed for a short time. No doubt the horses were eaten.

There was a story and, I remember, a picture in *The Illustrated London News* which Mrs. de Knoop sent to us each week, to the effect that the war dead were being processed to obtain the fats that the Germans were so short of. Maybe it was true maybe just another *Angels of Mons*[166]. I saw an impression of that too.

I think it should be put on record that an order was issued by the War Office at the outbreak of war that anaesthetics were only to be the privilege of officers. Operations on Other Ranks were to be done without such aids. They made the rule, but found that the medical profession refused point blank to carry it out and the rule was withdrawn. This always makes my blood boil and I think it should be put on record who these swine were. I suppose the swine who originated this idea finished up with a row of medals and a blighty job.

When war came, the parish hall at Bunbury became a hospital for the boys in blue[167]. The "swaddies" had come straight from the trenches, been patched up at the field dressing station behind the lines, and then carried by ambulance, boat or train to hospitals all over the country. Attempts were made to confine the more severely wounded to the big hospitals with professional staff but when big battles like the Marne, Ypres, and the Somme were on, the men came pouring out of the ambulances in all kinds of condition.

I've seen the wounded coming along the Highwayside at Calveley in Ford vans, canvas covered, about twenty yards apart, stacking up for miles, each with two men—they came two by two. The wounded that arrived at Bunbury may not have been the most seriously hurt but they suffered the disadvantage of having made a long journey with little or no attention.

Nothing had been done to their wounds perhaps for two or three days and the bandages were buried in their flesh and blood. Often the only treatment they had received, was a field dressing put on their wounds in France, then little or nothing done until they got to Bunbury.

The first job was to get the caked, trench mud off the men, and once the wounds were exposed, torn and clotted arteries had to be opened. This was done with a syringe and boiling water, without anaesthetic. The amateur nurses, responsible for holding the patients down, reeled over one after another, seeing the agony this process caused, with men screaming and writhing on the bed.

On one job several nurses fainted, but my Mother took her turn and saw the job through. "Sister Gore, you're a brick," Dr. Archer said to her afterward.

Thereafter he would ask, "Where is Sister Gore?"

It wasn't as if this business didn't upset her. She came home nearly crying at the agony these lads went through, but she was certainly braver than I would have been.

The wounded dreaded going back to the trenches, and put bits of copper wire in their wounds to prevent healing. This was known to the authorities and was dealt with as a very serious crime and was severely punished.

Mother saw one dressing was not as it should be, while the lad was asleep, and on undoing the bandage, she discovered a piece of copper telephone wire. The lad's scared look was pitiful. She slipped the piece of copper into her pocket and redressed the wound. She scolded the patient but never gave him away.

I had that bit of wire as a souvenir for some time. Reckon I swopped it for a badge or something. I had a leather belt covered with badges and buttons.

Two Scots in the hospital used to leap over the bed while they made it.

There were many casualties on the Western Front. Men in the trenches were getting killed; a large proportion with head wounds. One bright spark in the upper hierarchy of the War Office—an isolated case I should think—suggested that the men wear steel helmets as this was the only part of their anatomy regularly exposed to the enemy snipers. A metallurgist was employed to find a suitable steel and make a helmet. He came up with manganese steel[168] and millions of helmets were made. The helmet resisted the penetration of the bullet but became badly dented and this dent did more damage than the penetration. They all had to be scrapped and a new steel produced. I think this set folks off on the trail of making stainless steel which appeared on the retail market after the war, manufactured by Firths[169].

Once an entertainment was given by the "swaddies" at the Bunbury Hospital.

A soldier who had been wounded wore a vertical wound stripe low on his left sleeve. It consisted of about an inch of gold braid. Some had many such stripes.

Stitched inside the lining of their tunics were their emergency rations. I think they consisted of an army biscuit and bars of chocolate.

The first gas masks were black, bitumen-treated cloth bags with two eyeglasses and a narrow tube which the soldier kept in his mouth. The bottom of the bag was tucked well down under the collar.

My Mother was teaching every week day, so she did her stint at the hospital on Friday night and returned on Saturday morning bringing with her a whole batch of little boxes that had contained drugs and had strange smells. I was always eager for these. Inexpensive presents are often very acceptable to a child, not that I got many expensive presents.

The most expensive I ever got was a bicycle my Mother bought me from Wooldridges at Crewe. When we went to buy it, we found that unfortunately they only had a girl's cycle. As it was wartime, there would be an indefinite wait for a boy's bike. As this was a prewar model and, therefore, well-made, we decided to take it. I proudly wheeled it back to Crewe station.

I started learning to ride by going along the iron hurdles in the school-yard, but this was a bad way to learn. It is the knowledge that one has to go it alone that makes one try to keep one's balance.

I was wheeled up the road with someone holding the back of the saddle. But this too had the previous failing as I knew there was someone who would not let me fall.

At last I went on the road on my own and started off at the top of the little bank outside the school. Albert Major was talking to my Father who, every Friday night, swept the road outside school. They were in animated conversation.

I gave a gentle push and hurriedly got my feet on both pedals. I was away. The two talkers saw me in time and beat it for the hedge. I swept past. I could ride.

Back I went up the hill, pushing the bike this time, turned it and mounted with confidence. This time I made the descent without wobbling, and the two watched my progress with interest.

Later, Jack Key sold me his larger bike. This my Father must have paid for. And I sold my girl's bike to my friend, Raymond Hitch.

His assistant gardener was a fellow countryman named Sole. His first name was Robert and it did not take us lads long to put his initial in front of his surname. He threatened us with death but we only called the offensive name after him all the more.

The head chauffeur at the Hall was called Hebditch. Some said he was a German. His elder son had tuberculosis, and his mother had to sit up with the lad night after night. Mother, in spite of her many commitments, volunteered to give them one night's rest a week and they were very grateful. They gave her *The Glories of Northern France*[170] as a token of their appreciation, saying that, as the war progressed, many of these glories would fall under the German guns and so we should have a record of them in this book.

Hebditch was a well-educated man and remained a bit of a mystery. The family left and went down to the Thames estuary and we heard no more of them. Their house was taken over by a Scotch bailiff, whose younger son, Johnnie Duncan, became my greatest friend.

The elder boy was in the army, there were three sisters, the youngest Margaret, was younger than John, my pal, and we all played together.

We caught moles, skinned them and cured their skins with alum and pegged them out on a board. We made a raft with petrol cans and sailed it on a pit in the woods. It was very deep and our raft was too small; a slight movement and it tipped over.

Owen had bought me a .22 Remington rifle and we went shooting with it. Later we each bought .303 rifles—single-barrel bolt action. This was much more fun. Bullets were easy to come by. I found that Father had all the volunteer target ammunition and I soon swiped it, as cartridges had to be paid for out of a non-existent pocket money. Still we managed somehow.

THE CHESHIRE VOLUNTEERS

My Father volunteered twice for active service during the war but was rejected because of his age[171], so he started a volunteer corps—the Calveley Volunteers.

The Volunteers were local organizations which replaced the Territorials who had been incorporated into the regular army.

They were to fight on the Home Front if the Germans came, but had little in the way of arms or equipment. They were given old rifles which had the barrel at the breech half sawn through so they couldn't actually be fired, but were otherwise very similar to the current Lee Enfield. In fact they were Lee Enfields of an earlier pattern.

The Volunteers wore breeches and puttees. My Mother had to put my Father's puttees on. His pince nez kept falling off when he looked down, or so he said.

At the outset, the units were made up of men who were too old to join the army. Another type who found their way into the Volunteers were lads not old enough to join up. At first all were true volunteers, but then some men with "essential" jobs had their military service deferred on condition they joined such a unit. This brought most of the farmers' sons into the Volunteers and my Father was not too popular because he had brought them one step nearer enlistment.

The Cheshire Volunteers under Sergeant Gore tried to forget their 12-bores and handle a .22. A site was chosen for a rifle range just inside the Hall gates, in a valley on the left, and permission was given by Mrs. de Knoop. Sand had been dug from here at some time and it was long enough for twenty-five and fifty-yard ranges.

The young farmers fancied themselves as shots with guns but when it came to handling a rifle there were some red faces.

Mrs. de Knoop was asked to open the range by firing at the first target and she sprawled out on the raised earth bed and showed a good pair of legs. Unfortunately no one could find where her shot had gone. Was this an omen? Still the range was opened and all had been done by voluntary labour.

Raymond Hitch and I trimmed up the recess cut in the sand hill at the target end of the range. Ray got congratulated and was very bucked.

I had an old spade which had once been my Father's. It now had a very short blade and a handle I had put in myself. To cover the nail or screw I had put in, and which had a savage projection, I had wrapped a piece of sacking round the shaft.

The Volunteers met once a week and marched and counter-marched, left-inclined and right-inclined, dressed ranks, shouldered arms. You name it, they did it—the long and the short and the tall. Some of the older men were quite corpulent and, marching across the field that had always been grassland and so bore the ridges across it, the short men nearly disappeared from view when they went down into the hollows.

Once a German prisoner escaped and the Volunteers were alerted. I think their great weakness was the lack of communication. We hadn't progressed very far from Armada days. Then they used a horse, and now a bike was used.

I remember my Father marching past the cottages at the top of the lane, his swagger stick under his arm, on his way back from a Volunteer parade. Two corpulent old women, Mrs. Davies and Mrs. Gibson, saw him coming and, at a given signal, quickly came out of their gates and lined up at the side of the road and came to the salute as my Father passed.

My Father never batted an eyelid. He marched up to them, returned the salute, and marched on. Not a word was spoken. I was playing in the road and watched it all. The old girls were in hysterics afterward.

The de Knoops had a private bowling green near the Hall gates with a wooden shed and verandah attached at the side. During the war the green went to pot and Ray Hitch and I used to pedal the big lawn mower about. Later it was dug up as an allotment[172].

Well, the little hut had racks inside for the woods and Mrs. de Knoop allowed the Volunteers to use it as their storage depot. Father had the key and I remember being sent for some reason to take something to this place.

I lost the blooming key on the way home and one would think I had lost the war by the row I got into. I climbed over the fence into the woods as a short cut and ran between the trees making it difficult to retrace my steps in searching for the key. I suppose they fitted a new lock. I don't remember.

Calveley schoolhouse, looking north; the school is on the far side of the building.

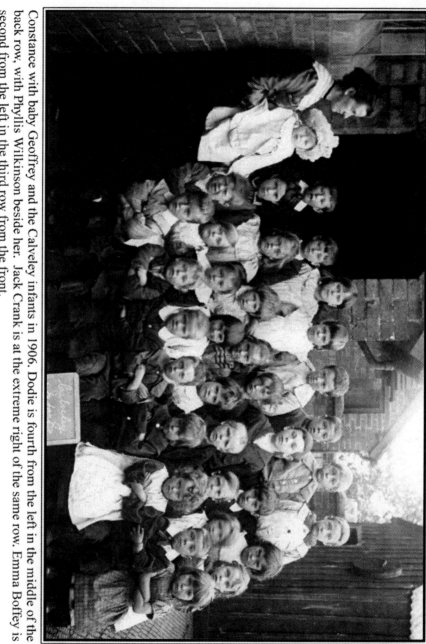

Constance with baby Geoffrey and the Calveley infants in 1906. Dodie is fourth from the left in the middle of the back row, with Phyllis Wilkinson beside her. Jack Crank is at the extreme right of the same row. Emma Boffey is second from the left in the third row from the front.

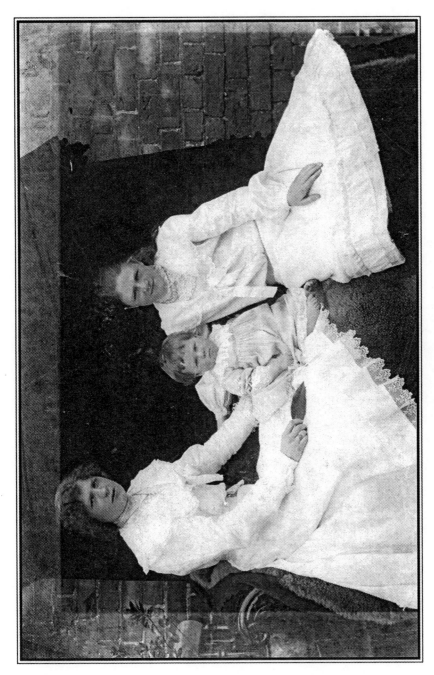

William Gore's three daughters, Mary, Dodie and Annie., circa 1902.

Dodie and Geoffrey, Rhyl, 1908.

Constance, William and Geoffrey, Llandudno, 1909.

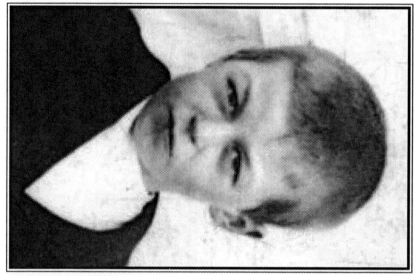

Geoffrey, circa 1912.

Harry Baker Gore, June 1902.

Owen Benison Gore, third horseman from left; Royal Engineers, 1915.

Constance's sister, Clara Annie Alcock.

Clara's second son, Charlie, January 1915. He enlisted at the age of 16 in the 4th (Reserve) Battalion, South Lancashire Regiment.

Constance as a Red Cross VAD nursing sister during the First World War.

William Gore in his garden at the schoolhouse at Calveley wearing his "trench cap" and Cheshire Volunteer Regiment lapel pin.

William Gore with Togo in the schoolhouse garden.

The Kennels, Calveley, where the family lived after William Gore's retirement.

Constance at The Kennels, 1920.

Geoffrey in Crewe Grammar School uniform.

Geoffrey at Queensgate, Northwich.

Levi Newman with Kipper.

Levi and Annie Newman, circa 1920.

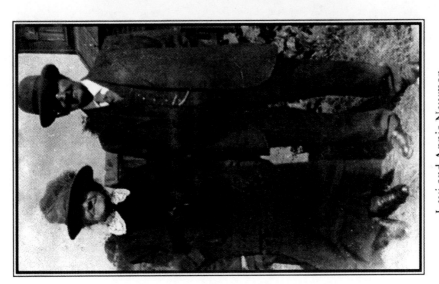

Levi and Annie Newman

The Heysoms College, circa 1925.

The Heysoms, west front.

Rose Ellen Newman.

Geoffrey, second from left, with the London University OTC Survey Unit, in camp at South Dibgate, Shorncliffe, 1930.

Geoffrey in clown suit as 1936 Rag Manager at Chester College, with "Polly" Carter in captain's uniform.

Geoffrey in his Austin, Heysoms, 1936.

Charles Edward Newman and his wife Gertrude, with Gyp in the Hartford
schoolhouse garden.

After Geoffrey and Margaret's wedding, 5th June 1937, with Constance and Charles at The Heysoms.

To raise money for war charities we held a concert at Calveley School. The school was used in the past, as many schools are used, for purposes other than education—voting, dances, whist drives and school concerts.

The children opened the performance and later a prize was offered to any of the audience who would like to come forward and compete.

For weeks we spent our spare time making artificial flowers. These I remember were intertwined with leaves and decorated with semi-circular bows which the girls held aloft when they danced. They carried hoops covered in artificial roses. They had pretty white ballet frocks too, made from crepe paper. I had never seen anything like it before.

I thought my Mother wonderful for the way she made all this stuff out of cheap but hard to get materials. It took two weeks to prepare that and other scenes.

I had to go on in a little play. I remember I came off stage in a hurry without saying my last piece. I was sent back to make amends. I remember it went something like this:

X (to me)	Can you say a piece of poetry, Y?
Y (me)	Yes, I know a piece of poetry.
X	Let's hear it.
Y	There was an old woman and she was as deaf as a post.
X	That's not poetry; it doesn't rhyme.
(I quit.)	
Y(after being sent back)	Yes it does: There was an old woman and she Was as deaf as a P-O-S-T.

I forget the rest of the performance but I remember that a youth I knew, called Harry, won the prize. He sang *Champagne Charlie*, and it went down well. I think some women entered for the prize but Harry was easily the winner.

We had been taught *La Marseillaise*, as we were great patriots and as France was one of our allies—at least we thought she was until she stood Doug Haig up.

A great catastrophe occurred during the show. The dressing room was the infants' room and the stage was immediately inside the big room. At the corner of the door, by what was then the fireplace, stood an acid-type fire extinguisher. We had not had this long and were very proud of it. Father had it delivered empty and I had to help him fill it. Water and sodium bicarbonate filled the big cylinder and a small bottle was clipped at the top holding acid. To start the extinguisher operating the whole thing was inverted so that the acid came into contact with the bi-carb and produced gas which forced out the liquid in a strong jet.

Well, all the girls were primped up in their dance costumes and went on stage. The folks behind, anxious to get a view of them, crowded forward and someone knocked the fire extinguisher over, setting it off. The darned pipe twisted and twirled, spraying everybody. It was heartbreaking. Everyone was drowned in it.

Mother was broken-hearted after all her work, but I don't think the audience noticed anything. The fire extinguisher didn't normally stand there, but had been moved when Mr. Lupton put up the stage.

I think the show went off well and all we kids enjoyed ourselves. It was my first school concert. I have seen many others, alas.

I remember one dance in particular in the school during the war. We all wore clogs in those days, even Baroness de Knoop when she cleaned the cows out. These clogs had irons on the soles and played havoc with wooden floors. The nails offered resistance to wear, so round each nail was a boss of wood standing proud of the rest of the floor. This was no good for a dance floor so on this occasion, Mr. Luke Lupton was consulted. He gave Tommy Lupton and me nail punches and hammers and we two boys were on hands and knees all over the room thumping down the nails in each floorboard in turn.

It was hard work; the cut nails were big old-fashioned, rectangular cross-section things with no point, such as they used in the 1800s, and took some whacking down. Following us came Mr. Lupton and his men with jack planes to level the floor by planing off the most protruding bumps. His work was given voluntarily as it was for war funds.

I suppose the dance music was supplied by a pianist. I don't know if this was Mother. I saw nothing of the dance. I had done my whack—you can say that again. The lighting would be from the two oil lamps which the school possessed. These hung from the ceiling. It was very primitive but I think all enjoyed the dance. It was war time and people were determined to make the best of it.

When I had the measles during the war, my half-sister Mary sent me a picture post card showing a young woman with a hobble skirt which was the fashion for that year[173]. The verse ran as follows:

Mary wore a hobble skirt
Tied tightly in a bow,
And everywhere that Mary went
She simply could not go.

Another card showed a small boy:

Cleanliness is next to godliness
but I'd rather be wicked and warm.

I suppose I was a grubby kid. We had no hot water except a rusty boiler at the fireside. The fire was out for most of the day so there was rarely warm water, and then there were many demands on it, so it did not encourage one to wash.

Another card that came when I had measles bore this verse:

The world is like a market, full of all kinds of wondrous things,
Sometimes it is a dog that barks, sometimes a bird that sings.
May barking dogs be far away and singing birds be near,
And pleasant thoughts and happy sounds, your path for ever clear.

During the war, Majors had two soldiers loaned to them for the harvest. These men were chosen because they said they had experience of farming, but most soldiers had never been on a farm.

These two were city fellows. One smoked his pipe while working as a stackman. Urchin heard him say he had lost his pipe. Well they pulled the whole stack down in an effort to find the pipe. All in vain.

Outside the school at Crewe a big traction engine parked itself at one end of some waste land, and after some juggling with cables, and a queer looking vehicle which turned out to be a digger plough, this waste land was turned over and later divided up into allotments in an effort to produce food, and thus combat the submarine menace of the First World War.

It was strange to see this big cumbersome thing heaving and tossing on its way across the very uneven ground without any apparent motive power.

A boy who went to school with me, and who lived in Crewe, had a father who had been disabled in the works and went about in a wheelchair. To eke out his pension, he kept one of the small shops that were built on the bridge over Crewe station. The wheelchair was propelled by an auto-wheel. There were not many in existence and I don't suppose many people today have ever heard of them. Only one company made them. They consisted of a wheel capable of being bolted on to the back axle of a bike with a stay to anchor it to the frame. An engine was mounted above the wheel and this drove the wheel by means of a chain. The back wheel of the bike and the auto-wheel ran parallel tracks.

Well when Hesketh's father died, my friend put the auto-wheel up for sale but found few with an interest in it. I happened to tell Mother about it and she bought it, saying, "It will give you an introduction to motoring."

She was quite right. After some trouble getting a new tire which was of an odd size, she had it fitted to her bike and used it quite a lot. She had been the first cyclist in the Whitegate area and now she was a pioneer in another form of travel.

Once she met Stocky in the lane and whether she was nervous or self-conscious at meeting this reverend gentleman I don't know, but she had a bad swerve which nearly brought her off and sent "old dog collar" up the hedge to escape.

Sometimes an irregular surface pulled the two wheels out of alignment and then they suddenly sprang together again making one swerve. What a pity our cop never got to know about it, he would have sat in the hedge all night to see if he could nobble her for something. I had many a ride on it. It's a wonder he didn't catch me.

Young Tricketts from the farm at the far end of School Lane had a little Levis motor cycle. It was a real beauty, the first of a new breed of lightweight bikes. Parker, at the shop, bought a Sunbeam with his war gratuity. These were the Rolls-Royce of bikes.

In a garage at Crewe was an A.B.C. bike. Clifford Cook, whose father owned the garage, took me to see it. It was a lovely bike but rather dear and I never saw any other of that make.

At that time, after the First World War, there were a great many ventures in this field. I suppose many men discharged from the army with a gratuity and no employment or likelihood of employment, decided to set up in business on their own. I think a lot must have failed.

It was along the Highwayside that Jack Crank, when he was a lad, was chased by the cop. Jack was coming from Alpraham without a light on his bike—a heinous crime in those days. The cop spotted him and a chase started.

Now the wounded were often moved in ambulances—small Ford trucks with two stretchers in each, as I've mentioned before. They traveled in convoy a regulation twenty yards apart, I think. They did not go fast by today's standards and Jack caught up with a convoy, with the cop on his rear wheel. In and out they went. The cop on his big bike was not as maneuverable as Jack on his semi-racer and Jack eventually shook him off by dodging in and out of the column of ambulances.

Jack joined the Royal Navy when he was old enough and was posted to HMS Tiger[174].

When lads were discharged from the Forces at the end of the war, certain gifts could be claimed. Jack was entitled to a box of tools and, being an apprentice joiner, he would have found them very useful. The form had to be signed by someone of standing in the village and so Jack came to Father. Father took the form and did nothing about it. Jack came to enquire several times about it but Father put him off. I could never understand this conduct. I suppose if he had been someone important this snob would have been running rings round him. Mother was very annoyed but we dare not say anything.

Jack had been in the infant class with Dodie and he had curly hair. Dodie snipped a curl off and Mrs. Crank came out to our house to complain.

The girl next to Dodie in the school photograph in which Jack also appears, is Phyllis Wilkinson.

Wilkinsons had a croft beside the rookery in School Lane, and Phyllis came night and morning to take the cow up to her home at the top of the lane for milking.

The croft gate had a strange fastener. I have never seen another one like it. One had to undo it with a spanner. A short chain went round a plug with a square head, the other end of the chain was attached to the gate. This croft had no proper water supply, but a pipeline under the road to a pit in the field opposite fed a small excavated pond in the croft.

At times I helped Phyllis to clean this pipe if no water came through, by poking a long stick up the pipe. I remember this hedge was the only spot where wild strawberries grew and we used to hunt for them. When Phyllis left school she went away to work. Later I heard she was in prison for theft.

One day Father had to go to Arderne Hall near Tarporley, to discuss Volunteer matters with Hamilton and others. He took me with him, and on reaching the Hall I was impressed by the military ironmongery in the big entrance porch. All a mass of rust, but I think much of the stuff went back to the Middle Ages.

We went into a large room and Father joined other men around a big table at one end. I nervously sat on the edge of a chair at the other end. A soldier with red tabs on his collar came into the room and, I think, was introduced as a brother of the host. He left the men and came smiling to me. He led me to the other end of the room.

"Mustn't listen to these important military matters," he said and sat down taking me on his knee. We talked but I reckon I had not much to say. Father told me when we were alone again that the man was General Sir Ian Hamilton[175]. Well! Well!

Another time, Father took me to a film show at Tarporley. It was in a hall with a flat floor and I could not see very well. I remember the film was brownish and indistinct. It was part of the recruitment drive for our county regiment and one scene showed the Cheshire Regiment capturing the Heights of Abraham, so just correct your history books will you[176].

There was a shortage of iron during the war and we all collected it. I must have had half a hundredweight of horse shoes I found in fields and on the road. Sometimes farmers had the ends of horse shoes beaten out at the Smithy into spikes and these were hammered into uprights so that a round pole could be anchored in them to serve as a gate.

The pheasant hatchery in the park ceased to operate when the keeper went off to war, but one or two pheasants which had escaped the guns still prowled about. I was taught a way of catching them. With a tin can or small trowel a cylindrical hole five or six inches deep by two inches wide is cut in the ground. A rabbit snare is then placed over the hole, the noose having the same diameter as the hole. Corn is then sprinkled round the trap and a handful dropped in the hole. The bird shoves his head down the hole to get the corn and on withdrawing it, his ruff catches the snare which tightens.

I caught one at Jack Key's like this. His farm was part of a game park. He nearly went mad, as it was the most dangerous thing that I could have done. The keeper had just been sacked for catching trout in Kinnersley's lake and Jack was frightened that his maid, who was courting the under-keeper, would tell. Anyhow she had gone to bed when I brought the bird in and no harm came of this act. The previous tenant of the farm had been given the push for some indiscretion.

At Crewe Grammar School there was a lad named Hoptroff. He was a German and his father had a butcher's shop in Crewe. This was resented by the loyal Crewe folk and, after some German atrocity during the war, his shop was raided and broken up. Hoptroff disappeared from school. I suppose they were interned.

One night German airships were seen in the London area and I believe the whole country was put on stand-by. There was a knock on our door in the early hours and there stood the Law in all his 6 foot 4 majesty. He informed my Mother (my Father didn't like getting up in the night if someone else would do it) of the German threat, and told her that all nurses and Volunteers were to be called out.

After some discussion, they dressed and Mother woke me to tell me they were going on duty.

I had other ideas, I certainly wasn't going to be left in that lonely schoolhouse especially with Germans about. Once more Pa and Ma talked it over. The Volunteers had .22 rifles at their disposal. What could they do against Germans?

Father slunk back to bed. Mother followed.

In the morning we read in the paper how one German Zeppelin had approached London and dropped a five pound bomb before being brought down in flames.

There should be a Roll of Honour in Calveley School somewhere. My Father had it made to record the names of all former students who served in the war.

During the war I started a football team at Calveley. I spent some time making out a subscription card in order to buy a football. Then I went round the place collecting the required twelve or fifteen shillings.

When the amount had been subscribed, I went off to a saddler named Butcher in Nantwich and bought the ball. Then I got permission off Jimmy Ravenscroft to hold our matches in his field. Lastly I collected our rag-tag team.

I think we played two matches which ended in utter defeat. There were only two of us who had ever played in a team before. The rest got into a pack and followed the ball wherever it went, leaving our goal wide open. The team dribbled away, losing heart. And I finished up with a football. Well, its an ill wind …

The end of the First World War was celebrated by a children's sports meeting at Alpraham. I was a scraggy long-legged individual as a boy and I beat all comers in the high jump. A man in the crowd wanted to be my trainer and to enter me for events but he had to approach my Father and the idea was dead before it started.

During the war Father got a circular asking for blackberries with which to make the famous blackberry and apple army jam. The children were offered four pence per pound and the school was the centre for collection. We couldn't wait to get out. We were millionaires until we found how long it took to collect one pound.

Father, Mother and I went out that night to collect. We agreed that the winner took all. Father of course thought the money was as good as his. I tied the can round my neck and worked with both hands. Of course I took the whole of the proceeds. Father never went again.

Toward the end of the war, food was getting desperately short and people in the country were in a poor position to be at the shops when limited stocks did arrive. We cooked nettles as a vegetable.

"Full of iron," my Father would say, to encourage me to eat the soggy mess. We had maize pudding too with fat floating on the top. Ugh!

THE KENNELS

I said the First World War affected my life. It was in this way. My Father was due to retire in 1917 but he was asked to carry on for the duration[177] of the war. In anticipation of this, and without a word to anyone, he went to Mrs. de Knoop at the Hall, and asked if he could take over the gamekeeper's house on the estate, that was then called The Kennels, and now has the more dignified title of Calveley Cottage.

So we moved from the "tied" schoolhouse, to The Kennels. The gamekeeper had been called up long before—there was no gamekeeper during the war which made my poaching efforts easier. His sister also disappeared, I don't know where.

Some Belgian refugees[178] were living in The Kennels at this time, but Mrs. de Knoop had them moved when my Father asked her if he could have the house[179].

This didn't worry my Father. His feelings were only skin deep. My Mother did not like this, she said: "No good will come of this. These poor people have suffered enough."

One member of the family was a girl a little older than me named Albertina.

Well, my Father had his term extended and we moved into The Kennels to prepare for his retirement. It was a nice three-bedroomed house and I was very happy there. But it was not a fortuitous move, as my Mother had predicted. Illness and other troubles assailed us.

We moved there about six months before Father retired and during this time I was alone in the house in holiday time. I remember once taking my Father's double-barrelled 12-bore, and loading it, I crept into the wood at the back. I saw nothing to shoot and, on getting home, tried to unload the gun. However, due no doubt to lack of use and attention, the ejector would not work and I could not get one cartridge out.

I was scared stiff. My Father at this time was in an abominable mood and I was both scared of him and of the gun going off with the breech open. Jack Crank, our nearest neighbour, did the same thing and his face was blackened with powder penetrating the pores and defying all attempts to wash it away. In the end I tied the gun to the saw horse with the breech open and shot at the end of the cartridge with the .22 Remington.

137

My hand was trembling so much and I was in such a tizzy that I could not aim straight and in the end I poked a stick down the barrel to remove the cartridge. I never touched that gun again.

Soon after this Johnnie Duncan moved to Spurstow and we cleaned and oiled Mr. Duncan's gun and eventually got him to let us use it. Prior to this we had each bought a double-barrelled .310 or .410 from a London firm, perhaps Gamages or Lilliwhites. We had some good fun with these and it was an easy step to a larger weapon.

We left a well-stocked garden behind us at the schoolhouse, and in war time this was of some importance, so my Father asked if he might reap what he had sown. And so it was that I made frequent journeys down there to fetch a cabbage or such like. The schoolhouse was now occupied by German prisoners[180].

On one occasion I took a short cut through the woods emerging at the hole in through the park wall where the brook comes through. Then, following this fence along, reached the schoolhouse fence.

Like most boys I had a catapult but found nothing to shoot at—that is until I reached the schoolhouse. There with his back to me tying up a boot lace was the fattest little Prussian I had ever seen. It was too much for me; the target was too perfect. I couldn't miss such a sitter. The next moment with a yell he was after me. I headed up the field to the Park Lane and here he gave up the chase.

The German prisoners had been billeted at the schoolhouse until a new headmaster was appointed, in order to work on the farms where there was a big labour shortage due to the call up of men.

Roland Yearsley, the son of our nearest farmer neighbour was called up, but his uncle who ran the farm with his sister, bought some sheep and Roland was designated "shepherd" and so escaped conscription.

He managed to keep clear of call-up until the war ended and then he was called up to clear the battlefields of ironmongery, which was a very dangerous job with many unexploded shells lying about. His mother was in a great fash, but we had to laugh.

At night the guard went round picking up the Germans in ones and twos from each farm and taking them back to their billets. It was unfortunate that this parade took place just as I was returning home from school and these Jerries used to spread themselves out across the road so that I could not get past. Once they even seized the handlebars of my cycle and I fell off, scrambled to my feet and scampered off home leaving the bike with them.

Shortly afterward I saw the party returning, they stopped at the gate and one of their number brought the bike back with such apologies that my Mother, who did not know anything about what had happened gave him a jar of home-made jam, thinking he had helped me when I had fallen off my bike. After that, all was forgiven and we were as friendly as it was possible to be under the circumstances. My parents never learned the whole story.

I often went and spent time with the men who guarded the prisoners. One came from London—a man named Bishop. He was a pleasant family man. The guards were always chosen from men who had been wounded. One guard had one wound stripe and I think the other had two.

I bought them some enamel and they enameled our bikes. They showed me how to line them, that is make a red or gold line along each bar of the frame by means of transfers. Mother often sent them a pie to relieve their army diet. They gave me army biscuits for the dog but I ate some myself. They were quite tasty once you had softened them up a bit.

They weighed out food for the prisoners. Their weights were clips of bullets. I was given a clip of bullets, but I took it to Knowsley and Cousin Edith made me throw it in the lake.

There was a strange smell about the Germans, it pervaded the house. One Jerry had a parcel from home containing the black bread. The guard tried to push his bayonet into a loaf but it was like wood.

Influenced by propaganda about the success of their U-boats, the Germans apparently thought we were starving and were sending food to their men.

Major Jersey de Knoop was killed in the Middle East. He had served on the Western Front and came home and spoke out, regardless of the consequences, about the paucity of shells on the Western Front and bad *matériel*—many of the shells didn't explode.

The Germans were sending over three shells for every one we fired at them. Men's lives were being sacrificed because of this. The High Command had tried to keep this from the British public, and Kitchener was very annoyed about the Major de Knoop's public statements. He sent for him, and then packed him off to the Middle East with the Camel Corps where a Turkish sniper shot him[181].

"I am on my way to Jerusalem," Jersey de Knoop wrote to his wife, Evelyn, in his last letter home, and so he was.

He left a son and three daughters. Wilfred, the son, went to Eton, and during the holidays I sometimes went shooting with him. He had a lovely double-barrelled 20-bore. The de Knoops were an Austrian family and the major's mother was a baroness. She was small and fat and one day I saw her cleaning out the shippons to show she was not afraid of work. Women were doing all kinds of work during the war.

It was strange how the war affected people's lives. In the case of the de Knoops they gave all: husband, money and home. The only thing the next owner of the Hall did during the war was to make a "bomb", and I don't mean the explosive kind.

There is a memorial to the Camel Corps in the Embankment Gardens near Charing Cross underground station. I found this memorial quite by accident when I was a student in London. I was sitting on a park bench by the memorial, and there was the name "Major Jersey de Knoop" at the head of the list.

Some people believe that Kitchener himself was got rid of on the Hampshire[182] for getting in someone's way.

Jersey de Knoop had been the Tory candidate for Northwich, opposing John Brunner[183], a Liberal. Of course, he had no chance in a Brunner stronghold—Brunner was king. However, Father went to one of his meetings, where the whisky flowed freely. A very drunken Father caused great amusement by cheering Jersey all the time. Mr. Major eventually got him out and home.

Well, Jersey died and it was a sad loss to us all.

We shed no tears over the loss of HMS Hampshire.

The Calveley estate was sold at the end of the war because Mrs. de Knoop could not afford to continue in the big Hall—she had to cut her losses. It was advertised as "an Elizabethan Mansion". It had its own electric generating plant with a battery room which made one's nose tingle on entering. A massive, gleaming, flywheel was in the doorway of an inner room, this was part of the engine which drove the dynamo.

The Hall, park and half a dozen cottages only fetched £12,000, and Evelyn moved to Portman Square in London. I never saw any of them again.

Farmers had to buy their own farms, and The Kennels was part of the estate. I think we could have bought The Kennels for £300, but my Father didn't.

Midwood, the new owner of the estate, was a war-profiteer. He was a cotton broker in Liverpool and with half a dozen fellow-brokers bought a shipload of cotton and had it shipped across the Atlantic.

The ship ran into a nest of German U-boats off the Western Approaches. Panic-stricken, all the partners except Midwood wanted to sell out. Midwood bought out the others at a discount and sat tight. The ship made harbour and Midwood made a "bomb"—he was a millionaire.

He bought the Hall and, of course, became owner of The Kennels. He gave my Father notice to leave the cottage, which he wanted for his bailiff. Although Father appealed against this at two tribunals, we saw that we had to go.

"How many cows have you?" Midwood was asked at one hearing.

He answered, and my Father capped his answer with "one pig".

This pig was notorious. It never stopped running up the drive, and along the lane, to School Lane. At the bottom, it turned through Jink's farm and back home, then off round again.

◆   ◆   ◆

If we had stayed at The Kennels, my life would have been vastly different. My Father had no love for me, and his other children, especially Annie's husband John Key, took every opportunity of presenting me and Mother in a bad light in order to get into his will.

John Key jumped the gun, however, and scoffed the lot while Father was still alive. He was always moaning about the loss of this beast or another, and once he blamed me for shooting a cow. My Father tackled me over this. I suppose he saw how taken aback I was when he mentioned it, and realized that there was no truth in the story. But that was the kind of thing we had to put up with, and a very ill-assorted marriage was further damaged by Key's tactics.

In the end, at The Heysoms, my parents lived in the same house but never spoke to each other. The maids brought any message he had to send. No doubt after his retirement his mind was slowly deteriorating.

At the time, I don't think Mother or I noticed it. We just put things down to his bad behaviour, but when I think back, I'm sure he was a nut case. He did so many things in his later life which were just idiotic.

At The Kennels, for instance, after I had left school, he sold the unexpired portion of my school railway contract, which ran for a year and had several months to run, back to the railway company. It wasn't long before the county education committee, which paid for the contract, heard of this and it looked as if he was going to be prosecuted.

My Mother went off to one of the county councillors to plead for him—not to prosecute or he would loose his pension. She got him off.

When the war was over, he took the two practice rifles belonging to the Volunteers to Monks of Chester—all on the quiet—and tried to flog them, but Monks would not buy them so he just left them there.

While on the subject of blunders, perhaps the biggest disaster of all was just after the war. The local farmers had just been forced to buy their farms or get out. This was going to be a financial burden for some years to come, although land prices then were not high.

For farming was not doing too well in those years. The farmers had been sending their milk in seventeen-gallon churns by rail to distant dairies. I used to help roll the empties back to the farmers' carts when I was waiting for the morning train to school. I got so adept that I could roll two at a time but I found to be quicker to take them singly.

Something went wrong with the economics of this milk business. When the war was over the big dairies didn't want to know the farmers, so they decided to convert an old brick or pipe factory by the station into a processing dairy. They put in a big Lancashire boiler, about twelve yards long, and big tin-plate storage tanks built *in situ*, etcetera. It took all their money.

My Father had to get mixed up in it.

The farmers' committee appointed a man named Leigh, who lived on the spot, to keep a cess-tank working. Now the effluent from the dairy went through this, including all the water that had been used to wash the churns. After the plant had been in existence for some time, Leigh came to my Father as a member of the Board of Guardians, and claimed that the tank in his garden, that he was responsible for and had to keep clear for a pittance, had resulted in much more work than anticipated. The washing water from the milk churns deposited a thick crust of foul smelling grease in the tank, which had to be removed each day.

My Father went to see it and saw that the man had a genuine complaint, but the manner in which my Father dealt with the matter was totally unjustifiable. In his grandiose method of dealing with a problem, instead of having a word with the farmers, he bounced off to Nantwich to tell his tale to the Board of Guardians. The result was that the financially pressed farmers had to lay a new drain. This would not have been such a problem but the difficulty was that it had to go under the railway which added greatly to the expense. It nearly broke them. The farmers were raging.

The next thing we knew was that one farmer after another refused to supply us with milk and we found that we had few friends left. Father had stood unchallenged as Board of Guardians representative for forty years. Now, when the election came up, he was challenged by Albert Major and was chucked out with a miserable thirteen votes.

To show the state of my Father's mind I could add the following. He had a good crop of cauliflowers and could not sell them locally, so he contacted a wholesaler in Crewe who sent two young people with a hamper. My Father cut all the cauliflowers for them and then started discussing the price. They offered a small figure and, as minors, could not alter the figure. The result was that they went away empty-handed. I think Father got his cauliflowers to Nantwich for sale at a loss.

To get out of the difficulty over milk my Father bought a goat from Togoland[184] and called it Togo, and also a dozen fruit trees. The two didn't mix, as any sensible person might know. In the end the nanny was chained up among the half-demolished fruit trees. He made a bed for her with leaves he gathered in the wood at the back.

In the morning, he found her dead with a twig of dead yew in her mouth. I believe dead yew is more toxic than the green stuff. He had the nanny skinned and we had the rug for years.

This misadventure didn't deter him, he bought another goat and then he heard that the field beside The Kennels had once been part of the property and was now being used by Luptons. But instead of going the right way about things and consulting the neighbour first, he dashed off to Mrs. de Knoop and asked her if he could have it. Of course Mrs. de Knoop asked the neighbour about it and then the fat was in the fire and we lost an old friend—the son-in-law of Mr. Hewitt with whom he lodged before the schoolhouse was built.

And we didn't get the field.

Once, when I was in the orchard at The Kennels, a fox jumped over the wall and looked hungrily at the hens. It ignored my dash toward it. The hens were scattering in all directions and suddenly there were fifteen foxes among the hens. I could do nothing. It appeared that Midwood wanted to hunt in a big way and he imported this batch of sixteen foxes from Scotland.

At this time they had not paired up but adopted a gregarious way of living and went hunting in a pack. We got the first onslaught.

I never knew foxes were gregarious, but these ones just invaded us, storming over the wall and grabbing a hen each and off with it. I just couldn't do anything about it, I was so amazed.

Of course this importation defeated itself, as so many foxes left more scent trails than the hounds could deal with. Half the pack went one way and half the other.

It was just about unthinkable for anyone to shoot a fox. I had heard of a tenant farmer losing his farm because he did.

Another, who owned his own farm and thought he was safe, found his cattle were boycotted at the auctions and his source of cattle food at the mill dried up, such was the pressure that the fox-hunting classes could wield.

All farmers who put up barbed wire had to display a little red board about fifteen inches long, nailed to the top of a post about two feet higher than the hedge in which the wire was placed. When the hunting season began, after the harvest, the wire had to be removed altogether, rolled up and left in the corner of a field ready for re-installation when wanted. The hunting season was preceded by the cubbing season.

The night before the hounds met in a certain district, the stopper-upper went round late at night and blocked up the fox earths with stakes and loose soil. Another man ran on foot with the Hunt, with a bag on his back carrying a couple of small terriers which were put down any hole harboring a fox to flush it. The hounds then pursued it. Such was the pleasure of fox hunting.

At the back of The Kennels was an elongated stretch of woodland and behind this was a patch of rhododendrons, several acres in extent, to give shelter to the pheasants.

I was in here once when I heard the hounds nearby. I was trespassing but could not escape as the Hunt was on all sides. Among the bushes were one or two trees and I hurried to the nearest which I had often climbed.

I reached the lowest limb when a fox with hounds on its heels dashed out of cover. I lay flat on the limb and saw the fox torn to pieces, first its rear quarters were ripped open, but it went on fighting the hounds, supported by its front legs, until the huntsman came and despatched it.

The open circle below me became crowded with followers and I was terrified and sickened. I lay still, and gradually they dispersed.

I knew then how Charles II must have felt[185]. I don't think he could have been more scared.

A lot of rubbish is talked by supporters of fox hunting. I once heard one fellow say that the fox enjoyed being chased. There was no fun for the fox in this little episode.

It was in a tree nearby that I found the squirrels' drey made of long ribbons of bark, and carried it home with glee, only to have Mother find I was smothered in fleas. She knew that all hibernating animals were flea-ridden. It is nature's way of preserving this branch of insect life during the cold weather.

My Mother had an awful job to get me cleaned up.

On very rare occasions we would go on a picnic. Delamere Forest was often the venue. I loved the smell of the pines. Mother had a small picnic stove consisting of a closed tin, like a large boot-polish tin. The bottom half was filled with absorbent material, asbestos very likely, and this was covered with a fine wire gauze. Methylated spirits was poured on this and then ignited. Some folding legs enabled the pan, or kettle in our case, to be placed above the flame and then I remember the prolonged wait for the kettle to boil.

When we moved to The Kennels we had a smoking chimney. Men came from the estate and pulled down so many nests from the chimney that the pile reached chest high.

The windows at The Kennels were made of bottle glass.

While we lived there, I had scarlet fever, as I have noted, and Mother bought me a silver watch. Both of us contracted the "wartime flu".

In July 1919 came the final leave taking and Father had his presentation from the school managers. It was an engraved, silver-plate tea service. He hardly got it home before he was off to Nantwich to sell it. All without a word to Mums or me.

My Mother continued teaching at Calveley until February 1922. Pickerill, the new head, told her he wanted his wife to take her place.

Mother tried hard to get another job, but married women were not allowed to teach in those days except in special circumstances. I heard later that Pickerill's wife only continued for a short time, so it was only a ruse to get Mother out. As most of the school managers were farmers it is obvious why she was asked to leave. And for her years of teaching she got no pension[186].

I think my Father only got a pension of £2 per week for forty-four years as head[187].

My Mother made a short visit to my Aunt Annie's at Warrington. It was unusual for her to go away and I wondered why. She saw my aunt's doctor, a man named Fox, I believe, who diagnosed breast cancer. So she came back with the distressing news that she would have to have her breast removed.

Her sisters Annie and Clara had both suffered in a similar manner.

She saw Dr. Frank Matthews, our own nice doctor at Nantwich—he had a wooden stethoscope—and it was arranged for her to go into the Cottage Hospital at Nantwich. She arranged with Roland Yearsley to take her. He came one evening with his Rover car and we all went to the gate.

The tires, I remember, were studded with round steel discs—they couldn't vulcanize rubber in those days so steel studs were used instead. Funny I should remember this, perhaps it was because my eyes were down to hide my tears. Mother was about to get into the car and then an astounding thing happened, which made Roland and me look at each other unbelievingly.

My Father went to her, was very effusive and, I think, kissed her and said, "You've nothing to worry about my dear—*I SHALL BE ALL RIGHT.*"

I was aghast and Roland hid his shock by getting into the driver's seat. I couldn't believe my ears, but it was typical of the man—no one else mattered. I'll never forget that.

The gate post had rotted off and we had dug the remaining part downward so that it became shorter than the hinge post. It is still there. I remember breaking down after she had gone and crumpled up on this post.

I cycled over to see Mother in hospital after the operation. I remember I was very scared of hospitals and doctors but I crept up the drive and saw Mother in bed with the French windows open, so I went to her.

I'd nothing to take her but we were glad to see each other. The sister called her, "My brave little woman." My Father never visited her. My Mother never looked back after the operation. They were grand old doctors in those days. Few drugs and simple tackle and yet they coped.

Well that was the first blow while we lived at The Kennels. Being turned out was the second.

When Midwood pressed us to leave The Kennels, my Father went to see Sam Williams[188] and he consented to rent us a back room at the farm where we would eat and sleep.

CRESSAGE

When the war was over, Mother continued with her poultry-keeping in a bigger way. With the help of a handbook, I made a small incubator which I still have.

Later I built a *pukka* Hearson type hot water incubator and the two worked side by side, between them hatching every fertile egg. I was a real expert on poultry in those days. When we had to leave The Kennels, John Key came over and took away the Tamlins incubator, *inter alia*. We brought the Hearson to Northwich but it was never used again.

Jack Key's first farm was at Stroud[189]. It was very wet. There were duckboards at the sides of the roads for pedestrians to walk on. When I was about twelve, they moved to Cressage[190] in Salop[191]. I went to stay with them on at least one occasion. I was very happy there.

Jack gave me free use of his gun and I always brought him some rabbits back to sell in Salop. I think he secretly matched the cartridges against the rabbits. He had nothing to quibble about. Once I shot a hare and he marched this through the streets of Salop much to the horror of the butcher who bought his rabbits.

"You want a game licence for that," he said. "Wonder you weren't stopped."

The country round Shrewsbury was divided into big estates with scattered gentlemen's houses, and game and poaching were of great importance.

There was a colliery at Coalbrookdale[192] not far away and the out-of-work miners were ruthless. They were hungry and went poaching in big parties. I nearly encountered them once and had to lie low, my heart pounding, until they had netted the field and moved on.

Jack had warned me about them. Lucky I saw them before they saw me, and I flattened out in the grass.

Jack was not on good terms with the people about and this made me uncomfortable. Every beast he sold was given an extra keen scrutiny for they knew he was a clever crook and a good vet.

He had a big chest of medicines. He would study their labels for hours at night as he hunted through the dozens of packets. He had bought the chest fully-stocked. He would buy an animal on its last legs and before long he would be selling it in prime condition. He was very clever in more ways than one. He and Annie had two children, Rosie and little Jack.

They sold milk to a dairy. It had to go by train in the usual seventeen-gallon cans. He took it to the station in an ex-army ambulance. The canvas body had been sprayed with green paint but it had not quite hidden the red cross painted on each side.

Jack was a last minute man. We always had a dash for the train. There were crossing gates at Cressage station and unfortunately we were on the wrong side of the track. Once I had to help him load the seventeeners. We were desperate as there was no one else about. The body of the Ford was rather high. I could get the can up so high with difficulty and then Jack would put his strong arms round the neck of the can and get it in somehow. There were four cans. Once the cans slipped back in the body of the van and burst open the doors.

"Stick to this," he said giving me the wheel. He got into the back just in time and yanked the cans forward. I drove for the first time in my life. The crossing gates were looming up—coming closer—I was getting worked up.

"Jack, Jack," I bleated.

He switched off the engine before we did too much damage to the gates. Phew! It was a close shave.

It was a very hot summer without rain and they depended on wells. There were two closed-in wells in the orchard which had gone foul. One in the back-yard was used for cooling the milk. I fetched the drinking water from a well behind the pub every morning.

We used a lot of water for cooling the milk and eventually the backyard well ran dry. Jack lifted the lid and looked down through the tiny trap door. It seemed a terribly long way down to the muddy mess at the bottom.

"We'll clean it out," he said. He went in the house, and then into the out buildings. I thought Annie looked anxious when she appeared at the house door.

Jack came back with a rope.

"I want you to go down," he said indicating the trap door. "You're the only one who could squeeze through."

I don't remember being scared. I trusted John's strong arms. He lowered me down to the second wooden framework spanning the well and supporting the pump pipe. I suppose the pump would only lift thirty-two feet, but it looked as if I was an awful long way down when I looked up at the tiny faces blocking out the only bit of daylight.

I filled one bucket after another with the ooze from the well bottom. Someone had to push the buckets down in it—me. The dripping buckets drenched me with the evil smelling stuff. At last I had done all I could do from the slippery sodden platform consisting of a 6 x 6 beam. I was glad to be out and Annie got me cleaned up.

One of the workmen—there were only two permanent—had been a stableman with the Duke of Westminster. He came to Jack without a reference so it was thought that he had blotted his copybook somehow. He was quite a satisfactory worker and had a tied cottage. He had been with Jack two or three years, just long enough to get a reference of some worth, and he had intimated that he would like to move on.

He was terribly scared of pigs. Jack's pigs were often turned loose to forage for themselves and if they came into, say, the stackyard when Hibbert was there he would be missing immediately. The other worker was only a teenager but Jack fell out with him after I had gone home.

We once walked a cow to Salop auction. It hadn't been milked that morning on purpose. Its full udder was swinging, I should think painfully, as we made our way to town.

On another occasion, I went to Salop auction with Jack. I went in the town while he was in the auction. When we met up he said brusquely: "I've bought some sheep. Want you to drive 'em home. I'll be with you until you leave the main road (to Wellington)."

This was nearly my Waterloo. The first problem was that I hardly knew the way. The second was Jack bought me a huge, heavy cake. Lovely to look at and very nice, but it created a great thirst before I had gone far. The third thing wrong was the thirty-odd sheep were out of several pens and from different farms. If you drive the bulk of an established flock in one direction the strays will soon catch up with you, but not these.

Each damned pen went a different way. I was getting one group out of a field when the others had decided to go their different ways. One lot made back for home, the rest sought pastures new. It was very hot and I ran miles. At last I came to an old crone leaning over a gate. She had a bucket of the clearest water I had ever seen at her door in the shade.

"Will you give me a drink, please?" I asked her.

"I had to fetch that water," she almost snarled. It was typical of Shropshire people. They have a terrible lot of the Taff in them.

I plodded on, dying of thirst, and then the greatest calamity of all overtook me—a motor cycle trial. We were in country lanes of course and here was a motor cycle, or motor cycle and sidecar every twenty yards. The sheep went this way and that. I got tired of chasing them and got cursed for not getting the damned sheep out of their way.

But I got the sheep home, eventually.

Jack had his troubles too. It was just before Christmas, so Annie told me, that a cow sickened and the vet was sent for. The cow was drenched with stuff recommended by the vet, but the animal died and Jack skinned it. Apparently the Ministry of Agriculture sent out a vet to inspect unexpected deaths of cattle.

This chap had a serious face when he encountered Jack. "Anthrax," he said. Now anthrax can be fatal to man and Jack had skinned the beast.

On Christmas Day there were twelve policemen to dinner, but not Jack, he was soaking in a bath of disinfectant. The cow was carried out to the field and, with two tons of coal, it was burnt.

Jack was going to sue his vet, but he had foolishly fallen out with the teenager I mentioned and, as it was the end of the year when farm workers change their jobs, this lad had left him so he could not rely on him as a witness.

Jack and Annie came moaning to Father, and I fancy they got money out of him, Jack worked the old man his way and I think he got a lot of money off him.

At The Heysoms, having been promised that he could go and live with them, Father made over all his money to the Keys. I don't think his other children knew this. Father was packed up ready to go and was actually waiting for the taxi when a telegram came to say it was all canceled—letter following.

The old man was penniless and completely shattered. I was at Hucknall then[193].

Owen and Mary came to my Father's funeral, as did Jack Ravenscroft and Roland Yearsley, and a Mr. Button, headmaster of the Aldersey Grammar School[194] at Bunbury. It had long ceased to deserve that title and was an ordinary council school. Admiral Beatty[195] went there when the family lived on Beeston Bank.

Jack Key had a sow which delivered a big litter, eighteen I think. Now each morning when we visited the sow, there was one piglet less. I suppose Jack had bought a "wrong 'un".

Soon after a young, posh, gentleman farmer called at the farm and Jack sold him the sow and litter. This chap was soon back moaning that each morning the piglets were getting one less. Jack looked so surprised he could have fooled me.

He bought another wrong 'un. It was a really beautiful-looking shire mare. The only thing wrong with it was that you needed a lid on the field to keep it in. He put it in the ley[196] between the River Severn and road. The damn thing swam the Severn.

I had to fetch it up once and, after it led me a dance, I grabbed its mane and got across its back. The damn thing went straight under a big tree with low branches.

Later I had to take it to be shod. I loved horses and to walk along the road with this beauty was a pleasure.

"Now go to the second smithy, to Johnnie the Twicer," Jack told me several times. He had fallen out, as usual, with the first smith.

Johnnie the Twicer was so called because in those hard up days, even when I paid him 1/6d for shoeing a horse, he could not afford to smoke a cigarette right through but stubbed it out and made it do twice.

As I approached the first smithy, the smith and his man came out into the road to welcome me.

It was most embarrassing. I hid behind the horse and walked past on my toes. I cast a look back when I dared and saw them scowling at me from the doorway.

The mare was nasty at being shod and the smith had to put a twitch on her which I held. This is a piece of cord on the end of a stick, the cord is doubled and the fleshy upper lip of the horse is held in this twist, the tension increased by twisting the stick. The mare was in great pain but allowed the smith to get on with his job.

I had been told not to ride the mare. I had taken a bucket of meal or oats to give the mare after the ordeal.

I got out of sight of the smithies, tied the empty bucket to the halter and tried to mount.

The animal had had enough of me. I got it against a gate, but again failed to mount and before I could grab the halter, away my proud beast galloped. It turned off the road and headed for the Wrekin[197]. I was wishing I could get the damn thing against that for a mounting step.

Unfortunately the fallen bucket scared the horse and away it went again. Then it stopped to graze and I crept up, but the downy brute knew I was there all the time, and when I got within a couple of yards, away it went again.

This continued until the Old Mole Heap, as they call the Wrekin locally, was right at our side. I grabbed the brute in the end, and the long trail back began.

"You've been a long time," said Jack.

"Damn thing got out of hand," I said and went off for a drink.

Owen came over when I was there and I lost the gun for a while. Still I had my laugh. He poked the gun through the bars of a gate and found he could not get the butt properly against his shoulder. He chanced it and fired. The gun kicked, and for days after he had a whale of a black eye to take home with him. He did not like my show of amusement.

I went fishing and one night I caught a perch. I was pulling it to the side—it must have been well over half a pound—when out of the reeds shot a pike and swallowed it. The line wouldn't handle that, so I went home very disgruntled.

Another day I went on fishing into the dusk. I changed my position now and again and on the last occasion something crept over my hand. It was a wasp. I jumped up and found I was smothered in them. I stripped on the river bank and searched well before going home. The things were stupefied and half asleep. I found later that I had been sitting on a wasp's nest. A few nights later I came down with the gun and poked the spout up the hole and gave them a blast. When I got back, Jack said, "Didn't I hear a shot?"

He saw I had nothing to show for it.

"Yes. I missed," I said.

When the hay harvest was on, Jack recruited some locals to help. One man was a notorious drinker. The previous year he offered to have his pay in beer. He was supplied with a big barrel and within a fortnight he had finished it and had to work the rest of the harvest without pay or drink.

I had to run between the harvesters and the house taking "baggin" and drink. This was sent in green whisky bottles. Every time I went, this man was demanding more drink. Annie got tired of his whines and filled the bottles with water. I took them down rather apprehensively. This chap came to meet me. He rolled up his sleeves, beamed all round, and was the first to take a swig. Next minute he was spitting as though he had been poisoned.

Jack suddenly told me he was going to Salop and had the van backed out.

"I want a drink first," I said, for I had just come up from the fields. There was a cider barrel in the sort of cellar, at the side of the kitchen. I filled something handy, and took a big drink. I staggered up the steps, my legs went weak and I staggered to the van. I got in somehow but I was drunk as a lord, and knew it.

In this semi-cellar was a hole in the floor about a yard square. In this they stood seventeeners over night. Jack wanted help to get one out. I gripped one handle and was surprised how easily I could lift it—that is until it came out of the water, suddenly the full weight registered and I nearly fell in the hole.

The farm was overrun with game. The land was chiefly boulder clay with handy roundish boulders turned up in the soil. I suppose this had long been grassland until the war made it imperative to plough. Well I often saw dozens of partridge in the furrows between the beet and I loved rolling these boulders downhill into them. I dare not pick up any I had laid out[198].

Jack bought a separator for the milk. It was second-hand and he had to get a new part for it. For years it had lain useless because he said the new part would not fit. I'm not boasting, but in a moment I saw what was wrong. It surprised Annie that someone in the family apart from Harry had brains.

John Key once told me how, when he was a lad at home, they were having their poultry stolen. Each night one or two birds would disappear from the roost. They informed the police and a copper appeared frequently at the farm. Well the birds went on disappearing and John thought he'd take a hand. He kept on the alert and one night something made him get up. He saw a bike tucked away in a corner and thought it looked familiar. He went to the hen house, where there seemed to be an undue amount of protesting among the birds for so late at night. He closed the door quietly and fastened it on the outside. They all went down in the morning and let out a dishevelled and shamefaced copper.

Once I had to help Jack deal with some foot rot[199] among his sheep. This is caused by damp conditions underfoot. I think the cloven hoof of the sheep accumulates mud under such circumstances and in this protective coat the fly lays its eggs which hatch into maggots which eat their way into the flesh between the toes. Jack turned each one over in turn and scraped between the hooves with a knife. When he found a grub he dug it out and then poured Friars Balsam into the wound. I had to hold the animal and it took me all my time as the Balsam hurt more than iodine.

In Leicestershire, Jack's home county, the farmers eat a kind of pudding before their main meal. This was very filling and the idea was that after this, one didn't make great demands on the more expensive meat dish which followed.

The previous tenant of The White House, as Jack's farm at Cressage was known, had been cleared off. Jack thought that, in revenge, he had killed a row of five walnut trees along the drive to the house. When Jack came to the farm the trees failed to come into bud and had to be cut down. To poison these trees was a rather dangerous game with so many wells in the vicinity.

For several days I had to use Annie's bike and take a bottle of milk to a lamb lying out in a field some distance from the farm. I think the mother was unable to feed it. Anyhow the lamb died about the third day. I don't know why it wasn't brought back to the farm, I suppose they were too busy with the hay.

One day Jack was busy with the harvest and found he had no sheep dip. I think this matter had to be attended to by law and, as a last-minute man, he was in a hurry to get the dip so that he could get the job done in time. I was sent on Annie's bike to Wellington. I went to the chemists that Jack had specified and was confronted with a poisons book. This powder contained arsenic and so I had to sign for it. I wonder where the drain off from this tank went. Still arsenic is a cumulative poison and I don't suppose a limited amount would do much harm.

Perhaps the best fun we had at Cressage was when the binder was about to make the last half-dozen swaths. The rabbits in the corn retreated before the binder and so accumulated in this narrow band of corn still to be cut. Then they would suddenly emerge. One had to be careful here with the gun. When a rabbit bolted and dodged this way and that between the sheaves and perhaps swung back on his tracks one could lose the relative position of others in the field in which there would be eight or ten men.

The estate keeper was usually there, one man on the binder, one often preceding the binder to poke up fallen corn if the weather had been bad, and seven stooking. I stooked once the corn had been cut and there were no more rabbits. I was inexperienced the first time. I had bare arms and the sheaves made the inside of my arms red and raw. The following day was the worst. I could hardly bear the discomfort. I kept my arms covered after that.

Next to the farm was the village pond and on the bank of this was the village school. There were only five infants there, but what a place to build a school. Anyhow there had never been any casualties. No doubt the infants had more sense than the folks who built the school.

Mary Gore, when she came to visit Annie which was frequently, made a pal of the teacher there.

Annie came to the station with me when I was leaving. Mother had given me the fare but Annie bought me my ticket. I mentioned this when I got home, and my Father pocketed the balance. My Mother always referred to him as Scrooge. Pity Dickens never saw him.

QUEENSGATE

In 1925[200], a lady who had a private school on Castle was attacked with erysipelas[201] of a contagious kind, and had to close her school.

Auntie Rosie wrote to Mother who dashed off and eventually got a house in Queensgate and started collecting the children from the disbanded school, and so we arrived in Northwich.

But my Father was just as stupid as ever and instead of helping Mother, as was originally intended, he became a nuisance and continued so.

It had been agreed that both my parents would be involved in teaching, but soon my Father adopted such harsh methods, reminiscent of his days of handling country yokels, that the children from nice homes were scared of him.

Mother realized that she would lose her children if this continued, so she gave him the push and took over the teaching herself.

Relationships between my parents became very strained, and Pa was doing much writing of letters.

Key saw his chance, I think, of supplanting Mother and me in Pa's will and he was oiling the old man for all he was worth. I think it was this man, behind the scenes, who made trouble worse.

For Mother's problems were not over when we came to Northwich. Mother and her sister Rosie both sold their houses and together bought The Heysoms.

I've told how their brother-in-law, Booth, was after Rosie's money, and after her death tried to contest her will.

One of Booth's sidelines was undertaking and he was responsible for the family grave at Hartford[202]. Because he couldn't get his way over her will, he did not say anything, but left the grave untouched after Rosie's funeral. It was in that state for months before Mother hired another man to finish the job.

We have had little to do with the Booths since then.

This Booth, who once sold papers barefoot on the Warrington streets, had grandiose dreams of power. He was a Rotarian and Mason and he and his wife wanted to dominate the family.

Most of the family never saw below the surface of the man and believed he was the John Bull type, which was just the illusion he wished to create.

◆   ◆   ◆

When he had told Mother that he would be all right, Father was really sincere. He was naturally self-centered, and had been all his life. From the time the bright boy of the village was made a fuss of by the noble Earl, who allowed him to go shooting deer in the great park with him, Father's only concern was for himself. He was the great Victorian father type who closed his eyes and ears to further learning, for he knew it all.

I saw through him when, at the grammar school, I called upon him occasionally to help with homework. I got into trouble at school with several of his efforts, and finally ceased to bother him.

At about fifteen, I inherited my first pair of 'longs'. Boys in those days wore shorts to a much later date than they do now. I remember how self-conscious I felt when I wore them for the first time to go to church. I went to school in them later and I remember the difficulty in keeping a crease in them. I put them under my bed at night to press them. This was a single bed with a diamond mesh mattress. In the morning my pants had a lovely diamond pattern all up one side. I remember trying to press them out but it was no use. I had to go to school in them.

When the cricket season came, I needed a pair of white flannels and cricket shoes. Owen gave me his flannels, which he no longer needed as he was by then a golfer, and Father gave me his cricket shoes. I was as proud as punch.

◆   ◆   ◆

I have been wanting to write about my early days in Northwich because it gives an insight into the courage and determination of my Mother who, faced with the hazards of those difficult war and post-war years, managed to fight off the greed of three men in her family—her useless husband, who became little more than a drag on her; her gambling, drinking, little upstart of a brother, Charles; and her despicable brother-in-law John Pendlebury Booth, ex-street urchin of Warrington who became wealthy by luck and cunning, and wanted more and more.

Strange that Booth wanted me to write him up in a Merseyside business periodical which told the story of a firm in the area each week. Well I never did write him up, but I will now, by heck, and I think he will make a novel by himself.

Johnsons, the Northwich-based furniture removers, came to The Kennels with their horse-drawn vans to take us to Northwich.

Previously, my Father had had the temerity to ask Roland Yearsley to take a lorry load of stuff to Northwich. I blush to think of the rubbish he took, bricks, old rusty corrugated iron, a hen house that I had made. We unloaded this stuff in full view of the street.

We hardly arrived with panache. My Father couldn't start the clock as the pendulum was missing. Johnson had thoughtfully removed it lest it did damage, and put it in the top drawer of the desk. I had to foot it across the town to Station Road to ask where it was.

The firm is still extant. I think it must be run by the grandsons of the old man I knew. I can still see the team of four shires pulling the big van while we rode ahead on our bikes. It was a wonderful time for a boy who had spent his life in the country.

We varnished all our kitchen furniture with combined stain-varnish and brought it to Northwich.

The school that had closed had been located "on the front"—that is on Chester Road. Queensgate was a *cul-de-sac* with no outlet, except across a small field owned by our milkman Mr. Gaunt, who came that way each morning with milk for the street. It was very nice there, among nice people.

Next door we had Bert Sproston, headmaster of Victoria Road School, who had been at Chester College with Harry Gore, and to whom I was sent as part of my college training.

My Father got me fixed up at the Technical College on London Road. Tommy Stuart was in charge of me. I had to work in a big room on my own and steer my own course. This was mad. Tommy would help me with any difficulties—he was the science master at the Tech, and one of Charles Edward Newman's fellow Masons. I had to take five subjects in Matric. There was a practical physics class and a French class; the other three subjects I had to study on my own and I neglected them badly.

Coming to a town after a life in the country, I found that there was so much new to see and this didn't help my studies.

I spent each morning in a room by myself at the Tech, or with one other student, doing my own thing, without any guidance or encouragement. Tommy Stuart came in at the end of the three hours to ask if I had any difficulties, and then I went home.

The Tech was a one-horse college. The I.C.I., the main employer in the town, had its own education facilities in the works, run by their own trained staff and this undermined the local Technical College and made the classes so small as to be not worth while.

The I.C.I. was no asset to the town except for employment.

The schooling I got at the Tech was no use to a lad of my age and I slipped back rather than made progress, but this was the one-horse education system we had in those days. I later enrolled with the University Correspondence College which was quite good, but I had no competition and was left far too much by myself.

There were too many wonderful things going on around me, and my grandparents were alone all day and getting feeble. My Aunt Rosie taught in the same street as their home at Farndon Villa—Darwin Street—but she couldn't keep an eye on them. Grandma's mind was getting confused[203] and she had a persistent yen to go in the Hartford direction, perhaps it was her old home at Chester or perhaps Whitegate. Anyhow she was very cunning and when Grandpa was having his after-dinner nap she would slip out and away she would dash.

Uncle Willie from London came over and seeing a chance of getting me off my grandparents' doorstep offered to take me to London and send his daughter Connie, named after my Mother, to look after our grandparents.

It was a grand plan in theory but the Cockney sparrow was no help to Auntie Rosie. She kept getting herself locked out of the house without a key, and not looking after the old folk.

I went to East London College where Cousin Madge studied. I had all the help at my elbow but lacked a steering committee. The first year lectures for a degree were far above my head and failed to cover the whole syllabus.

The arrangement broke down at the Northwich end and I was glad to come home. I struggled on, but it was not until I got to The Heysoms that I settled down to serious work, but even at The Heysoms there were distractions.

One night a week at the Northwich Tech we had a Physics practical based on the Lancashire and Cheshire Institute exam for engineers. It was the most interesting part of the week.

The college was not much use to anyone studying for Matric. I wanted guidance and I got none of that. I was working among students who were doing intermediate level work, much above my head.

When I came back home, I got through the Cambridge School Certificate which qualified me to teach as a pupil teacher, and so I helped Mother.

After Con Newman had packed her bags, Aunt Rosie asked Dorothy Alcock to come and help. Dorothy was young but self-possessed and capably took over the household which consisted of both grandparents and Aunt Rosie.

I went across each morning for a short time to see if Dorothy wanted any shopping doing. Grandpa was bedfast and needed a commode by his bedside. The pot, or top-hat, in Aunt Rosie's chair was broken, so one day Dorothy and I went to Witton Street to buy another. She made me carry the darned thing.

Another day she had to chase Grandma up Hartford. The wily one had even dodged the sharp-eyed Dorothy. Dorothy had a swell frock with swinging tassels. Aunt Rosie joined the chase and met one of her class. She asked the little lad if he had seen her niece. "What 'er with 'angins down each side?" he asked.

We often laughed about it.

I was given a little pup at Queensgate. It was a black and tan mongrel full of life and mischief. However it jumped up at the children, and one milk sop of a butcher's son cried, so I had to get rid of it. We called him Bud.

Well my Father had a habit of sucking his teeth when he was annoyed which was often. It annoyed Mother and me very much. My Mother now being liberated and able to visit her parents in Darwin Street, he had much to be annoyed about; no longer was his slave at his beck and call.

One night when Mother was at her usual haunts—her parents were in failing health and Aunt Rosie needed help—I was in the front room reading at the table with the pup sleeping on the rug. My Father was sitting back in his armchair with his newspaper stretched out in front of him, giving it an irritable shake at times to show his displeasure.

The pup became very interested in all this but I managed to provide a counter-attraction. Then my Father started sucking his teeth. The teeth sucking made Bud raise his head, he got up for further examination of the source of the noise, for neither of us could actually see my Father.

Then, without warning, the dog dashed at him and shot straight through the paper which he was holding at arms' length.

It scared the hell out of the old chap. He jumped up and picked up Bud by the scruff of the neck and rushed to the front door and flung him out into the rose bushes. I was close on his heels. No one touched my pup. He was in the act of shutting the door when I gave him a push.

"You come in when the dog does," I said and slammed the door. I was blazing.

The door opened and the dog dashed in. I stood just inside waiting for trouble, I was in a real temper and one word from the old man and he would have got what was coming to him, but he slunk past me with his head down. Relations with my Father were never the same after that. He knew that there was another man in the house and we saw even less of him.

Communication broke down between him, and Mother and me.

I made my first effort at papering a room. I didn't do so badly, but started off out of plumb and by the time I had finished one wall, the pattern was getting on to the ceiling.

I made a well for the mat in the back kitchen so that the door would pass over it.

One bedroom had been converted to a bathroom but the geyser[204] was defective. For a time I slept there. Below was the back kitchen containing the gas cooker. Between the cooker and the wall was an improvised rack where my Father kept his boots. One night, when putting his boots away, he must have knocked the tap on the line that supplied the geyser, for in the middle of the night my Mother dragged her almost unconscious son from a bedroom filled with gas.

I was sufficiently conscious in the morning to hear my Mother turn on her old man and call him things which couldn't have bolstered his self-esteem. Whether it was this which caused his departure, I cannot remember, but my Father packed his bag and disappeared.

Grandpa told Mother that if anything happened to him, she might get into trouble if she hadn't report him missing, so I had to get down to the police station to explain matters.

The sergeant patted me on the back and said, "Never mind, lad. The silly old bugger will turn up. They always do."

Sure enough, after many moons he came back.

Near us lived Danny Guy, the Welsh headmaster of Darwin Street School, where Auntie Rosie taught. His wife's sister was married to Dalton, the optician in town. There was never a more sinister pair than the Guys, silently slinking through the streets looking for what mischief they could make.

Because Danny was Auntie Rosie's boss, Mrs. Guy tried to dominate Mother and give unwanted advice on all matters. Mother was a gentle soul and didn't like to offend her. Well this went on for a few years and there is no knowing what harm this woman did us. Eventually Willie Dalton, who lived on Chester Road, got pneumonia, and the street outside was covered with a layer of tree bark from the timber yard.

I have never seen, before or since, traffic noise being reduced by this method although I had heard of it.

Well, Dalton died. Soon after, the Daltons had a burglary and, *inter alia*, a suit of clothes was stolen. The burglar was caught and the suit he was wearing was restored to the Daltons. Shortly afterward, Mrs. Guy swept down on us and told

Mother some yarn about Mrs. Dalton having a suit which she did not want. Would Mother like it?

We were hard put to it in those days as Father only got a Fisher pension of £4 a week, which he did not turn over, and so Mother said she would be glad of the suit, not knowing it was the one that had been stolen.

She passed the good news on to me and I immediately saw red. As soon as Mother understood the history of the suit she too saw red, and went hell-bent for Mrs. Guy. After that, relations between us were strained, to say the least of it.

Before opening a school, Mums had to apply to the council for permission to do so. We were in a state of apprehension for some days until the meeting of the council which readily gave permission. Then some leaflets were printed and distributed each night by my parents to let the natives know that a progressive educational establishment had invaded the town. The first pupil was a girl named Mills who came from a back street on Castle and was the biggest nuisance we had. She could get on with nobody and her parents were bigotted Methodists.

◆   ◆   ◆

At night I used to creep into the town, with its gaslights and cobbled streets. On market day I loved going round the outside market on Crum Hill. This was the old, open-air market, with puddles and dripping canvas covers on the stalls. Flickering kerosene lamps, with their long snouts, hung from the frames of the stalls.

In the old days, the market started where Crown Street and Applemarket Street met but now it runs from Chester Way to Sheath Street alongside the police station. The council has often retained a street name but altered the position of the street. For example, Watling Street once was an entry by Weston's shop, and now it is a two-lane motorway from Chester Way to the Bull Ring.

One chap who was at the market every week had a pottery stall. He broke more stuff than he sold. He gave his audience a split second to bid and then bashed two plates together above his head.

I remember one vehicle that came to the market. The back opened and a man, stripped to the waist, showing good physique, juggled with tubes through which a ribbon of light ran when he held the ends.

I suppose they were Geissler tubes[205] but I couldn't fathom how the juice got into them, there seemed to be no wires in his hands.

The market crowd was well-behaved, although it was the depression years of the twenties. I never heard of pickpockets.

But we had our beggars, wrecks from the war no doubt. Each had his pitch and squatted on the pavement with his begging can.

Buses were just becoming common, with solid or cushion tires, and these brought in people from the surrounding districts, many with their garden and dairy produce. In the old market hall, the floor was at two levels. On the higher part was a row of forms on which these heavily petticoated market women sat with their baskets at their feet.

Some looked about them to catch the eye of a customer.

Others sat stolid, waiting no doubt for their regular customers whom they knew would come to them.

The popular song of this period was *Peggy O'Neil.* Everyone whistled it including the errand boys, with big baskets on their arms or pushing bikes fitted with large carriers which held the big basket.

The favorite game of lads at that time was to fire a blank cartridge pistol behind one in the street. One could buy these starting pistols for five bob.

I used to go for a walk every night and had a walking stick. I was crossing Hayhurst Bridge, along the footway which is boarded with one inch spaces between boards. I put the stick under my arm while crossing so it wouldn't anchor in the cracks between the boards. There was an old chap hobbling along in front of me, and a gang of noisy lads coming in the opposite direction, so that I could not overtake for the time being. The pointed end of my stick was very near the old chap's back.

As the gang passed, one boy fired his gun, and it made a terrible row for such a small weapon. I jumped, and the inevitable happened. The end of my stick gave the old chap a sharp jab in the back.

Before I could apologize, he crumpled up shouting, "I'm shot."

The gang fled and left me to handle the matter. He was quite convinced he was shot and when I got him to his feet, he went down again. Someone else who knew him came and I became swallowed up very quickly by the darkness.

The school was prospering, and two rooms in our semi-detached house were getting filled up. Mother wanted to build a school room but the I.C.I. owned every bit of vacant land in the district for miles out. It was their policy to prevent other factories coming which would compete with them for labour and also they pumped away the brine, causing much subsidence for which they had to pay compensation to property owners. If these property owners were kept at a minimum, and gradually reduced by the I.C.I. buying property when it came on the market, then they had less to pay in compensation.

Mother made the most of her Red Cross service to contact Lady Jarmay, the chief of the Red Cross in Cheshire and the wife of an I.C.I. director[206], and to appeal to her for help.

Her sister, Annie Booth, also reckoned she was well-in with an I.C.I. *wallah* and she promised to use her influence, but nothing came of these back-door efforts.

I should mention that it was not until 1926 that the chemical industries amalgamated to form Imperial Chemical Industries. It was Brunner, Mond up to that point.

I remember having to go to Belmont Hall at Great Budworth to take a letter to Lady Brunner[207]. I was scared, for there were many tales of this woman's temper. She was alleged to have seized a painter who answered her back, by the arse of his britches and scruff of his neck and thrown him down the steps at the front door. My knees creaked all the more as I crept up those steps.

My letter was taken in and soon Lady Brunner came out to me beaming and smiling. She was a very pretty woman. But nothing came of the letter.

Shortly afterward, in 1925, their niece, Shelagh Salome Houston, married Prince Ferdinand Andreas of Liechtenstein—a real do. Later, sad to say, Sir John and Lady Brunner[208] were found dead. I forget who killed who. Belmont Hall is now a private school.

So Mother was back at square one, and eventually she hired the Castle Bowling and Tennis Club room, and here she continued with an ever-growing register. Father and I were members of the club, and later Father was put on the committee.

Father and I went several nights a week to the club. I took a fancy to bowls but the old fellows on the green said a young fellow like me ought to be playing tennis. I think I was too good for some of them.

Tennis never appealed to me. All the cissy boys played it when I went to school. I played in the bowling team and usually brought home the bacon.

However my Mother must have heard of this for after a visit to town she came home with a swell tennis racquet. It was a fifteen-ounce, which I found rather heavy.

I couldn't wait to try it out, but I often wished afterward that I had a lighter racquet. She also bought me some K Shoes with moulded rubber soles, most unusual in those days. I wore them for years.

But I never cared very much for tennis. I suppose it caught on because it can be played in a reasonably small space, and one doesn't have to collect twenty-two men to play it, as in cricket.

At Queensgate I did up the old bike I had brought from Calveley. I put racing handlebars on it, and several other new parts, and painted it olive green. I was very pleased with it but Dr. Terry intervened and said I must stop riding it. So I became earth-bound once more.

Bert Sproston lived next door, as I said. I put a workshop up and nailed it to what I thought was a boundary wall. It was his washhouse wall and he came round opened the back gate while I was there and scowled at it. He didn't say anything and being just a kid, I didn't know what I had done wrong.

It was his hedge down the front path and it had been lazily cut for years so that it covered almost half our path. I cut it back right to the boundary.

He had another scowl at that but didn't say anything. Poor old Bert. Still we had to put up with his daughters' five finger exercises every night. When one finished the other started.

Our neighbours on the other side were Charlie Carter and his wife, and her sister who took in sewing. Charlie was an old soldier of Indian Army days. He walked as though he was carrying a big pack over hot sand. He went down to the gas works with his barrow and brought back a can of gas tar with which he daubed a joint shed on our other boundary.

One morning I got up early and went to Holy Communion at Castle Church. I was the only one there and the priest came down the aisle and said something. Too late I gathered it was to tell me if no one else came there would be no service. I sat it out and the poor devil had to go through the service just for me. I bet he cursed. I never dared go there again.

There were no clothes line posts at Queensgate when we went there. I suppose solicitors wives could afford to use a public laundry. I was in an inventive mood and rigged Mother a new-style clothes line. As a prop would have to be poked into the vegetable patch, I made Mother a line hauled up with a pulley. It worked fine when hauled up, but unfortunately the inventor hadn't thought of how to get the line down again.

It was discarded in favor of the more usual method of supporting the line. This reminds me of Bud. We left him loose in the back garden one day when we went out. Mother had just spent weeks knitting herself a grand, coral, silky, blousy affair. She couldn't afford to buy such a thing and was very proud of it. Well she left this to dry on the outside line while we were away. When we got back the thread was stretched round every bush in the garden. The pup had managed to reach it, he had jumped up and caught a loose thread and eventually unwound the whole thing. I think there were two helpless sleeves flapping miserably in the breeze when we returned.

Bud had never had his tail lopped but, by jingo, he nearly lost it that time. It's a wonder Bud survived.

There was a family at the end of Queensgate named Hough. The father owned a barge on the River Weaver. They had two daughters Vashti and Zilla, Vashti was at Sir John Deane's and I think she had her eye on me.

I didn't know who she was at first but she used to wait till I crept out of the *cul-de-sac*, and rush up and take my arm. She was fleshy, dark-eyed, and very pretty. I could have liked her, but after school, if I passed the house, she would dash out and link her arm into mine and walk with me wherever I was going.

This was terribly embarrassing and I tried all ways to sneak past. When I went to Newmans in London for a term, I got a telling off for not telling her. Just think, I might now be pushing a barge down the Weaver had we not moved to The Heysoms.

Mrs. Guy didn't approve, so I was in a predicament. I couldn't get rid of Vashti, and was very shy of girls anyhow. Her mother too made herself pleasant. I think they were nice people but Mrs. Guy didn't like them as they lived next door to her.

At Queensgate, we had a visit from my greatest boyhood friend, John Duncan. He now lived at Thursley Park, near Winchester, and was on his way to Ruthin to see his sister, who had married an ironmonger in the town.

He begged me to write a poem for his girl friend. I did my best. When we first came to Northwich a cycle dealer in the shop next to the Library, which became Dawson's music shop, was going out of business.

John and I were pretty good with cycles and Father and Mother were prepared to back us in taking over the shop if John and his parents would do likewise. The canny Scot said we were too inexperienced. Well after all, we were sixteen. We had a neck.

Castle[209] was a close-knit, long-standing, little community at that time. Shops rarely changed hands and, when they did, they went to another member of the family. We soon got to know every shop and what they sold. They soon got to know us.

Willie Preston was at the post office. His late father had been a baker and young Willie used to come round Whitegate with the bread cart so my Mother knew him well. He had never married and kept shop with his sister who, I thought, was no Gainsborough.

He nearly got into trouble for having the Bobby off the beat for a drink in his back room. My Father called there every morning as he had had his mail redirected there—soft old chump, as though we'd touch it—much.

Willie told my Mother everything that went on. It was rather laughable.

THE HEYSOMS

My grandparents died in 1924 and 1925, so Auntie Rosie was left on her own in the Darwin Street house.

Harold Moss, the solicitor, had been looking out for a larger place for my Mother as the semi-detached house on Queensgate was getting overcrowded as the school grew. One day he called her and told her that his cousin, Johnnie Weston was thinking of selling The Heysoms. He was asking £2,000.

Johnnie Weston showed her round and she approved of it as being suitable. My mother and aunt sold their houses for a total of £1,000, took a mortgage for the balance, and bought The Heysoms.

I remember the night Mother went to Moss with Auntie Rosie to get the matter settled. I went to the Castle Picture House and wrote a poem. I did so want her to get The Heysoms.

It was something like this:

Oh Heysoms, shall thy portals be the entrance to my home?
And shall thy shady lawns be soon the place where I may roam?
Then happy be, for you I'll always cherish
And never shall my love grow cold or liking ever perish.

Well it's not quite Tennyson is it? But it expressed my feelings at the time.

Johnson's big vans with the horses, which brought us to Northwich, came for us and took us the short distance to The Heysoms.

Father and I stayed to supervise the loading. I suppose Mother was at the club room with her bairns.

When we walked to The Heysoms we found the big vans standing there and no attempt at unloading being made. The driver explained: "Mrs. Gore said that we were not to unload until all the Westons were out."

I suppose the place was very dear to them. The two Miss Westons were sitting tight in a bedroom, but their peace was rudely broken when a tigress stormed into the house. Mums was in a real paddy, although she had been expecting something like this to happen.

The Miss Westons left in a flurry and some tears. I can understand their feelings and felt sorry for them.

I don't think that this termination of their life at The Heysoms brought us any luck: two suicides, the family disrupted, I was dragged off for two years in hospital, and Charles Edward Newman got himself into trouble by drink, and vexing an unscrupulous person. All this happened in about a dozen years.

Still I love the old Heysoms. It is a very old building and was in the way of road widening so the council, in pre-motor car, days wanted it removed but obstinate John Weston Senior would have none of it, and reacted by facing the outside of the house with locally made bricks of good quality, but I found them not very durable.

The Miss Westons took a house on "the front". One was quite mad and used to parade along the street in a bride's outfit.

I found a blackthorn tree in the garden. These trees are reputed not to like strangers. I can quite believe it ...

Mother went up to a building firm at Hartford, whose proprietor she had known as a girl. The name escapes me, possibly Willie Wood. They came and did a lot of work, putting in new toilets and so on. Then the electricity people came and ripped up the old pine floors because they did not know how to take a floor board up. They wired every room for electric light and power.

When Woods were doing the plumbing, they removed a pipe carrying the earth wire and wrapped this round a chisel and stuck it temporarily into the end of the remaining part of the severed pipe. I was poking round and saw this cold chisel and picked it up. I soon dropped it when I plunged the house into darkness. Had I been on a stone floor, I would have been *kaput*.

The Heysoms had a double gable with a central trough to catch the water. It escaped at each end into a down pipe. The place was surrounded with trees and this system was a constant trouble. We went to Anglesey for a month once and Rosie came home first as her school opened before The Heysoms. We got a frantic letter from her saying that water had reached the downstairs rooms and the decoration in half a dozen rooms was spoiled. We came home in a hurry and after tidying up the decoration, I made two funnels with raised, perforated sides and a filter top, to fit into the pipes that drained the central channel. I kept these under observation and we had no more trouble.

Charles Edward Newman copied the idea for Hartford School, which had the same problem.

Most of my time at The Heysoms was spent in decorating. As the place had hardly been decorated since it was built, there was much to do. Mother got Robinson, whose son was a pupil, to do the hall, landings and stairs. Then Rosie got him to do her two-roomed flat.

This was all he did. I had the remainder to do, and they were big rooms.

My Father tried to get me a job at Imperial Chemical Industries but in the 'twenties people at the I.C.I. couldn't even get their own sons in. Of course this visit to Mackarel, one of the managers who lived in Chester Road, was done secretly. My Father could never do anything openly.

I think with his bumbling, I would have done much better on my own. He later wrote a long rambling letter to Colonel Saner the chief engineer at the Weaver Navigation. He let me read a copy after he had sent it and I blushed at the trifling rubbish he had included.

Later Booth took a hand, and came over to tell me of a job going in the council offices at Warrington and I duly applied "in my own handwriting" for this post. I thought my Uncle Jack was very thoughtful.

It wasn't until some time later that it became known that a young fellow in such a job had been revealing the confidential estimates for building work which the council was considering. My Mother and other members of the family never saw through this man, but I had a first glimpse of the man's nature.

I suppose he wanted to plant me in the building offices so that I would tell him what estimates his rivals were submitting. All very nice, but unfortunately for him I never heard any more of the job. Perhaps, as he gave me a testimonial, someone saw through the game.

◆   ◆   ◆

Years of neglect during the war had left Northwich in a poor way. The original subsidence due to pumping brine had lowered the land level so that the bed of sand on which the town was built had become waterlogged. Houses continued to tilt away from the river as the sand flowed riverward. Dredging the river to remove this intrusive sand only encouraged more to shift.

"The dredger's in the river," were ominous words when whispered about the town.

Eventually the council took on the gigantic job of raising the town six feet. Drains, bridges and buildings were all raised and hundreds of tons of clinkers were tipped in the main street and thereabouts.

All the buildings in the town were built on rafts or timber frames made of baulks with a square cross section of nine or twelve inches. Hydraulic rams were placed under this frame at intervals of a few feet and the men, crawling about like miners, pumped away at these rams apparently making little progress, as the lift was terribly powerful but very slow. I have seen these machines "sweating" as the cast iron leaked hydraulic fluid under compression within them, through the pores of the metal. Men were not expected to work under buildings which were dangerous.

The 300-ton post office was the biggest lift and was one of the last buildings to be reached, as they started at the Bull Ring and worked up High Street. Boards were placed across the lower parts of shop windows as the street was raised higher and higher. Improvised steps led down into the shops, until they were raised. Notices in the windows proudly announced "Business as usual".

Where there were side streets, ramps were created by raising the main street but not the side street. You can see this at Leicester Street and Meadow Street.

There was a row of slum cottages down the right hand side of Meadow Street and the ramp covered much of the front of the houses closest to the main street. The doorway was reduced to a couple of feet at the top through which the occupants had to climb.

One night, just as men were coming off work, I went with Uncle Charlie (we must have been at The Heysoms) to the Plaza Cinema.

About this time a trade union leader named Cook had organized a miners' strike and this was in the news. Well, a gang of workmen were walking in front of us as we went up Meadow Street by a footpath leading from the old police station corner. One chap dropped out of the gang and commenced the difficult task of entering the end house. Suddenly the whole gang started shouting: "Blackleg, blackleg," much to his amusement. It certainly looked as if he was entering a mine.

The raising of the Town Bridge must have been one of the biggest jobs, because the shops in the Bull Ring were not only raised but were moved laterally, changing a sharp-cornered crossroads into the wide thoroughfare it is today. The frames of King's Café and others were placed on great baulks of timber flat on the top side and well-greased, and then the slow process of sliding the buildings backward began.

Of course, some building disappeared in the upheaval. This was true throughout the town.

A ramp was created on the west side of Town Bridge, to the inconvenience of the Electricity Shop and others around. This is still recognizable today in the slight drop away from the bridge. Traffic, of course, had to use the Hayhurst Bridge when work was under way at the Town Bridge, but a ferry was established alongside the Town Bridge and one could cross the River Weaver at a penny a time.

The footpath to the Town Bridge was via a narrow covered way through a pub building. This was a terrible squeeze on market days.

Anent the Northwich bridge, it was Queen Elizabeth I who gave timber from Delamere Forest to build or to repair the first bridge across the Weaver at this point.

Salt wains[210] which broke down in the town area were fined and there was no better place to break down than in the old ford which was used before the first bridge was built. Wains from all over the country would make a nice sticky mess of the ford. To avoid this danger I think they kept their wains at Wainington (Winnington) on the high land above the town and had a shuttle service from the salt houses in the town to the wains, avoiding the danger of getting stuck or having their salt swept away in times of flood. This is only my idea, but I've known a lot of wagoners and they are a canny lot.

Left comes from the Old English word for worthless. I reckon the salt from Leftwich[211] wasn't so good.

The canny wainers heading for mid Wales or the border country would make for Wainsford (Winsford) where the penalties for breaking down did not apply. Having lived at Whitegate, my grandfather knew a lot about Winsford.

A five-bar gate attached to Northwich's George Hotel, at the entrance to the car park at the rear, was inadvertently left *in situ* and was raised six feet with the building, with the strange result that cars went under it when entering or leaving the car park.

We had a flood when we lived at The Crescent, and the whole town was under water. What it would have been like had the town not been raised I dare not think.

There was a chemist in the Bull Ring who had exploited everyone during the war and had his cellars full of black market stuff. Then came the flood. And Platt, the greengrocer, who waded through the water to rescue his cabbages. And Mrs. Driver[212], next door to us at The Crescent, who hitched her skirts up and fished some dead hens out of her henhouse at the bottom of the garden and returned with bees clinging to her bloomers.

It was dark when the flood came. I walked into it going round to the back toilet, then I warned the neighbours.

◆   ◆   ◆

With Charles Edward Newman being headmaster of the Church of England school at Hartford, and very friendly with Canon Pitts, we attached ourselves to Hartford Church, although it was a long way to walk from The Heysoms.

Canon Pitts came down to visit us and found me making a desk for the school. I made several. I made the wooden undercarriage of one five footer but had nothing to make the top part with so mother got Fred Whitehead, who was just starting up in business, to make it and he charged her fifteen shillings. I thought it a large sum.

Each year they had a fête at Hartford on the vicarage field in aid of the church and I made a roulette board and wheel and Mother found a firm to supply prizes, so we set up shop on the field to aid church funds.

The nigger money box that I have is a "prize" which we held back, because I wanted it. We had to shift a piano from school to the field. We borrowed a Boy Scout handcart and took it up the drive. At the top we had to turn into the field through a narrow gate. It became difficult on leaving the gravelled drive and I thought I might be more use pulling than pushing so I was about to squeeze through the gate past the piano when the wheel came off the cart and I had to jump back, had I had the post behind me I should have been trapped and crushed.

The Booths made frequent visits, with John always making a great fuss of Auntie Rosie. I was later to find out why this fuss was made and why they visited so frequently. They never brought their welcome with them and I'm sure Rosie was hard put to it to entertain them, with having to pay her parents' medical expenses.

One night, I was on my way to the Tech over the locks as usual. The gangways over the locks are not very wide and two people can only squeeze past each other with difficulty. Well it was a dark night and I reached the first gangway when I saw a young woman at the other end.

I took my eyes off her and looked down into the inky blackness of rushing waters waiting for her to cross. She seemed to be taking her time, I looked again and she was not there. I went across and looked left and right but there was no sign of her. I laughingly told Auntie Rosie when I got back. She looked concerned, almost alarmed.

"What's the matter?" I asked. With some difficulty she told me that a young servant girl, expecting a baby, had drowned herself there. I treated the locks with respect after that, but I never saw the little lady again.

A girl named Burrell, who worked in Williamson's cake shop just opposite Queensgate, got pregnant. The other girls would not work with her, so she was sacked.

The sister of a teacher at Danebridge School had an illegitimate child, and the teacher was sacked.

There was such a thing as public opinion in those days.

Dr. Terry was our doctor. He lived on Hartford Hill. When I went to see him he sat in a swivel chair asked me a few questions and then swung round and put his feet on his desk and talked to me offhand over his shoulder. His wife was a Quaker. When they first came from Yorkshire, his wife pushed their baby about in an old pram with a tire off one wheel. His son did three years as a medical student and then packed it up, upsetting the old man. No doubt his father had forced him into the course.

Young Terry started a second-hand motor racket from his home. Mother was sorry for him because one could see his father was overbearing and a bully. She bought a little Austin Seven from him. It had been converted by an amateur into a sports car. The front bumper was 15 inches from the radiator which made swinging the engine very difficult as one leg within this fender impeded the swing and to stand outside it was awkward too. The steering wheel went a full ninety degrees before it took up the bite with the result you were very busy swinging the wheel from side to side when driving.

An attempt had been made to chain mount the engine. I didn't realize this until late on. This insulated the engine almost, so that there was no earth return for the ignition. It was impossible to start the thing sometimes, but push it a yard and then try and it would start quite easily because it was then making earth contact. I sweated over this thing till I found this out.

I should have put an earth wire from the engine to the frame as on modern cars but I did not know this then.

Well young Terry wanted a local garage but could not get one and I don't know what became of him. He should have made sure of one job before he tried his hand at another. Well, in his hunting for a garage he found that triangle of land which Lloyds have their nursery on, where Hartford Road meets the By-Pass at Davenham, but the powers that be said it was dangerous to have a garage on the By-Pass so he was not allowed to build.

I had about a bob for pocket money each week, from my Mother of course. I never remember my Father giving me any money. I spent it on ten Sarony cigarettes and a mechanics paper. At that time I dare not let my Father see me smoking.

I often begged another bob to go to the pictures once a week. This was wonderful after living out in the wilderness. The Pavilion was the only decent picture house in the town then. The Central was a plain, flat-floored barn of small dimensions, and showed some lurid films. I went once but the show was hardly worth the price of admission.

There were three picture houses in the town before the Plaza was built. At the Pavilion we had visiting troupes of actors. One outfit under Terence Conlin was very good, they had a different show each week. Terence and his wife, his leading lady, were very popular and the nobs at Hartford vied with each other to put them up.

Some time later there were court proceedings and we learned that Terence was not married to this woman. There was egg on the faces of a lot of people at Hartford and much washing of sheets.

At the Pavilion we had *Nurse Cavell* and *Ypres*. It was not long after the war, of course, and films were silent. I enjoyed these very much.

At the showing of the *Ypres* film, a young fellow of some local repute sang *Whistling up to Wipers*. The latter word representing the Tommies' pronunciation of Ypres. We saw George V on the battlefield.

"Our backs are to the wall," he said.

Since Dettingen[213], when the Cheshires were given their spray of oak leaves by King George II—this became their badge—it was the only occasion when an English king had gone near a battlefield.

During this period, the Rudheath School was built and the I.C.I. was formed. All the Brunner, Mond managers had been officers with some sinecure in the army. When one big noise came over to Brunner, Mond to inspect the organization prior to the 1926 amalgamation, he is reported to have muttered, "This damn place is more like an army barracks ..."

He set to work to put all these *wallahs* on retirement pay.

This was the town into which we had to adjust ourselves.

I had to have a medical exam with a view to going to Crewe College. Dr. Mannering White was the local medico for such things. Now he had a surgery-cum-nursing home just past Timber Lane, Northwich. Between the nursing home and the Chapel—it was called the Salt Cellar when it was used as a café during the Second World War—was a cobbled entry from which the stage coaches once started.

At the time of my exam it was the fire station, and while I was having an auscultation[214] the fire engine turned out with the horses champing, the bell ringing and sparks flying from the horses' hooves as they got moving across the cobbles. Well, what would your heart do under such circumstances? I had never seen anything like this before. White said I had palpitation—140, I think.

Terry grabbed at the chance to get such a patient and so he told me I must climb stairs which I did, not ride my bike, etc. I used to take my own pulse and it was always near normal when I took it.

◆   ◆   ◆

Lord and Lady Delamere were at Vale Royal; the eagles had gone, and according to Nixon's prophecy[215] there would be no heir.

Nixon made many prophecies which have come true. He said that "Ridley Pool shall be sown and mown." It is now farmland.

Nixon said of the bridge over the drive from Chester Road to Vale Royal, that when Lord Delamere went under it, a brick would drop; next time two bricks would drop. The third time the bridge would come down. Well, Lord Delamere had some respect for this Cheshire prophet from Whitegate and only made two trips under the bridge and then had it sealed up and another entrance cut.

We had a copy of *Nixon's Prophecies*. I wish we had it now. He seemed to talk a lot of rubbish but much was true.

I met a lad at the Tech, when I went to classes there, who lived on Castle and bore the famous name Billy Cotton. He knew the countryside well and on Sunday afternoons we went long walks along footpaths I should never have found myself. We crossed the Flashes[216], went through the woods and emerged at Vale Royal Abbey and then crossed the park in front of the house, discovered a lake in the woods, and so on.

He took me along Shipbrook Lane before it was bisected by the By-Pass, and out into the country beyond. He knew something about all the places we visited. Down by the Flashes we inspected an old salt works long since out of commission. I remember a pile of pipes there made out of wood and consisting of two halves of a tree trunk hollowed out and then put together again and held in position with iron bands. I suppose they couldn't use metal pipes for brine.

One day the road collapsed at the corner of Hayhurst Street and London Road. It is in the triangle formed by the Dane and Weaver and they thought that underground currents were cutting a channel across this Vee.

I must have got through some suits in that period. Soon after we got to North-wich, both parents took me to Beatty's shop. It was nearly opposite the post office and was a big place. They bought me a clerical grey suit—damn near black. When I went for walks with Bill I remember I had a blue serge and had a red silk hanky in the top pocket, of which I was very proud and then later, I had Grandpa's suits which he had hardly worn.

My Mother maintained her connection with the Red Cross and one day, at our humble home, we had a visit from Lady Jarmay, the divisional organizer. But after the war the Red Cross was played in a lower key.

KING'S COLLEGE,
UNIVERSITY OF LONDON

At King's, I joined the rifle club and the Officers' Training Corps. The rifle club was down below the college and one could nip down there between lectures for a dozen shots.

Later women asked to join and, squirming about on the mat to get in a comfortable position, they tended to displace their clothes.

One of our members was a theolog and he must have carried this back to the faculty for immediately we were besieged with theologs. They didn't want to shoot. They only came to see the women's legs.

They sang dirty little ditties and disgusted us all, but that we ever ponder.

The president of the women's union got to hear and the women were banned from the club. The theologs departed immediately and once more we could get a chance to shoot in a reasonable time.

We had inter-college shoots and I was chosen to go to Princes Risborough and be in the team for Bisley. This was during the summer holidays and the family were going to Llandudno. I'm afraid that Happy Valley won.

The range at King's was part of an underground railway tunnel; the trains rushing past on the other side of a wall. Their approach was so sudden that you often got a shriek at the critical moment. I sent some of my target cards home to my Father. He commented, "The hand has not lost its cunning."

The OTC had shooting practice too. We used a Lee Enfield with a Morris tube[217]. I could steady this heavier weapon more easily but the open sights left much to be desired.

I joined the Survey Unit of the OTC. This unit was in charge of Captain Flint and Major Worsnop, the former our physics lecturer and the latter his boss.

There was no radar, of course, and these two were conducting research in the labs on flash spotting and sound recording of guns.

In their counter-bombardment role, our guns were used to destroy enemy guns, which were concealed. Only the muzzle flashes could be seen. These are hard to pinpoint, when there are many of them, but each gun was found to have its own "record" or signature. The vibrations from each shot fired were channelled on to a film on which a needle scribed the graph.

When two graphs were identical, you could conclude that both shots had been fired from the same gun.

Flash spotting was difficult too. I suppose the invention of radar put all this work in the bin.

We worked in cooperation with the artillery. The Royal Artillery were always hidden in a hollow and couldn't spot their targets. They fired blind on our info. We were on a hill or spot where we could see the enemy and where the RA could see us.

By triangulation, etcetera, we found the enemy positions, and by triangulation the RA found our position. The two triangles had then to be superimposed. This was all done by referring to the official data. For instance our triangulation was done a base line of 100 yards. We used the theodolite to get a line on the enemy, wearing our peaked caps back-to-front, to avoid knocking the theodolite. Then we ran a base out at right angle for 100 yards. For this we just swung the theodolite through an angle of 90 degrees and put out a marker.

We measured off 100 yards along the line and moved the theodolite to that point and took a new look at the enemy. This second angle in the right angle triangle solved the triangle.[218]

We had only to refer to the book and we had the range of the enemy. We conveyed this by runner to the RA and they adjusted their range and direction accordingly.

We went out one day to Aldershot to undergo a practical test. Troops were lent to us by the regulars—how they must have loved this. When we swung the theodolite round to get the base line there was a sapling in the way. One man on the theodolite one on the base, and the rest of us hung on to the sapling which we could just bend out of the way. This delayed us and the RA were angry.

Zero hour was approaching when our calculations were finished. I dashed off to the guns with the figures. I was coming back leisurely—our work was done—when a gun fired.

The RA loosed off a salvo and the wood beside me became alive as half a dozen tanks bore down on me. I ran like hell.

We had a look at the tanks afterward. They were pathetic things. One entered by a hole at the top. A fat chap couldn't have entered. There was one gun on a cupola on each side—each about 12-bore. That was the total armament. The British built a steel box and put guns in it as an afterthought.

The Germans chose a good gun and put a steel box around it. That's why our tanks were no good. One wonders where the high command finds all the lunatics[219]. It must be an awful strain to keep the vacancies filled.

When the battle was started we went over to join the rest of the Survey Unit who were laying a telephone line for flash spotting, etc. They started off tying it firmly to the trunks of trees but had to go back and undo it.

We were told that loose wires laid across branches stood a far better chance of survival in a bombardment than a fixed wire. The wire ran along the edge of a spinney but this ended and there was a 70 yard gap.

We were not allowed to cross the open space as it was exposed to the enemy. There was not enough wire to go round. We were in a great hurry as the general was on his way round. There was a manhole in the middle of the paddock and, on the far side, a small brick building.

We rumbled that there was a drain of sorts across the paddock—we searched the wood for another manhole and found it. There was a two foot pipe running from manhole to manhole. I (daft-like) volunteered to go down it and regretted it the moment I got in the pipe. I had gone in head first with the wire. I gawkily emerged, pulled my tunic off and went in feet first. I took with me a 12 pound hammer.

I reached the second manhole and frantically belted it, and wasn't I glad to get my head out for a moment! I hurried on, hoping there was another manhole. There was, and the cover had already been removed.

The cistern was too small for me to enter and I was frantic for a moment, but strong hands seized my legs and I was pulled out. I was covered in muck. Someone took the wire and made the necessary connection. I was just recovering from my trip when a red-faced officer rushed up to me in great alarm.

"What the devil have you been doing? You know this place is the smallpox hospital for the camp?" And I'd crawled down the drain.

I went off to get cleaned up. The camp medical officer came over to me during my ablutions. He allayed my fears. There hadn't been a case in the hospital since the First World War, so I had no need to worry. He offered me a vaccination. I had enough for one day.

In the summer we went to Shorncliffe Camp on the Downs between Hythe and Folkestone. I went to camp on my Ivory Calthorpe motor cycle, but broke a valve rocker at Banbury and had difficulty getting to Shorncliffe. All the roads ran to or from London and to go west to east was a nightmare.

The Government was on an economy drive again and the OTC was to be closely examined for likely extinction. The London outfit, I suppose because it was handy to the War Office and Whitehall, was chosen as the unit to be examined, so General Sir John Milne came down to the camp to see us at work—all except for one M.Sc. who was asked to state Ohm's Law and couldn't.

My pal and I were dragged off by one of Milne's officers.

"You've got half an hour to sundown and a battery of guns has got to be on target by that time. Tell me how you would go about it?"

I forget details, but while the light lasted one had to establish one's own position first from distant fixed objects. Churches and beacons, etc. using a plotting board and back bearings. This is not too accurate, and you get a triangle of error which has to be eroded by a further reading.

From your own position you can establish the positions of the guns just behind you, and by triangulation can get them on target. Well between us we scored four marks.

At the end of the day we took the salute. There was much tidying oneself up and inspection by the sergeant major, who was a guardsman—there were no flies on him.

When all was ready, by some parade work we were sorted out for height so the tallest were at the front and back of the column.

South Dibgate Camp was a First World War camp. The huts had gone but the roads remained. The chalk had the bad habit of dissolving and leaving small deep potholes. Well we set off to take salute, eyes right six paces before to six paces after, and don't stare him out, the SM warned.

I was in the rear rank and the SM followed. We had to take our eyes off the road to give the "eyes right" and so dropped into the potholes. I heard the SM swear behind me: "Are you buffers marching or ...!" I couldn't keep my face straight.

One night we had a storm—a real belter. Now chalk is as hard as concrete when dry and turns to soft spongy stuff when wet. All our marquees blew down, to say nothing of our bell tents.

I had a motorcycling coat which resembled a military one and everywhere I went the lads took me for an officer in the darkness.

On the morning of our departure, there were high spirits of course and the bugler blew *Dawn is braking and a new day has come* from *The Desert Song*, instead of *reveille*. We had to go another day in camp as a punishment.

I was shocked at the church services held on Sunday. All the well known hymns had vulgar parodies. I didn't like it.

Bishop Charles Gore[220] was a person of some importance at King's. On one occasion he sent for me.

"I think these belong to you," he said, handing me some letters that had found their way into his pigeon hole in error.

Random Thoughts:

—Surveying on terrace. Shot tower. Brewery chimneys, and how they swayed.

—Dean Inge[221].

—Snowballing.

—Somerset House[222].

—Lord Mayor's Show[223]. Elephants lifted up little kids.

—Sundays, Corner House Café[224], St. Paul's Cathedral.

—Old Nathan, TOC H[225], St. Ethelfreda's[226], Putney, Bridge Road.

Mr. Ryle wrote me one holiday to say Emily, our landlady, was dead and the boarding house was closed.

I never saw any of my friends there again. Emily was a funny little woman. Her aunt had owned the house and Emily was her maid of all work—she was a bit simple. When the aunt died she took over and muddled her way through her work. I went into the kitchen once, a big table in the centre of the room was piled high with everything you could imagine. There was no working space at all, and nothing washed up.

This place was recommended to me by the YMCA and they were supposed to inspect these digs. All the house was full of dingy Victorians. There was a horn gramophone with one record. One side was *In a Monastery Garden* and the other *In a Persian Market*.

The food wasn't bad, although Emily only had an old iron range to cook it all on. When I went there first, she showed me round and took me upstairs and showed me the bedroom. Here she suddenly rushed at me and shook my hand vigorously. I was quite taken aback.

My next digs were in Highbury and here I met a fellow countryman named Manley, from Chester. He was connected to a family building firm. The firm is still there.

Like Mr. Ryle, he took me around. He was a woodwork master under the London County Council. He took me to see Crippen's house[227]. It was still standing empty and overgrown. It made me shudder, it looked so desolate.

Another time he took me to see Dirty Dick's, this shop or pub had never been cleaned since early in the previous century[228]. There was a plate of cakes or something in the window and cobwebbed stuff hanging from the ceiling although it was hard to say what.

SECOND WORLD WAR

I joined the Royal Artillery before the actual outbreak of war. The 112th Light Anti-Aircraft Battery was a Territorial Army unit resurrected for the emergency and converted to light anti-aircraft duties.

The government, for once, showed some prescience in seeing the necessity in moving children from the big cities if they were likely to be bombed[229]. They intended to have an adequate supply of teachers to do this job, and so a bill before Parliament included a provision banning the calling up of teachers over a certain age. This would have trapped me; I was 33 and teaching at Hucknall, Nottinghamshire. It was this that prompted me to enlist quickly.

Normally I would have joined up through the London University Officers' Training Corps. I did approach them later but they could do nothing to get me a commission once I was in the army.

My unit had no anti-aircraft guns at the beginning of the war, but we were told by the old hands that one opened fire with a rifle thirteen lengths of the plane in front of it. That had been the rule in the First World War. We never tried it. How one estimated thirteen lengths in front of a plane, even of a Swordfish (with a top speed of eighty miles an hour)[230], puzzled me.

Our headquarters was the Trent Bridge Cricket Ground, near Nottingham, and after tramping the sacred turf for two days, we were told to march elsewhere—under the stands. It was a boring job for all concerned, and we got very slack.

We marched round and round the blasted place while the officers dined and wined at the local boozer.

We were *pukka* guardsmen when we marched across the gaps between the stands but we stopped for a 'drag' when we were hidden from view. If the cigarette wasn't finished, we carried the fag hidden in our palms until we were behind the next stand.

We were supplied with canvas palliasses and turned loose into a stack of straw. We were all too greedy and put far too much straw in the bags so that it was like sleeping on a sausage. We discreetly unloaded some of the straw before the second night.

Next we were supplied with uniforms. These were flung in a big pile in the centre of the Cricket Club committee room and we all waded in, picking trousers and tunics. Underclothes came some time later, but as the army laundry never returned one's underclothes, even to the right unit, it did not matter what size one had.

Army boots were not to be had so the stock of a local manufacturer was bought up and I got a good pair of posh boots, but the join across the toe cap did not facilitate marching. It bit into the toes, especially when coming to a sudden halt or change of direction. My toes were nearly severed, and I was glad when we left Trent Bridge with little cardboard boxes on our backs containing our gas masks. We did feel daft with these things. I've seen pipe and baccy appearing out of them occasionally.

We did not get water bottles. I can only imagine what secondary use these would have been put to at night.

Some scruffs brought a dustbin into the sleeping quarters so they wouldn't have to go out in the cold to the urinal. This thing began to leak and we kept awake that night watching for whose palliasse the trickle made for. In the end there was a row and the bin went outside. The sergeant major was notified in the morning, so we had no more of that lark.

The army had run out of blankets, so we were issued lengths of suiting material cut off a bolt of cloth as a substitute. All the lengths of cloth disappeared in twenty-four hours, flogged or sent home for a new outfit for the wife.

That lot would flog anything. Our entire butter supply went one night, and I've no doubt we did not get our proper rations.

The War Office issued an appeal to the public to supply books to any local units. We had an abundant supply, but I came in one night and a gang were sitting round a fire stoked up with books. Other books were lying around with pages torn out to be made into spills to light cigarettes.

When the next lot of books came, I checked them over and brought several home, leaving behind such gems as *Lady Chatterly's Lover* and one or two others I thought the family would not approve of.

◆   ◆   ◆

At the beginning of the war there were plans to send us to Norway.

Our equipment was sent on ahead and we were moved coastward and then suddenly moved back again. We read in the papers that Jerry had reached Norway before us[231], and our equipment fell into his hands. That is why we had to wait so long for a new supply of Bofors[232].

Our colonel[233] was a Nottingham solicitor. He was old and could only walk about twenty yards before he had to sit down. I only saw him twice and then he disappeared.

Oates, our battery commander, was a quiet resolute man from Nottingham and it was said that he was of the ilk of Scott's companion in the Antarctic[234]. I could believe it.

He had that kindly, resolute face that one immediately trusted. The lads, of course, called him Titus[235] corrupted to Tight-arse. One night very late he shoved his head round the orderly room door and surprised me. One of his eyes was blackened—a huge ring of black round it. He saw my shocked look but, not finding in the room who or what he wanted, he withdrew. I heard next day that he had walked into something in the blackout.

Another thing that was done early in the war, was to plant posts in every bit of open land where a plane could land. This was a stupendous job, but in our part of the country it was done.

I remember we were sent a map. It had no compass points on it and so we were stymied for a bit and then yours truly thought he was a clever dick and, noting the outline of a church with a tower at one end, pointed out that the east window of a church was at the opposite end to the tower. We oriented the map from that one detail, but (would you believe?) it was one church in a thousand that wasn't aligned east and west. I got some black looks after that.

One thing I did see on this map was a leper colony. I never knew there were such things in England.

The brass hats had another idea in those dark days when we were so short of weaponry that some of our rifles dated from the Boer War.

They ordered us to convert our truck into an armored vehicle with sheets of corrugated iron. I wonder if they ever shot at corrugated iron. At Calveley I had put a .22 lead bullet through a sheet. An army bullet that would go through twelve inches of oak, or so the sergeant major told me, would go through corrugated iron as if it were paper.

Well, the men got some second-hand corrugated iron and made a hut on the lorry. The noise it made had to be heard to be believed. They made holes in the iron with nails and then lashed the sheets together with wire. I began to despair of the War Office, but good old Churchill soon shifted the nutters.

When we heard that our new Bofors guns were coming, some of the lads were sent off in batches on courses—good old courses, the army was full of 'em.

The men were trained on actual Bofors guns but the number of these trained men was insignificant, so *inter alia,* I was commissioned to make a dummy Bofors for training purposes.

I mounted a log cut from a young sapling on a framework so that it pointed upstairs somewhat. Then I attached a crosspiece carrying the sights for line and elevation.

One sighter sat at each sight, and by turning a handle could move the barrel. One handle moved it up or down (elevation) and the other could move the gun right or left.

These were open sights. When predictors became available they were preferred to open sights in most situations.

However, our unit was being trained to defend a moving column of vehicles. Every sixth vehicle was to be an AA gun, and predictors could not be used to advantage under these circumstances. When a convoy is being attacked it is close-quarter work and open sights are better.

Predictors were a new thing then. No doubt they have been improved since 1940. Anyway, our lads took their stuff to North Africa; I don't know how they went on at Tobruk[236].

◆   ◆   ◆

Our first assignment was at Ransome and Marles of Newark, the ball bearing people. We slept in the band hut[237] and our First World War officerdom went to work getting gun emplacements dug in the beet fields round about.

They were flooded in no time and we had men coming in soaked after standing in deep water all day. What fools we had running things in the first days of the war.

It really wasn't until Churchill came on the scene that this lot was cleared out of the War Office. I think Churchill's success was due to his ability to assess the value of anything and discard anything whose value was based on humbug or tradition. He got rid of the humbugs in the War Office and made the officer class open to all ranks and devised a scheme for assessing ability of rankers.

The Trent Bridge (Nottingham) cricketers were in our mob—Hardstaffe, Rhodes and Harris. These and others went before the officer selection boards and came back with tales of the grilling they had had—it was a new thing then, and it was Churchill who initiated it.

I was over the age limit for these boards, but Captain Jimmy Irvinge came to me one day—he kept six pubs and six wives in Nottingham—and told me to bide my time.

We had been made a training regiment and our own men were promoted to take charge of the conscripts. Most of the latter came from London, and when we were stationed at Spondon and had to patrol country lanes, guarding the Rolls-Royce aero engine works[238] and Qualcast, the lawn-mower people who were now making tanks, these lads came running back to headquarters in tears just frightened to death of the dark. They were a poor lot. I saw one lad scrubbing a table top and he was blubbering so much he didn't need water for the job.

When our lads got two stripes, they had to go out of our unit with these newly-trained gunners. The result was that after a couple of intakes had passed out, and others gone before and passed the selection boards, our unit was depleted. New men were brought in. As I was responsible for personnel and disposition, *inter alia,* I had to continually learn new names.

During our first air raid, one of the lads went bonkers and started firing his rifle right and left flattening the men on the gun.

They turned a lot out of Lincoln jail and sent them to us. One, who quickly became a sergeant, was built like an ape, his huge body bent forward and his long arms terminating in huge hands which hung below his knees. He disappeared during that first air raid.

I was writing about Jimmy 'the Twicer' Irvinge. We called him Jimmy the Twicer because he would say "Yes, yes," or "No, no," and so on. Well he told me to bide my time in my pursuit of promotion; they didn't want to lose me. If I got two stripes I would have to move out with the conscripts.

Anyhow I crocked up before the continual stream of conscripts was trained and I never reached that Paradise that Jimmy had in store for me.

I did hear, when I was in hospital, that six ATS girls were doing my job in eight-hour shifts.

I worked non-stop for forty-eight hours many a time during those early days with telephones all round me. When the air raid signal came in over the General Post Office (GPO) line, I had to notify HQ at Trent Bridge and then contact all ten gun sites and get an answer from each that they understood the message and were standing to, on Red Alert, which meant an attack was imminent.

Later, I had to give them the Stand Down. Some nights we had no sleep. I had a grid in front of me—a squared map—and was given the coordinates of each plane observed in Lincoln and Nottingham. I had to plot it with a special Chinagraph pencil on the celluloid covering of the map.

When an enemy plane headed our way I got into action and gave the height and direction to the guns.

Well one of our huts was hit—that was when I got razzored—but Rolls-Royce and Qualcast escaped injury while I was with the 112th LAA Battery.

◆   ◆   ◆

At some time in the early days of the war, we were sent to a new camp somewhere south of Nottingham. I had my motor cycle with me and went home on leave once. It was an adventurous journey back. There is a big traffic island on the road into Nottingham, and here I happened to look up and saw the sky was full of blimps[239].

I was so taken aback that I nearly ran onto the island trying to sort out what these balloons were for.

Then, just past Nottingham, I was in for another shock. A whole field was lit up with lights hanging from trees. I learned afterward that this was a decoy 'town' to mislead enemy bombers looking for Nottingham.

It was on this trip that my motor cycle lights failed and I had to ride on without them. The dynamo had packed up.

At one point, someone shouted at me. I don't know whether it was a civil cop or a military cop, but he threw his torch at me when I didn't stop.

When I got back to camp, one of the lads asked me if I had met a cop. I was mum. I don't know what he knew.

We weren't long in this *pukka* camp. The builders were not yet out of it. It consisted of a concrete square with new huts all round it.

A Royal Engineer unit had one wing.

The huts were newly varnished when we went in and they turned the central heating on. For days we had to endure the smell of fried copal varnish. The earth displaced by the leveling of the square had been spread over the land on the south side. It was wet clay and here we had to pick our way down over duckboards to the latrines.

One morning there was great excitement. The officers hurried us out of camp and we climbed a rise on the opposite side of the road. Then they told us to lie down while they searched the countryside in front of them with field glasses. We had to lie for ten minutes or so in vegetation about six inches high with a heavy dew on it. Of course we had only one outfit and had to endure the rest of the day in soaking wet uniforms.

We did some square bashing on the square. This time it was the real stuff with the sergeant major in command and all the officers watching. Among our crew we had two podgy twins named Gibson. They were every inch mamma's boys, pleasant and cherubic. One had a growling appendix, and mamma came down to see him. She wouldn't let him be operated on. At Spondon he had more trouble.

One day, one of them had to bring a prisoner across the square in a fog. The 'jail' was in the opposite corner to the newly-erected toilets which superseded the primitive latrines. Well Gibby lost his prisoner in that hundred yards.

◆   ◆   ◆

Next we were sent to Lowdham. Our headquarters was a charming old house with a covered gateway—a rose grower's house.

This was the battery HQ. Titus, Jimmy and two others slept upstairs. The janker[240] lads were sent here and made to pick up rose cuttings. They slept at night in the machine shed, duly locked.

My job was dealing with the post, and filing copies from the out tray. I slept alone in the office and was on phone duty all night. The office was a nice room overlooking the lawn and having a French window over which an ancient wisteria drooped.

The rose cuttings were brought to the garden at HQ and attempts were made to burn them but, being green, they resisted combustion, or so we thought. The attempts to burn them went on for days until one night there was a hammering on the French window. I slipped my army boots on and went to the window. It was one of a pernicious breed, the local Air Raid Precautions *wallah*.

The ARP warden indicated the pile of cuttings now blazing merrily.

Clad in pyjamas, washed until they were almost white, I went in the back place with its ancient stone sink and pump and filled two buckets of water. Again and again, I went out in the darkness, bucket handles clanking. At last I was satisfied that the fire was out and went back to bed.

A night or two later, I decided on a walk. We were at a big cross roads with masses of telegraph wires crossing so that one lot was very high indeed.

Well, I went eastward. I knew Nottingham lay to the south. One road went north to Scotland; the other remained to be explored.

I came to a gate and stopped for a rest. In the field, or market garden, a man was pushing a single furrow plough in great heaves that moved it two feet at a time. When he got to the end of the furrow he stood up. I began to believe the

Darwin theory because this chap just looked like a gorilla, both in shape and movement. There was a black shed in the field in which, I was told later, he lived.

I went on and met Titus, who bored me with his cold eye[241]. I saluted and continued on my way. As I was coming back, a car tooted. I thought it might have been Titus keeping an eye on me but it was a man named Spiller[242] who lived in a big house near us and had a dog biscuit factory.

He beckoned me, and I got in the car beside him. He was smiling. "We had some fun at the pub the other night," he said, and explained. A young lad, too young for the army, had been on local defence duty and was crying hysterically outside the pub. They took him in and gave him brandy and eventually he told them he had seen a ghost at our HQ—a figure in white, flitting about the garden, rattling chains (bucket handles).

One man in his time plays many parts but I had never been taken for a ghost before. Of course I told Spiller the whole story and he was very amused.

I tried to find means for Margaret to come over to Lowdham but none of the inns wanted to know about her. Anyhow she came and found herself some nice digs in the village—just for a few days.

One day a blowzy blonde, smelling strongly of *ersatz* scent, came to our front door and asked for Captain Irvinge.

I knocked on the sitting room door and called him.

He came out very embarrassed. "Yes, yes, and now where can we go?"

Titus and another officer came out of the room, never looking at the woman, so I gathered she wasn't Irvinge's wife—not that I ever thought so.

Titus and his companion went out. I heard Spondon mentioned as I withdrew but I didn't know where Spondon was in those days.

Then I heard Titus and party drive away. We always liked them off the premises so we could put our feet up. However we hadn't had our feet up long when someone walked down the corridor and tapped on the door.

Not waiting for me to get to the door, the real Mrs. Irvinge opened it and asked for Jimmy.

"He's just gone to Spondon with Captain Oates," I lied.

"Oh, I met Captain Oates' car but I didn't think it was my husband with him—still I may be wrong. Thank you." And she walked back to the door and I followed her praying that Jimmy would keep quiet.

"Shall I tell him you called when I see him?"

"Tell him to ring me at home." And with that, she walked off, looking in the office window as she passed. If the other two hadn't left the sitting room, Jimmy would have been forced to take his dame in the office and would have been caught.

I watched her pass through the gate and then turned to enter the door. Jimmy was standing inside.

"You're an acme of tact, Gore," he said. "An acme of tact."

He was scared and very grateful.

On another occasion a lineman had been up the high telegraph pole. He hurried down as I stood watching. His face was a mixture of excitement and incredulousness.

"Have you got a little bloke with grey hair and a grey 'tache?"

I nodded, thinking of Jimmy.

"Well he's got his pants off in the corn field. Cor, he's rolling her over he is. Coo, never seen anything like it." Poor Jimmy. He couldn't go anywhere for privacy.

Behind the HQ was a post on which a Lewis gun[243] could be mounted and here the sergeant major took a party of men each morning, to get them used to being dived at by aircraft.

They had to stick to their gun while a light aircraft dived at them, coming within a few feet of them at times.

Once the tail skid hit the post and gun. Even as the machine started to pull out of its dive, it was still losing altitude. On this occasion, the pilot didn't take enough account of this.

After each lesson the pilot would do a victory roll over the house. One day, I don't know if it was always the same pilot, he flew around the cross roads and then turned to come over the house. Too late he saw the high telegraph wires and could not get over them so he dived under them.

We were on the lawn, as we usually were when the pilot did his roll. He made an inordinate amount of noise on this occasion, which disturbed the sergeant major who dashed out of the French window just in time to see the plane's tail clearing the house.

The plane only just missed the roof and the draft ripped the ancient wistaria from its hold on the house and it fell on the sergeant major. There he stood, his cap brim round his neck.

His head was firmly wedged in the mass of creeper and we went to his aid. We saw a chance to get our own back on Cyril for his various misdeeds and, as one helper lifted, the other pulled down. Lower and lower came the creeper as more of the nails supporting it gave way.

At last the sergeant major got himself free without our help and rushed inside to cover his embarrassment and to get cleaned up. It was a sight though, to see his head sticking out of that mass breathing fire and fury like a young dragon.

We had a guard posted in the gatehouse, a biggish square building with small doors in two opposite sides. When a guard went off duty he had to present his rifle to the duty officer for inspection.

To unload the rifle, the guard had to operate the bolt five times and the five bullets would fly out onto the ground.

Then the man would pull the trigger to show the gun was empty.

Well, some of our bright sparks had learned from First World War veterans how they put a clip of five in their Lee Enfield and then put an extra round 'up the spout'.

Jimmy made the inspection on a day when there was one 'up the spout', unknown to the guard. When the man pulled the trigger, the bullet went ricocheting round the four walls of the guard room several times, I believe, and Jimmy was jumping up and down like a yo yo.

The commanding officer received the colour code signals over the GPO line, as I said. I was the stooge who had to take these messages upstairs at night when it was a Red Alert, meaning a raid was imminent.

The officers spent their evenings in the boozer across the road and were in no fit state to handle matters of importance. The first night I got a Red Alert, I put my boots on and made as much noise as I could on the uncarpeted stairs in order to wake the officers. It didn't have the desired effect. When I knocked on the door, I got no reply and eventually walked in.

Three officers lay in camp beds, which consisted of a canvas sheet stretched across a wooden frame.

I found Oates in the semi-darkness. First I spoke, then I tapped his shoulder, then I shook him but he went on sleeping and snoring.

The other two in the room were now awake. Jimmy sat up as well as one can in that type of bed and put the light on. He cast a bleary eye at Oates and studied the big bulge of his bottom stretching the canvas to its limit and then, after I was almost despairing at waking him, Jimmy looked once more at his bottom and then at my army boots.

"Kick the bastard," he muttered.

I did eventually wake him and gave him the Red Alert, but he just muttered something and then resumed his sleep. I had mixed feelings as I went downstairs. I felt we'd never beat the Hun with men like this—very efficient when sober, but this is not enough.

Still I kept on reporting Red Alerts and hoped that the other two officers would find a solution.

◆   ◆   ◆

I was in charge of the orderly room at Spondon. Men with office jobs were cut down to a minimum to get every man they could muster on the guns. I looked after personnel, sent them to the baths, issued passes and food coupons, reported the sick, and kept track of those sent to hospital, attended on the Medical Officer, who called every morning and found him a clean towel after his mucky labours. We were good friends.

The men were in tents on some sites during that awful first winter of the war. I had to supply them with coal to build fires outside their tents. Once there was no one to fetch coal and a critical stage was reached.

Our lieutenant looked after the shop and I took a two-ton Bedford to the railway goods yard, loaded it with coal and distributed it to the needy. After this, a big effort was made to get the men indoors. One gun team was housed upstairs in an outbuilding. Here a big dog had long had his quarters and, when the gun team moved in, elected to stay.

Jerry usually came over at dawn and dusk and the men had to be on the gun during this period.

We were using Lewis guns then. I was a Lewis gunner. I could take to pieces and assemble a Lewis gun blindfolded and, believe me, there are dozens of parts from tiny springs to the pans.

As I was troop quarter-bloke and it was my job to check the guns at intervals. I went to this place late one night. I was tired and this dog lay sprawled across the fireplace and was in my way.

I brushed past him, picked up a newspaper lying by a bunk ignited it in the fire. The huge beast came at me, snarling viciously. I rammed the blazing paper in his face. He fled and I chased after him and threw the blazing bundle down on him as he bolted downstairs. I believe the men had no more trouble from him, and I was able to check the spare gun parts and replace any missing.

Another gun site was near the railway line and the railway authorities gave us the use of a hut beside the track. As the men were now under cover, they got no more coal ration, so they placed bottles and tins on top of the post along the line and encouraged the slow goods train drivers and firemen to shy at them.

Then they picked up the coal after the train had passed and replaced the tins ready for the next train. That was how they kept their fire going.

There was a big house near this site. Some lord, whose name I forget, owned it. He and his family were not at home, and they leased the castle to a teacher training college evacuated from Nottingham.

Once an alarm was raised by a girl at the college. She said she had seen a parachutist drop into the grounds. The Loot[244] called up all the men he could muster and, as I was the only driver on the premises at that time, I went out on the front lawn too. We lined up and when the Loot came to me he started laughing.

"What have we here—the Foreign Legion?" I usually wore a grey and red checked lumber jacket under my tunic and I had forgotten, in my haste, to put my tunic on over this Joseph's coat.

We loaded up the lorry with armed men, some of whom had never seen a rifle before, and went to the castle. The old place was in ruins and they had built a mansion alongside.

We went under the arched gateway, through the yard, and onto a track through the woods where, here and there, a stream ran across our path. It was even darker in the woods, and I drove too fast. Everybody was shaken to pieces.

When the Loot hit the cab roof with his head I thought it was time to slow down. We saw no sign of a parachutist nor of his discarded harness. The sergeant major took a party out next day to make a thorough search, but found nothing.

In Holland and other countries overrun by Jerry, the Germans first dropped a few parachutists. They looked out for a site suitable for their purpose and, when they found it, signaled upstairs, and more parachutists were dropped on the spot indicated. A perimeter was established and, as other men arrived, it was extended. Finally, when the perimeter was big enough, armored vehicles were brought in.

When this stage was reached it would take a major battle to overcome them. Our brass hats were aware of this danger, and so we were warned that the moment a parachutist dropped, we were to eliminate him, hence the scurry out that night.

It was good practice, but I would have liked to have smacked that girl's undercarriage for sending us on a wild goose chase.

We had to supply and erect our own communications system to the gun sites. Fortunately Ericsons were in the vicinity, and they made telephones. One of our sergeants, who was an agent for Metro Goldwyn Meyer and a good talker, got us ten phones and some wire.

His name was John Stables and the commanding officer said men had got the Order of the British Empire for what he did.

Supplies were slow coming through but Stables anticipated them by getting the material and installing the whole system connecting the local headquarters to each individual gun site. Before that, we could not convey information on the grid to the guns; they just had to keep a look out and then decide if a plane was one of 'theirs'.

At night, our own planes flashed three colours. This code was sent over the GPO line each evening as a listing of three men for duty. For instance if the colours were red, green and yellow, then Roberts, Gregson and Yearsley were posted for duty. Poor old Yearsley was nearly always on duty, due to the shortage of names beginning with the letter Y.

Later we were supplied with a grand tilting and swivelling chair and a damn big pair of field glasses to enable the gun site spotter to keep a better lookout.

He had to know the points of the compass relative to his site and he measured the position of the plane by finger widths. He held out his hand the lowest finger resting on his horizon, then fingers of the other hand were added to estimate the plane's altitude: "Plane to the north, travelling east to west, three fingers, estimated height 1,000 feet."

We could estimate with some accuracy the height of planes close to, but distant planes posed more of a problem.

Later men were sent away on courses on how to operate "Predictors AA"[245] as well as the Bofors guns, with which we were eventually supplied. The Bofors had four shells in a clip and if one of these misfired the gunners had to scamper for their lives. A second barrel was kept by the gun, with a tool for unscrewing the hot barrel. The barrel was changed at intervals when it got hot, to avoid pre-ignition.

When we moved to Spondon the HQ staff consisted of a cook—an old soldier with Indian Army experience and very fond of curry, and an almost-blind ex miner. To have our eyes tested, we lined up and each man read the large print of a newspaper heading; we all knew it by heart by the time our turn came, so this chap easily slipped in. Also there was an assistant cook, a batman, and some sergeants.

Wright, the blind chap, came in laughing one night after the commanding officer's visit. He had had a woman against the back gate and as the CO pushed to get in, Wright pushed the other way.

A rather cross CO won the battle of the push and confronted Wright and the woman.

"Wright," he said, "if you want to have your bit of fun, have it somewhere else."

We had another old soldier who was court marshaled for giving his wrong age when he enlisted. He had actually served in the Boer War forty years earlier.

We were expecting the red tabs[246] to visit us, and the CO came over to see all was ship shape. Now we had a lawn in front of our bungalow and the grass was long and lying down where it had been trodden by many feet. We had no tools but an axe, spade and yard-brush. Titus ordered the grass to be brushed with a parting in the middle and the two halves swept in opposite directions.

I dug up this lawn at a later date and planted potatoes.

Our bungalow was situated in an old clay pit and was reputed to have been built by an Australian. It was called Floradale. The canal ran along one end of the property and the main road to Nottingham at the opposite side. Now the canal had flooded this property on several occasions and the floors had been under water for long periods, with the result that the floors were rotten and powdery and enameled advertizing boards were liberally spread about the floors to cover the holes where army boots had gone through.

We slept on these floors and the blankets of course extended beyond the palliasse and swept over this dirty powdery wood.

One's blankets got turned about each night, for the room was used as an orderly room by day, and the mucky blanket would get turned so that the part that had been on the floor one night was under your nose the next. It was no wonder I picked up a lung infection.

The Anglers' Arms, a big newish pub, stood opposite Floradale, and here we resorted when possible. There was always an unsavory gang of young women round this place and it was a job to avoid them so I didn't go as often as I would have liked.

One very foggy night I was working on the grid: a squadron of Jerries was coming in our direction.

The Loot had gone to Nottingham and I tried on the phone to contact him at his favourite boozer. I failed, and tried HQ at Trent Bridge, but there were no officers there.

I wanted authorization to open fire, if necessary. The Jerries were on us so I assumed command and gave the order to fire. The incident over, I dozed off to sleep, but was awakened early in the morning by a bleary-eyed Loot who had driven through the fog on hearing that Jerry had pressed home an attack on us.

"Who gave the guns the order to go into action?" he asked.

Half-apologetically I admitted to it.

"Thank God," he said. "Now remember, I was here and I gave the order. Good night."

I never wanted to be left in that position again, but I remembered the case of one of our troops stationed on a Lincolnshire airfield. They were quartered by the

RAF on Ministry of Agriculture land, and fed by some other unit. They didn't know who was in charge of them.

Our bombers came in from a raid on Germany and, unknown to them, were followed home by German bombers. As soon as they had landed, Jerry bombed them to hell, right on the muzzles of our guns, which had no authority to fire.

I was prepared for the situation I found myself in on that foggy night and knew what I should do. We couldn't see Jerry, but we scared him off.

A sarky sergeant came in a day or two after and said he had heard that our troop had a new CO.

I looked concerned for I liked our chap, then he laughed and pointed at me as he went through the door. I could tell from the attitude of the other officers that they knew what had happened and our Loot had been given a wigging for being away from his post.

◆ ◆ ◆

Somebody in the hierarchy thought up a test for our troops. We were given the GPO telephone number of a cache of ammo.

At a certain hour, all four troops were to order a lorry and ring up the cache, collect the ammo and return to troop HQ.

I thought things over and, as there was only one lorry, I decided when zero hour arrived to grab the lorry, suspecting that the others would go directly for the ammo.

I was right, and I got the lorry and sent it on to the cache. There was only one thing that the officer at the cache could do, as we had the only lorry. This was just one of the half-baked tests of initiative they devised.

The loots were being trained on the job, and each week ours had a question sent him, to which he had to submit a written answer. He discussed these problems with me as I was the only one in the orderly room most of the day, but it was obvious he had discussed the problem with other officers.

I remember one question was what would he do if the enemy had blocked his path to his objective by felling trees across the road. There were other matters to be taken into consideration, but I forget them.

At Spondon we were guarding four factories or other installations important to the war effort, although there was also a battery of heavy anti-aircraft guns[247] in the district. One night when I was asleep, the heavies drew up outside Floradale and opened up.

The firing charge in those heavy AA guns is terrific. The noise is terrific.

I mentioned Rolls-Royce and Qualcast (I have a Qualcast lawnmower at the moment, which brings back memories), then there was the big Notts and Derby power station and an I.C.I. factory, alleged to be making dyes, but I rather think it was something more important. They were using bacteria obtained from the nearby sewage beds and had a private guard on the factory.

One day I got a call from the gun near the power station that a man in a car was behaving suspiciously. The Loot said take the lorry, and he gave me a section of men with rifles to sort the matter out. I saw the car half hidden in a hedge and got more suspicious. As we passed, the man was taking off earphones. We pulled up across his bows and the eager lads with rifles at the ready surrounded him.

It turned out that he was a GPO *wallah* following up a complaint that the power station was interfering with radio reception.

Our lads had not yet been supplied with battle dress[248] and had to clean their brass buttons every day. As soon as the lads on this power station site cleaned their's, their buttons turned purplish. They were indignant when an officer complained about their appearance.

Yes, we were in a lovely spot with the sewage beds and the I.C.I. filling the air with stink and then the power station emitting these fumes.

It was at Spondon that I met Cox. He was a Fascist—one of Oswald Moseley's men, and I think someone was after him. A few days later he tried to shoot himself and I never saw him again.

We had one Bedford two-tonner in which we took out the gunners, who slept at Floradale, for the dawn vigil and brought them home after the dusk stand-to.

They were a daft lot. How such a daft lot got together I shall never know. They had a felling axe to keep themselves provided with fire wood. One decided to test the efficiency of their steel helmets. Of course he couldn't do it with the helmet on the ground—he had to take a swipe at a chap's head. The axe didn't penetrate the metal but the dent cracked the man's skull and put him in hospital.

One gun was near a small farmhouse on the opposite side of the main road to Floradale. I think the men spent most of their time helping on the farm. The farmer and his wife were very good to them. One day they decided to sweep the chimney for madame. They cut a bush out of the nearby spinney tied a rope to it and one gunner shinned up the roof and dropped the rope down the chimney and stuck the end of the bush in the opening ready to follow the rope when the men below pulled.

But the bush was too big and wouldn't go down, nor could they pull it upward.

The lads working on the chimney called on the rest of the ten gunners to come and help. They all pulled on the rope with the result that it came down with a rush and a ton of soot smothered them.

At this juncture, a party of red tabs passing along the road and seeing the gun deserted decided to investigate and met the ten emerging with faces and clothes black. They lined up in front of the red tabs, who, I'm sure, had a lot to say to Titus.

Men were coming and going all the time. One of our new recruits, chosen because he could drive, became our permanent lorry driver, which made things easier for me. He was only a school kid.

A new regulation had been issued by the War Office that all military transport must carry a rifle in the cab. When young fellow-me-lad got his rifle he went out to the Home Farm site and tried it out. Unfortunately the sergeant major was in the vicinity and he said he heard the bullet whistle past him.

This lad had to drive across fields to get to the site and he soon got fed up with opening and closing gates. The Bedford was well-behaved and would tick over nicely. Well at one muddy gateway young fellow-me-lad steered the truck at the gate and then jumped out and ran ahead to open the gate. He slipped in the mud and the truck ran him down, and so he soon left us.

Another driver came to take his place. He was a borrower. He had half a dollar off me but I was on the spot when he got paid and I got it back. Others were not so lucky.

As troop quartermaster, I was responsible for transport and had to keep a record of mileage. After a week or two his mileage figures started creeping up and he was never there when wanted. I was not responsible for ordering his journeys but became a bit suspicious of him.

One morning the GPO telephone rang and an irate old crone with a cracked voice asked me how long that lad would be who was shifting her furniture.

I handed the phone over to the Loot who had just come in, and was tickled at his incredulity as he grasped what the old girl was telling him. We needed another new driver after the court martial.

One day I got a message over the blower that all guns were to be warned not to shoot at an orange plane that was about. This was just before Holland fell[249] and at the last minute the Dutch royal family came to England. We saw this in the papers next day.

Another warning that we got was of strange green objects suspended from parachutes. These were not to be shot at unless they were still two thousand feet above sea level. We learned later that these were land mines. One dropped at Weaverham. Another smashed a shop window at the foot of Castle Hill.

When we were at Spondon, Jerry made his push to the coast and reached Abbeville on 20 May 1940. Then between 26 May and 4 June, 300,000 Allied troops were evacuated through Dunkirk, abandoning most of their *matériel*.

That caused a flurry in the dove-cotes. If Jerry came for us, we had not much to defend ourselves with. The high command realized that we could not defend the whole coast of southern England, so it was decided that a fall-back line should be established. This was to be on the Trent and Mersey rivers, and this line was to be held to the last man.

Had the Germans invaded, at the last minute our battery was to move to the north of the Trent and be responsible for guarding Gunthorpe Bridge. We were taken there in batches so that we would be familiar with the site.

We were told: "You stay there to the last bullet. You stay there to the last man. You stay there."

On the road I met a police inspector. "Well, soldier, what do you think of things now?"

"Pretty grim," I said.

I remember Jock Huxtable—John Player's gamekeeper—and our battery quartermaster, lying in the middle of the road with a Vickers gun[250]. It was a pathetic looking thing when you thought of the might of the German army. I couldn't understand why the quartermaster was in the front line.

Jock was a great lad. I brought him home once to Papplewick. Like me, he had trouble with the Nottingham dialect. During the period of high unemployment in the 1920s and '30s, Nottingham was the only place where new pits were being sunk. Rather than accept ten shillings a week dole money, Welsh, Scots and English miners flocked to Nottingham. The local speech became one untidy, polyglot dialect.

One uncouth fellow came into Jock's QM store and flung his old shirt on to the counter. "I want a 'shot'," he said.

The little Scot bristled. "I'll gie ye a shot up the arse if you come here wi ye bad manners," he said and refused to serve him.

I mentioned a chap from Lincoln jail who deserted the first time we went into action. Well the police caught up with him and brought him in. I was one of his escorts when he was taken before the CO: "Prisoner and escort left turn".

Just then Churchill was making one of his dramatic speeches: "We shall fight on the beaches ... "[251]

We had been issued with a plain radio, specially made for the Forces with no frills. There was one on the CO's desk as he considered the prisoner's case, so he suspended proceedings to listen to Churchill.

The set jibbed just at the critical juncture. The CO scowled and twiddled the knobs but no result.

The prisoner stepped forward helpfully. "We allus thump ourn," he said and with that he brought his great bundle of five down on the set which shattered.

I had to bite my lip hard as Oates' cold eye turned on the culprit. I forget the sentence but I don't suppose that there was any mitigation for breaking the set.

I was finding it difficult to get all my jobs done in a day. The worst thing was when, owing to the lack of men who could drive, I had to leave everything and take the lorry out on a quartering job.

The Loot we had then was a nice chap. He kept a pub on Donnington car race track and as there was no racing during the war, he joined up.

He tried to help me by appealing to the troop for any man to come forward who could drive a lorry.

One man admitted to having driven a cattle truck. I was detailed to give him a test. I took the lorry down to the site near the I.C.I.

I took it across the field and handed the wheel over to him. He seemed angry and I didn't like his attitude at all. However, I was obeying orders. He raced the lorry across the field and had to swing through a narrow gate into a still narrower lane. He managed it to my surprise, and I wiped the sweat off my brow.

Over the station bridge he raced, up to the roundabout on the main road. He barged right into the traffic to the sound of squealing brakes, and then tore off for home.

The old Anglers' Arms, now replaced by a new Anglers' Arms, stood on the corner of the lane leading to the back entrance to Floradale. Two big doors enclosed the back yard of the old pub, where the delivery men used to draw in.

Just as we were at the lane end, I saw a car approaching. Our lunatic swung across the road in front of the car, over-steered for the lane, and went right through the double doors.

The Loot was wrong in ordering me to take a dubious driver on the main road and not checking his licence.

The fellow was in a temper from the start. It was obvious he had driven before, but I think he was scared.

There were two courts martial. I wanted him to be accepted, to get me off the job of driving, and I didn't want to get the Loot into trouble, so I swore at the courts martial that I thought he was competent to drive. After all, anyone could make mistakes in a strange vehicle, and it was a giant van obtained under the requisition scheme. Owners of several vans or lorries had to surrender one to the army, and you can be quite sure that they did not surrender the best.

I stuck to my guns and refused to be browbeaten by the half-dozen on the other side of the table. The brewery that owned the Anglers' Arms refused to accept the findings of the first court martial, so another attempt was made to get me to admit that the man was unfit to drive. I stuck to my guns.

I don't know what the verdict was, but this Loot disappeared from our ken, for which I was very sorry.

One day we were taken to Chilwell. A naval gun had been fixed up there on a rubbish tip outside an ordnance factory. It was in the early days of the war and a guard was pacing the 'iron curtain' round the factory, carrying a pick-axe handle. The gun was placed there I suppose so that many units could practice on it.

It was surrounded with a wall of sandbags and a cave like structure in the bag wall was the ammo store. We were taken on the gun in batches of ten, and lined up and given a number. I forget details, but each man relieved the man in front of him at a command from the officer. I don't suppose I can remember all the ten positions, but on the gun was the loader. I reckon that on an AA gun pointing upstairs, this is the hardest job of the lot because with one gloved hand he has to push a heavy shell up the spout and snatch his hand away when the next chap operates the breech, which rises and falls when desired.

If your glove gets trapped, and when you're exhausted this easily happens, you snatch your hand out quickly.

So that accounts for two men. Another man stands by the loader with the next shell. The empty cases drop at your feet when the breech comes down, and form a death trap.

Then there is a firer with his lanyard.

There are gun layers for line and for elevation. There's another man in the ammo store getting a shell which he hands to the carrier. I think the others are involved in shell carrying or shifting the empties.

We stayed there all day among the scavengers who were stacking paper in bundles. These were wet and stank of mustiness. We went in the rag gatherer's hut and sat on forms at a table which had once been white. The same musty smell invaded this room, no doubt obliterating the smell of the rag gatherers, who gave us some professional advice on military matters.

I told how Johnnie Stables fixed us up with a telephone system. The wire had to run along hedges and, in the field between the castle and the railway, the cows took a great delight in chewing the wire.

An irate—that's too mild—estate manager rang me up one morning and I gathered something was wrong on the estate. We left the batman to attend to the shop and the Loot and I walked down the road to the railway which was only a hundred yards from the castle grounds.

What a sight met our eyes. The lads were tired of mending the chewed wire and tired of driving off cows so, in the night, they took the felling axe provided to each site, and chopped down a dozen fifteen-to-twenty foot high saplings.

They dug these in across the field to hold the cable aloft. They were delighted with their effort, and looked disconcerted when Loot told them that they were naughty boys. I forget how the matter ended.

Another complaint came from an irate female. She was screaming at me. That lorry driver of ours who cleverly got himself run over, had driven into her Austin Seven and pushed her off the drive.

Now it was a long, sinuous, gravelled drive from the Borrowash road, and was blind all the way. There was no room to pass and the lad, no doubt, was driving too fast. We had him in.

"Silly old cow should have sounded her horn," he said, and then he blubbered.

The Loot went round to cool her off and inspect her car. One of our men had worked in a scrap yard, and he had fitted new front springs to the Loot's car.

He didn't use jacks because we hadn't any; he used half a dozen men.

Well we got him on the old girl's car and he replaced the bumper and wing and headlamp and she was smiling again.

I got this driver lad to take me to the Home Farm site—the one behind the castle. Coming back, I saw something in the woods through which the drive passed, which made me curious.

We parked off the road and followed an overgrown path to a yew hedge in which some topiarist had cut an ornamental gateway, but which was now overgrown.

We pressed through and behold, it was an ornamental garden with white marble figures every five yards. In the moonlight it looked very spooky.

"I've never seen anything quite like this," I said and, getting no reply, looked round. I was alone. I found my companion in a state of near breakdown in the cab. He was scared to death.

The cook called me out one day to see a delivery of fish we had received: great cod about a yard long, four or five of them lying on the back path. They stank to high heaven. This was the only fish we ever saw while I was in the army except for some kippers I bought.

The cook wrapped these in greasy paper and put them in the oven. It was Spencer, our ex-Indian Army *wallah,* who had also been in the Robin Hoods[252] and played the clarinet.

I was dubious of his cooking, but the fish were delicious.

On my travels with the lorry I often brought bits home. Curry was what he loved and it was not on ration.

One of our louts raided an old woman's hen run in a fog. The hens made a row and the old woman belabored him as he couldn't find the way out of the pen.

We had a sergeant sent to us who was a real uncouth swine. He made the conscripts' life a hell. He had come from a boxing booth and was one of those sparring partners that boxers train on when not using the bag, so his nose was driven into his face.

He had only come to us to help with the conscripts. When the batch passed out, he went with them.

I ran over a cat one day and threw it into the lorry intending to have fun with the cook.

Now the unit had organized a boxing match for the evening and our pulchritudinous sergeant considered himself to be the star. He had bought himself a rabbit and gave orders in his uncouth way to the cook as to how he wanted it cooked, in order to keep his strength up for the evening performance.

The cook resented this and when I encountered him he was in a very unhappy state of mind because this fellow lived on the premises and was always in the cook's way. I showed him the cat.

He showed no interest but walked back to the cookhouse door. I threw the cat on the garden and was about to go when the cook ran back to me. "Don't say a word," he said. "I've got an idea." There was an evil look in his eye.

Well after a day of bullying the recruits, our pompous sergeant returned and bellowed at the cook that he wanted his meal. I was out that evening as I had to bring men in from our various scattered sites for the night's performance. When I returned there was a HQ full of smiling faces, the cook included.

When I had shaken the Loot off, the batman came into the orderly room. He told me how the cook had cut the head off the cat and cooked the rest of it. Roasted potatoes as well. Well the sergeant scoffed the lot and came into the kitchen to lord it over the cook once more.

The worm turned, saying, "You've eaten the rest of it; you might as well have this and he threw the cat skin and head at the sergeant, and then he threw him his own rabbit. The fellow went outside and spewed and spewed and spewed.

He showed up at the match. He had to as all the officers were there, and he just got knocked to hell. He walked about very shamefaced after that and became a reformed character.

An outbreak of scabies occurred in the unit, manifesting itself by a rash between the fingers. It was very contagious and when men got it they were whisked off to hospital—Derby workhouse, which was where our lads were sent. The old women inmates acted as nurses and to the delight of some of the scruffs they would get into bed with their patients. I was pretty well on my own in the orderly room and felt no alarm as man after man was sent to Derby.

They trusted me and if they had any valuables it became the rule that I kept them until their return, because things had a habit of disappearing in the workhouse.

I little realized that I was handling infected articles until, one night, my hands itched and I saw the tell tale spots between my fingers.

I didn't want to go to hospital. I had a bottle of Dettol[253] in my kit and I rubbed neat Dettol on the spots. The itching went and, after a repeat of the Dettol treatment, I was okay, and yet men were being kept in hospital for a week.

There was nearly a tragic sequel to the story because a friend of mine on a site near the I.C.I. works was taken straight from hospital back to the site, and so he phoned up to ask if I would send his effects to him.

I had sealed them up in an envelope and I didn't trust anyone to take it down as suspicion would fall on me if anything was missing, so I decided to take it to him myself. I told the Loot that I was going to this site, and he said it was time I got out of the place a bit.

So off I went, down the road, over the main railway line and past the railwayman's hut, now deserted because we had been supplied with brand new huts.

We were not allowed to make a bee line for the huts or guns because tracks across grass are very visible from the air, especially if several converge, so when I came in sight of the hut which I had not seen before, I hesitated.

At this moment, the air raid sirens blew and, away in the distance, the Heavies' anti-aircraft guns opened up. The searchlights got busy and I saw them stabbing at one spot in the darkened sky.

Of course, one isn't allowed near a gun when it's in action, so I stayed on the perimeter and watched the fun. I don't think our lads saw their victim but they knew it was in a certain bank of cloud from the concentration of searchlights, which didn't depend on visual sightings.

Our lads fired a burst on open sights. Shortly afterward, the searchlights eagerly concentrated on one spot, and then we saw a dark object, a wing, twisting and twirling in the searchlight beam.

I was so fascinated, that I became deaf to other sounds. Suddenly there was a hiss and, before I could hit the ground, the whole place blew up. When a loaded bomber is about to crash, bombs are jettisoned for obvious reasons. They found me in the morning light, half-buried and spitting blood.

The wrecked bomber was close by. Its burst fuel tanks had sprayed me with diesel oil so that the dye had come out of my khaki uniform and stained me like a Chink. They gave me a cup of tea and, very groggily, I went back to the orderly room.

I had no external injuries but, unknown to me, a lung was damaged. For some time I carried on but I didn't pick up my strength, and went off my food, which didn't help matters.

Eventually my leave was due. As Margaret had moved back to The Heysoms, I was bound for Northwich. I had a BSA motor bike and the HQ gang gave me a push start. I couldn't use the starter, I was so groggy.

I clung on to the bike for dear life, but due to my worsening condition, I over-worked the clutch instead of changing gear.

After fifty miles, at Holmes Chapel, the clutch packed up.

I don't know how I did it, but I pushed that bike another four miles to Middlewich. I could hardly get over the station bridge. A woman had a second look at me and gave me a push. She was the only one to offer help.

I found a baker's shop open and left the bike there to be called for. The young man saw how groggy I was and pushed me in his van and dropped me at Northwich bus terminus. I got a Hartford bus, and people kept turning round in the bus to look at me. It was most disconcerting.

I reached The Heysoms and staggered upstairs. The next thing I knew Dr. Duff was leaning over me. He and Mother struggled to remove my harness and get my greatcoat undone—we had long cavalry greatcoats

Duff put his stethoscope down my coats as well as he could.

"There's no air going into that lung," he said.

Strange how this remains very vivid to me and yet things that happened at the same time or thereabouts are vague.

Margaret contacted my unit at Spondon, and they asked for a military doctor to see me, so a Dr. Faulkner from a local anti-aircraft unit came over once or twice.

He was very nice and eventually got me into Davyhulme which had been turned into a military hospital. The family gave him a bottle of whisky on his last visit.

Well that ended the Gore, Gort and Gamelin trio, and now our Forces had a chance of winning with this triple exodus!!!

◆   ◆   ◆

At one point we were, for a time, encircling Derby with our ten Bofors guns. Here were Rolls-Royce making aero engines and Qualcast packing up their lawn-mowers to make tanks, but neither took a hit while we were there.

Dawn and dusk were the danger hours when sneak raiders came in. So after dusk we could relax. It was my only time off.

If any mail had come in for friends of mine, constantly being moved from one site to another, I used to dodge the Home Guard patrols and walk across country, cross the river by a footbridge, deliver the mail, have a chat, and so home. It was often so dark I had to follow fences to get back.

It was during these trips that I noticed that on some nights, the birds in the hedges would be disturbed. A blackbird would fly screaming down the hedgerow and flocks of small birds would start chattering animatedly in the bushes.

I soon began to couple this conduct with an impending raid. Sure enough, on these nights, the sirens would go.

How did these birds know? Could they hear the distant *burra-burra* of the German diesel engines, or was it distant gunfire? I never found out, and then my army days were over.

After two months at home, an attempt to get me into Moston Park military hospital failed because Jerry got there first. Then there was another long wait, and then Davyhulme.

When I was in Davyhulme military hospital, I heard our mob was going to North Africa.

I cursed my luck at being left out, but in those days I didn't feel much like fighting. I never heard any more about them.

I was discharged at Davyhulme during the Manchester blitz, and so home. But, no doubt another bomb blast in Davyhulme when the hospital was attacked, had contributed to a worsening of my condition.

At last I got to Market Drayton Sanatorium. Here my morning temperature was 102 degrees as regular as clockwork. What the night temperature was was no one's business. I was washed down with cold water when it reached certain levels.

Well here's the story: I used to lie at night—I had five pillows in an arm-chair—and I'd look out across the heathland where one pine tree taller than the rest was bent over and, against the sky, looked like a witch on a broomstick, which was our divisional patch[254] when I was with 112th LAA.

In this spinney was a cock pheasant and some nights he was very vociferous. On these nights the sirens went and we were rushed to the shelters. One night this bird started screaming just as the night nurse came past.

I said, "They are coming, Sister."

"What are?"

She had hardly got the words out when the sirens went. She had no time to bother with me but looked at me strangely later, when she tucked me in my little iron bed. A few nights later the pheasant shrieked again and I rang the bell.

She came rushing.

"They are coming," was all I had time to say before the sirens went.

Folk began to look at me strangely but I was in no talking mood, even with a journalist, Bert Simcock of the *Staffordshire Sentinel,* a few beds away. Well this happy warning system went on for a few weeks and the strange looks passed to the doctors who were puzzled.

Well, in a land suffering from an acute meat shortage, and only a few miles from the Potteries, an inevitable ending came to my pheasant. After this I had to lie doggo and pretend to be asleep when I heard footsteps in the night. I've never told this tale to anyone before, but the thing was good while it lasted.

POSTSCRIPT—THE
SECOND HALF

GWWG made a good recovery from the lung injury and tuberculosis that knocked him out of the war in 1941 and confined him for a couple of years to hospitals at Davyhulme (where he was bombed again), Wrenbury and Market Drayton.

As more interesting work was hard to find in Northwich, he reluctantly went back to teaching after the war, and settled down with his wife and son in a damp old house which kept him busy for a number of years.

Constance and Charlie moved into a small house in Davenham. Constance died of Parkinson's disease in 1949 and Charlie of cancer in 1956.

GWWG taught briefly at Moulton and Davenham and then secured a permanent appointment at Winnington School, where he remained for eleven years. In 1957 he moved to Church Minshull, a small country school less than four miles from Calveley, where he taught until his retirement in 1970.

During the Second World War and subsequently, he applied his imagination to practical matters. He held a patent for a tool storage system, and was a member of the Society of Inventors, although he never made much money from his many and varied inventions. He also tried his hand at writing and completed several manuscripts.

He was devoted to his wife Margaret, and she to him, and their greatest joy was in the time spent with their grandchildren, Louise and Richard.

Margaret died at home in 1984, and Geoffrey on the eve of what would have been Margaret's eighty-third birthday in 1986.

ENDNOTES

1. Born Adlestrop, Gloucestershire, 7 April 1845; died Castle, Northwich, Cheshire, 23 April 1925.

2. The black sheep of the Newman family, John Henry Newman (1801–90) was a prominent Anglican churchman who converted to Roman Catholicism in 1845 and was elevated to the College of Cardinals in 1879.

3. Levi's youngest son, Charlie, was a pupil teacher at Hartford School and subsequently headmaster there for about 25 years from the First World War to the Second.

4. Chemical manufacturers. John Brunner and Ludwig Mond went into partnership as Brunner, Mond & Company in 1873 to manufacture soda ash, the trade name for sodium carbonate. Brunner, Mond combined with other chemical companies in 1926 to form Imperial Chemical Industries (I.C.I.), but the Brunner-Mond name resurfaced in 1991 with a reorganization of the chemical industry. Sir John Brunner was a generous benefactor to the area and built a public library and salt museum, and a school.

5. The Green. With Chester Road and the northern end of School Lane, The Green forms the triangle in which Hartford Church and the Church Hall stand. Constance Gore leased the Church Hall for a short period for use as a schoolroom after The Heysoms was requisitioned by the government in 1942 to accommodate the bombed-out Liverpool Lighterage Company.

6. There is no record of any brother who would have been of military age in the 1850s. Levi's siblings were born between 1844 and 1862. A brother Ivo? is, however, recorded in the 1871 Census as being nine years old, and was therefore born in 1862. Levi, born in 1845 was the oldest boy. However, his father. Abraham (born 1816–17), had several brothers: Richard (born 1819), William (born 1826) and John (born 1829), any of whom could have served in the Crimea (1854–56). An Ivor of this generation may have escaped bureaucratic notice. Charles Edward Newman knew of

209

this story, without offering the name Ivor, but added the detail that the individual concerned served in the Black Watch.

7. The story was presented as evidence of the already well-substantiated stupidity of the British military establishment, but wearing enemy uniforms might be expected to result in deaths from friendly fire in the best-regulated armies.

8. A popular print of Sir Edwin Landseer's picture of a bloodhound and a terrier, still on the market in 2001 at $50 US.

9. Abraham Newman (1816–1914), farm laborer, groom; Adlestrop, Gloucestershire.

10. Following the marriage of Levi and Annie Wainwright on 1 May 1869. They later lived at Davenham, Hartford, Needwood and Castle.

11. GWWG contracted tuberculosis during the Second World War and so became an unwilling expert on respiratory problems.

12. Levi's youngest daughter, Rose Ellen Newman, 24 March 1878–8 November 1932.

13. Herman Eugen Falk (1820–98) was born in Danzig and came to England at the age of eighteen to join his brother in the timber importing business in Hull. They supplied Robert Stephenson with sleepers for railroad construction and shipped salt as return cargo to the Baltic ports. By 1856, Falk had taken over a salt mine and works at Winsford. In 1888 he achieved his goal of uniting salt industry interests in The Salt Union, otherwise known as Falk's Salt Union. His wife was a Hadfield and his son Herman J. Falk (1857–1941) was with John Maynard Keynes on the team of economic advisors at the 1919 Versailles Conference.

14. Northwich had two shipyards, built beside the River Weaver: Pimblott's, south of the town, and Yarwood's, close to the town centre. The river was canalized in the eighteenth century, and from that time provided passage for some fairly large river and coastal craft. Vessels of 300 tons could sail as far upstream as Winsford.

15. Born at Saltney or Handbridge on 1 January 1843; died Castle, Northwich on 21 July 1924. Annie was baptized at St. Mary on the Hill, Chester.

16. GWWG's account is not consistent with census data. Annie's parents, Job Wainwright (1811–83) and Martha Joinson Wainwright (1815–99) lived at Stoney Bridge, Saltney, in 1841, and at 55 Hough Green, Handbridge, in 1851. Hough Green is the main thoroughfare between Saltney and Handbridge. As Martha outlived Job by sixteen years, there was no wicked stepmother. Job is variously described as a labourer, carter and coal agent, and as he fathered eleven children, it is unlikely that the family was well-off. There is some evidence that Annie suffered from Alzheimer's disease in her later years. This may explain various inconsistencies between what she told GWWG and the record.

17. Frederick Temple (1821–1902), the reforming Anglican bishop who became Archbishop of Canterbury (1896–1902). His son William Temple (1881–1944), was successively Archbishop of York (1929–42) and of Canterbury (1942–44).

18. See footnote 15.

19. There is evidence that they were married at St. Oswald's Church, Chester, on 1 May 1869.

20. Her grandmother was Susannah Reynolds (1769–1840). She married Timothy Wainwright (1766–1843) in Chester in 1790, and their son Job (1811–83) was Annie's father. Sir Joshua Reynolds (1723–92) was born in Devonshire.

21. A distance of fifteen miles.

22. A pitchfork.

23. Voluntary Aid Detachment, British Red Cross Society. The VADs were introduced in 1910 to provide an emergency volunteer reserve for the Territorial Force Medical Services, but heavy casualties during the war meant that they were called on to staff many hospitals in the United Kingdom, and some units served at the Fronts, including Russia. The best and brightest women of that generation were VAD nurses: Enid Bagnold (1889–1981), Agatha Christie (1891–1976), Vera Brittain (1896–1970), etc. Constance was very much involved in Red Cross work before and during the First World War.

24. A village south of Prestatyn, Flintshire, within walking distance of the sea.

25. In fact, Annie Wainwright was at Warrington (Teachers') Training College in 1861–62, and so was better qualified than most for a teaching

appointment. It's unlikely she would have had to rely on patronage, although a recommendation wouldn't have done any harm. She was the first member of the family to have a college education.

26. Second wife (1860) and widow of Hugh Cholmondeley, 2nd Baron Delamere (1811–87). She died in 1911. It was their son Hugh, the 3rd Baron Delamere (1870–1931), who played a prominent part in the history of the Kenya Colony.

27. A *cul-de-sac* off Chester Road, where the Gore family lived between leaving The Kennels at Calveley, and acquiring The Heysoms, which was on the other side of Chester Road.

28. Polly Harrison (1883–1977) married George Wainwright-Newman (1879–1953) in 1908.

29. Daughter of William Newman and Matilda Cole.

30. Probably Clara's daughter, Violet Dorothy Alcock (1900–88), who married William Isaac.

31. The Beach, Hartford, was one of the better houses in the district. Beach Road ran from Greenbank to Weaverham.

32. More likely King Frederick IX of Denmark (1899–1972).

33. The Heysoms was an old 1640 farmhouse at Greenbank, west of Northwich, which had been refaced with Ruabon-type brick during the Victorian era.

34. At St. Wilfrid's Church, Davenham, 18 July 1900.

35. Alice Anne Owen died of progressive pernicious anemia at Calveley, 19 December 1893. She was thirty-six and left four children ranging in age from six to eleven. The term *progressive pernicious anemia* was first used in 1872 to describe vitamin B12 deficiency. In 1934, Minot, Murphy and Whipple shared a Nobel prize for their work on liver therapy for pernicious anemia. During the 1930s, scientists extracted and crystallized a chemical essential to enabling the body to utilize both vitamin B12 and vitamin B6. Originally called "factor M" or "vitamin M", this chemical is now known as folic acid. It was not until 1945, however, that researchers actually crystallized vitamin B12.

36. On a map dated 1910, Huxley Street, Castle, is shown as having seventy-nine houses. Huxley Street may have had a relatively high rate of volun-

teer enlistment early in the war (to account, in part, for high casualties) as a drill hall of the Cheshire Regiment (Territorial Army) had been built just round the corner on Darwin Street in 1911. The regiment's thirty-eight battalions had 8,000 men killed during the war. Actually the system of county regiments survived, but some attempt may have been made to avoid high regional concentrations of casualties lest public morale be affected. Despite forecasts of heavy casualties on D-Day, several county regiments had multiple battalions engaged. The Royal Ulster Rifles, however, was the only British regiment to have both regular battalions in action: 1 RUR was with 6th Airborne, and 2 RUR with 3rd British Infantry Division—'the Iron Division'—on Sword Beach.

37. Wars of the Roses, 23 September 1459.

38. Hundred Years War, 26 August 1346.

39. The Cheshire archers made a come-back. Sir Edward Stanley's Cheshire and Lancashire archers made up almost one third of the English army at Flodden, 9 September 1513, and played a decisive part in destroying the Scottish host. A further 1,200 men from Lancashire and Cheshire served under other commanders at Flodden (including Abbott John Buckley of Vale Royal who led a force of 300), so almost 10,000 of the Earl of Surrey's army of 26,000 men came from these two counties.

40. The wax museum was opened in London in 1835.

41. The Rev. John Roy Newman Booth (1899–1968).

42. The Pembroke table was a small, drop-leaf breakfast table with a drawer. It is unclear exactly when this type of table was developed and the term Pembroke applied, but it has been suggested that it was conceived by Henry Herbert, 9th Earl of Pembroke (1692–1750), or by an early 18th century Countess of Pembroke. One of the earliest examples appears in Thomas Chippendale's *Director* (1754).

43. *Diabetes insipidus*, a rare disorder of water metabolism and an entirely different disease from common *diabetes mellitus*. It involves excessive urination, dehydration and severe thirst.

44. 21 December 1908.

45. John Pendlebury Booth (1869–1950).

46. Bridge Foot is the side street at the south end of Bridge Street, Warrington, that leads to the Greyhound Track. A prime location for a pawnshop.

47. Roy married Charlotte Woods Houghton (1901–1978) on 13 February 1923. Their daughter Charlotte was born 14 October 1923, so she could hardly have known she was pregnant when she was married.

48. George V (1865–1936) married his cousin Princess Mary (1867–1953) in 1893. Mary was the daughter of Francis, Duke of Teck and of Fat Mary, as she was known.

49. Dorothy Gwendoline Newman.

50. Opened at Leytonstone in 1903 as a hospital for paupers, successor to the workhouses of an earlier period. Inmates were not to have any communication with the opposite sex; were only allowed official food, and no strong drink. Non-religious reading material had to be approved by the West Ham Union Guardians. Shortly after the opening of the hospital, the Guardians' financial affairs were investigated. As a result, one of them killed himself and five more were sentenced to penal servitude.

51. Annie Wainwright's sister, Elizabeth (1839–1919), emigrated to New Zealand with her husband, Thomas Evans, a tailor. Lynsey Melville of Wellington, New Zealand, confirms that the antipodean visitor in the 1890s was her grandfather, William Edgar Evans (1869–1932). He had followed his father into the tailoring business (not newspapers) and his visit to England was, in part, professional development, and partly to visit relatives, including his grandmother, Martha Joinson Wainwright (1815–1899) who still lived in the Chester area.

52. GWWG omitted to mention that Philip means *lover of horses.*

53. GWWG taught at Winnington School, Northwich, from 1946 to 1957.

54. This must certainly refer to Lizzie's son.

55. *The Good Companions* by J.B. Priestly was first published in 1929 by Heinemann.

56. The family lived at 18 The Crescent, Northwich, from 1942 to 1946.

57. Born Whitegate 1876; died Calcutta 1936.

58. William Johnson Alcock, Member of the Institution of Civil Engineers (M.I.C.E.) and of the Institution of Mechanical Engineers (M.I. Mech.E.), born Northwich 1876, died Calcutta 1940.

59. A mile south of Tarporley on the Nantwich road.

60. Richard Alkoke, Chaplain, Clerk of works.

61. On one occasion, William Gore met a woman in old-fashioned dress on the stairs at The Heysoms. Geoffrey was waiting for him at the top of the stairs, and saw his father pause and turn half way up, as if meeting a stranger. "Who was that woman?" he asked Geoffrey, who had seen no one. Parts of The Heysoms dated from at least 1640, as a beam removed from the house during the Westons' renovations bore that date. Geoffrey subsequently built the inscribed part of the beam into the top of an oak bookcase.

62. Ammonium hydroxide is a caustic alkali that can cause burns to the mouth, throat and stomach.

63. Born Whitegate 1879; died Stretford? 1953. At some point he decided to hyphenate his name as Wainwright-Newman.

64. A northern suburb of Crewe.

65. Gertrude Pennington, 1879–1925.

66. She died of Parkinson's disease, 3 September 1949. Dr. Constantin von Economo (1876–1931) claimed that *encephalitis lethargica*, which reached epidemic proportions between 1915 and 1926, when the causative virus suddenly disappeared, could lead to Parkinsonism years after the original flu-like infection.

67. A public house on London Road, Northwich, near the north end of The Crescent.

68. The Army Cyclist Corps was formed in 1915 and disbanded in 1919. The corps included cyclist units from other regiments, including one Scottish unit that had served in South Africa, 1900–02.

69. Possibly Kirkby. There is no Kirby near Knowsley.

70. John Gore (1824–58). He died of phthisis (tuberculosis) at the age of thirty-four on his fifth wedding anniversary.

71. Edward Geoffrey Stanley (1799–1869), 14th Earl of Derby, succeeded to the title in 1851, two years before William Gore was born. GWWG was called Geoffrey for him. The 14th Earl, was Prime Minister three times (1852; 1858–9; 1866–8). As Whig Colonial Secretary he sponsored the bill abolishing slavery in the British Empire (1833), but subsequently joined the Tories under Peel, and led the protectionist Tories after the 1846 split over Peel's free trade policies. In 1862 he was offered the throne of Greece but turned it down. (From the 15th to the 18th centuries the Stanleys had been kings of the Isle of Man.) As William Gore was growing up there, the 14th Earl would have dominated Knowsley, almost as a god. Knowsley Hall was the seat of the Earls of Derby from the 1400s and the Gores had lived in Knowsley since the mid-seventeenth century at least.

72. The Derby family name.

73. GWWG's own *alma mater* and now a college of the University of Liverpool.

74. Work started on the Manchester Ship Canal in November 1887. The canal was opened on 1 January 1894.

75. His first wife was Alice Anne Owen (1857–93), daughter of Thomas Owen (1822–75), a blacksmith and a neighbour at Knowsley. He may have been the uncle of the blacksmith Owen that GWWG worked for on his vacations at Knowsley.

76. Born in 1882 and died in British Columbia in 1974.

77. The site of St. Oswald's Church at Winwick was chosen, according to legend, by a pig who carried and laid its foundation stones. His likeness was carved on the west front of the church.

78. *Sans changer* is the motto on the Derby arms. It was Sir Walter Scott who wrote the lines:
    "*Victory!—*
    Charge, Chester, charge! On, Stanley, on!"
    Were the last words of Marmion.
    They come from *Marmion*, of course, and refer to Sir Edward Stanley's distinguished role at Flodden Field in 1513.

79. And also in the Zeebrugge Raid in 1918.

80. Catapult or slingshot.

81. In some sources, Aron; 1850–1924. His wife was Caroline Brown (1850–1928).

82. Probably Simonswood Moss, north of Knowsley.

83. A possibly mythical ancestor who fought with the army of William of Orange at the Boyne in 1690, there saving the life of James Stanley (1664–1735/36) who became a major general and, in 1702, the 10th Earl Derby. The grateful Stanley brought Gore to Knowsley and gave him a law-enforcement job. One of his horse pistols, dating from approximately 1710, is still in the family. But there is evidence that the Gores were at Knowsley at least a generation earlier and no member of the family can be identified with this John Gore.

84. Edith Mary Gore (born 1884) was John's second wife. They married in their later years, probably after she retired from teaching. He had a son, Hartley, by his first wife. Hartley had two daughters.

85. In the mid-twentieth century the perimeter of the estate was about ten miles. The great boundary wall was built in 1845–50.

86. Owen Benison Gore, second son of William and Alice, born 1884.

87. The Prince of Wales, later Edward VII, married Princess Alexandra of Denmark (1844–1925) in 1863.

88. The 17th Earl of Derby (1865–1948) was Director General of Recruiting in 1915–16, War Minister in 1916–18, and then British Ambassador in Paris. He is described as a fat ruddy-cheeked man of the greatest good-humor and integrity.

89. Sappers are private soldiers in the Royal Engineers.

90. One of Bruce Bairnsfather's celebrated cartoons, entitled *That Evening Star-shell*. The lines are from Wagner's *Tannhauser*.

91. Mabel Richardson Gore (1887–1974). She and Harry were married in July 1914.

92. Four miles north of Calveley.

93. Constance was twenty-eight when she married in 1900. Her husband was forty-six.

94. Older daughter of William and Alice, born 1884.

95. Charles Peace (1832–79) spent much of his criminal career in Sheffield but lived and taught music in Cheshire at one time. He was living in Sale around the time he shot and killed P.C. Cox at Old Trafford. It is possible that William Gore met him early in his own teaching career.

96. A type of gig; a small, one-horse, two-wheeled carriage.

97. William Johnson Alcock's only known uncle was George Alcock (1820–1901). It seems likely that GWWG was thinking of George's son, Willie's cousin, also named George (1850–1942). His wife was Isabella Guthrie Neaves (1846–1930).

98. Elsewhere in his text, GWWG has Willie working for Mr. Major at harvest-time.

99. The 1896 edition of *Kelly's Directory of Cheshire* lists De F. Pennefather, Esq. as occupant of Calveley Hall. The de Knoops must have arrived later.

100. Youngest of the four children of William and Alice, born 1887. Annie Louise Gore studied cheese-making at the Worleston Dairy Institute, and subsequently married John Key, son of a Leicestershire farmer.

101. Actually the Boy Scouts aren't quite that old. The camp on Brownsea Island took place in 1907 and *Scouting for Boys* appeared in 1908.

102. Sir Hugh Calveley (c.1320–94) resided at Lea, 3½ miles north of Chester, when not campaigning in Europe, which he usually was. He bought the advowson of Bunbury in 1385 to establish a collegiate church where prayers might be said in perpetuity for his soul. Calveley was the estate of his cousins, the senior branch of the family.

103. A concealed fence, usually in a dry moat.

104. Built about 1838, according to *Kelley's Directory* (1896).

105. A kind of soil consisting mainly of clay mixed with calcium carbonate, used as a fertilizer.

106. There had been rinderpest outbreaks in 1714 and 1745, but these bones would probably date from the devastating epidemic of 1865–67 which resulted in the establishment of state veterinary medicine in the United Kingdom.

107. For young chicks.

108. The Irish Mail had run daily between Euston and Holyhead since 1848.

109. Bunbury was hit several times by bombers on their way to or from Liverpool or Crewe. On this occasion, a land-mine packed with explosive and dropped by parachute so that it exploded at ground level, severely damaged the village. Local people believed that it was unloaded by a German plane that had been attempting to reach the railway junction and yards at Crewe, but was frustrated by the heavy anti-aircraft defences there. A row of cottages was demolished and the roof, windows and one side of the church were demolished. The Gore grave, on the other side of the church, was not damaged. Some sources date the incident to 1941.

110. Minoru won the Derby in 1909.

111. Edward had his appendix out in June 1902.

112. A local name for Nantwich, probably from the Welsh who came there to trade for salt in the Middle Ages.

113. *Victoria Regina.*

114. Canals or canalized sections of rivers were sometimes colloquially known as *cuts.*

115. The land girls were members of the Women's Land Army. As the Western Front meat-grinder consumed immense numbers of men who had worked on the land in peacetime, shortage of farm labor threatened the national food supply. So the Women's Land Army was formed. Initial resistance by farmers (and by farmers' wives) was overcome by Board of Trade propagandists who toured rural areas, and by 1917 more than 260,000 women were working as farm labourers. The Women's Land Army was mobilized again in 1939 and finally disbanded in 1950.

116. Nut of the horsechestnut tree (*Aesculus hippocastanum*), which is not a true chestnut but a buckeye.

117. RAF squadrons were operational in Afghan border areas from 1919 to 1925, and again in the 1930s.

118. The 1944 Education Act introduced the concept that the government provide the children of the masses with secondary education...up to a point. Twenty per cent would go on to state-run grammar schools and have a shot at a university education; the others would go to secondary modern schools until they joined the labour force at the age of fifteen. The 11-plus examination, which included questions to measure intelli-

gence, was used to separate the sheep from the goats. Many children took this rather important examination before they were eleven years old.

119. Sir Roger Gilbert Bannister, MD, was the first man to run a four-minute mile, Iffley Road, Oxford, 1954.

120. About five miles.

121. A young eel.

122. The OED defines a ferret as a half-tamed variety of the common polecat (*Putorius foetidus*).

123. Hedge sparrow.

124. Popular television entertainer of the 1960s and 1970s.

125. Colostrum or green milk.

126. Geoffrey taught at Church Minshull School, four miles east of Calveley, for the thirteen years before he retired in 1970.

127. An expensive ten-volume reference book edited by Arthur Mee.

128. Lord High Admiral Howard knighted Beeston and several other captains on 5 August 1588, while the battle still raged. Sir George died at the age of 101 in 1601, having lived through the entire sixteenth century.

129. Fêtes have been held in Beeston Castle grounds over the years and GWWG's description is consistent with other accounts.

130. GWWG taught at Hucknall, in Nottinghamshire, from 1937 until the beginning of the Second World War.

131. Celebrated on Queen Victoria's birthday, 24 May.

132. The birch was made from a bunch of lightweight branches, usually from three to five feet in length, tied together at one end to make a handle and leaving a spray of twigs at the business end. It was applied to the bare backside to maximize the pain and humiliation.

133. Clara's son, George Edgar Alcock (1902–75).

134. Son of George Wainwright-Newman (1879–1953) and Polly Harrison (1883–1977). Gerald died in 1970.

135. An archaic term for a shoot or sprout, or here, the process of removing sprouts.

136. Pte. Charlie Alcock (1898–1922), 4th Reserve Battalion, South Lancashire Regiment (Prince of Wales Volunteers), survived the war but died in Calcutta at the age of 24, apparently from the effects of having been gassed.

137. Actually seven years younger. The war ended before GWWG reached his teens.

138. As a full member of the Church of England.

139. 10 March 1921, when GWWG was fifteen.

140. The Rev. Edgar Stockdale, perpetual curate of St. David's, Wettenhall, and curate at Calveley since 1889.

141. Welshman. *Taffy* is the English perception of the Welsh for David, patron saint of Wales.

142. Tom Foy (1879–1917) was a Manchester music hall and pantomime comedian of Irish parentage. He was noted for his act with a live donkey.

143. Cattle sheds, from the Old English.

144. Handle.

145. Under a pile of earth which would preserve them.

146. The sharp, curved, heavy-bladed knife of the Gurkhas.

147. That part of the field close to the hedge or fence which machinery could not mow effectively.

148. Jingo was probably a euphemism for Jesus used in the patter of 17th century conjurers, but the song was written by G.W. Hunt at the time of the Russo-Turkish War of 1877–78, when anti-Russian feeling ran high and Disraeli sent the Mediterranean fleet to Constantinople.

149. Field Marshal Frederick Sleigh Roberts, 1st Earl Roberts of Kandahar (1832–1914).

150. Not true, although the Roberts family was the first to achieve the distinction. The brother and son of Major C.J.S. Gough, VC, 5th Bengal European Cavalry, both won VCs; the brothers during the Indian Mutiny, and the son in Somaliland in 1903. Captain W.N. Congreve won a VC in the Anglo-Boer War and his son was awarded a VC in the First World War. Both were Rifle Brigade officers.

151. Powell, Geoffrey: *Buller: A Scapegoat?—A Life of General Sir Redvers Buller VC* (1839–1908); London, Leo Cooper, 1994. Powell's biography, using

fresh material, argues that a near-conspiracy of the press, politicians, landed interests and military rivals succeeded in destroying a fine officer and in permanently damaging his reputation.

152. David Lloyd George (1863–1945) was Liberal chancellor of the exchequer (1908–15) and prime minister (1916–22). Rejection by the House of Lords of his 1909 budget, which sought to finance old-age pensions, led to passage of the 1911 Parliament Act, curtailing the power of the Lords.

153. By the 1960s, the Barony had become a maternity hospital. William Gore's great-grandson, Richard, was born there 7 July 1963.

154. Elsewhere, GWWG gives the name as Pritchard.

155. Elsewhere GWWG says he was nine years old when he went to Crewe. He would have been nine in December 1914 and, on this basis, would have gone to Crewe in the summer of 1915.

156. Guy Fawkes Night had been celebrated annually on 5 November since the seventeenth century.

157. Crewe station was one of the most important rail junctions in the country. It was already the junction of three railway lines by 1837 and over the next thirty years became the hub of six systems. Locomotive manufacture became a major industry circa 1840, and the Great Junction Railway had built 200 houses for its employees by 1843. Much of the station that GWWG knew would have dated from the 1860s. By the 1960s, all the country stations between Crewe and Chester had been closed.

158. Before cheap alarm clocks became available, many companies sent knocker-uppers around to the homes of their workers each morning to make sure they got to work on time.

159. The DCM is a second-level decoration for NCOs and ORs, ranking between the Victoria Cross and the Military Medal.

160. Freckleton, a small village near Preston, was the scene of one of the Second World War's worst aircraft accidents. A B-24H Liberator of the U.S. 8th Air Force crashed while attempting to land at Warton in a severe thunderstorm on 23 August 1944. The plane, with a crew of three, was on a test flight and unarmed, but spilled fuel from its tanks ignited. A total of sixty-one people died, including thirty-eight children in the local school, and two women teachers.

161. The British Empire lost 900,000 dead in the First World War and many of the two million wounded passed through Crewe station on their way home to live or die. After a major battle, the hospital trains were full and frequent. Sixty thousand men were wounded on a single day, 1 July 1916, when the Somme offensive opened, not counting the dead.

162. Harry Lauder (1870–1950), an extremely popular Scots entertainer, was knighted by George V in 1919 in recognition of his work in recruitment and in maintaining morale during the war. His only son, John, a captain in the Argyll and Sutherland Highlanders, was killed by a sniper on the Western Front in December 1916.

163. According to her certificates, Constance Mary Gore became an Associate of the British Red Cross Society in July 1910. She passed a St. John Ambulance Association first aid course with Dr. S.H. Langston Archer at Bunbury in May 1911 and a St. John course in home nursing a year later. She was a member of the Red Cross VAD by May 1914 and was reexamined in home nursing. In May 1919 she completed five years of VAD service and was elected Member of the British Red Cross Society. One of her medals was for ten years Red Cross service.

164. The first Zeppelin raids on Great Yarmouth and King's Lynn in January 1915 caused considerable alarm in a population that had felt more or less secure, as each dirigible could carry a two-ton bomb load. However, the Zeppelins' vulnerability to explosive shells which ignited the hydrogen that filled their envelopes, and to interception by faster aircraft, meant that seventy-seven of the German fleet of 115 Zeppelins had been destroyed or badly damaged by 1917 when the last raids took place. More than 1,500 British civilians were killed in German air raids during the war, but few, if any, as far west as Cheshire.

165. *From John o'Groats to Land's End* by Robert and John Naylor, Caxton, 1916. Privately printed. The book is an account of a journey the Naylor brothers made on foot in 1871.

166. Arthur Machen wrote a story called *The Bowmen*, which was printed in the *London Evening News* of 29 September 1914. To summarize: A soldier of the hard-pressed British Expeditionary Force, retreating from Mons, murmurs an ancient prayer as his unit is about to be over-run by the German horde—*Adsit Anglis, Sanctus Georgius!* And a ghostly host of English archers appears and mows down the Germans, their arrows leaving invisi-

ble but lethal wounds. Despite Machen's assertion that his story was wholly fiction, it was soon widely believed that the salvation of the BEF was due to angelic intervention and even A.J.P. Taylor appears to give credence to the story in his book, *The First World War* (1963). Oxford historians of that period, however, thought A.J.P. Taylor was a flake.

167. Convalescent wounded wore blue uniforms with a white shirt and red tie.

168. The British Mark I helmet, developed from the Brodie Type A, was stamped out of a single piece of 12 per cent manganese steel.

169. The first true stainless steel was invented by Harry Brearley of Brown Firth Laboratories, Sheffield, in 1913, but the war delayed commercial development.

170. *Summer Holidays Among the Glories of Northern France: Her Cathedrals and Churches* by T. Francis Bumpus (London, 1905) was a well-illustrated book on ecclesiastical architecture. Years later, GWWG gave it to Felicity Alcock as a token of friendship.

171. William Gore was 60 when the war began; 64 when it ended.

172. Allotments were plots for the growing of vegetables, usually by people who did not have gardens of their own.

173. The hobble skirt was the height of fashion between 1910 and 1914, but the war rang down the curtain on that impracticable garment.

174. The battlecruiser HMS Tiger sustained heavy punishment at Dogger Bank in 1915, and took fifteen direct hits at Jutland in the following year. If Jack Crank was in Dodie's class, he would have been born in 1900–01. Jack Cornwell VC (born January 1900) joined the navy at the age of fifteen and was just four months past his sixteenth birthday when mortally wounded on the cruiser Chester at Jutland (31 May 1916). A filthy and tattered White Ensign used to hang in Chester Cathedral—the battle flag flown by HMS Chester at Jutland. Beneath it was a shrine dedicated to Jack Cornwell, which doubtless inspired many boys to join the Royal Navy.

175. General Ian Standish Monteith Hamilton (1853–1947) had been Kitchener's chief of staff during the Second Anglo-Boer War and, during the First World War, when given a command in the Mediterranean (including the Dardanelles), he had trouble standing up to his former chief on resource issues. He was recalled in October 1915 and not given another

command. He is, however, described as decent, heroic, courteous and kindly. He was a competent tactician, but lacked the ruthlessness and ability to remove incompetent subordinates that would have made him a great general. Given the abysmal quality of the British officer corps, Hamilton probably ranked as above average, even if he didn't beat Mustafa Kemal.

176. While the 22nd Regiment of Foot, subsequently the Cheshires, was not with Wolfe at Quebec, the regiment's grenadier company was one of the constituent companies of the Louisburg Grenadiers. Wolfe was leading this force when mortally wounded, and Benjamin West's celebrated picture of The Death of Wolfe shows Lieutenant Henry Browne of the 22nd tending the dying general, while a tall grenadier of the 22nd stands close by wringing his hands in anguish. West (1738–1820), a Pennsylvanian, was a friend of Sir Joshua Reynolds.

177. He finally retired in July 1919.

178. Between August 1914 and June 1915 about 265,000 Belgian refugees fled to England, most with only hand luggage. Their plight aroused much sympathy.

179. It appears that the Gores moved to The Kennels at the end of 1918 or beginning of 1919, by which time the Belgian refugees would have returned to their liberated homeland.

180. As the war would have ended by this time, it would seem that these were men awaiting repatriation. Once the British troops were demobilized, there was no shortage of labour.

181. Captain John Julius Jersey de Knoop, Cheshire Yeomanry/6th Company Imperial Camel Corps, was reported killed in action 7 August 1916, presumably during the Turkish rearguard action at Oghratina (northwest Sinai). The Yeomanry were awarded a battle honour for their role in the Battle of Romani on 4–5 August 1916, which blocked the Turkish advance toward the Suez Canal. De Knoop's rank of captain may have been substantive; that of major, acting or temporary.

182. Horatio Herbert, 1st Earl Kitchener of Khartoum (1850–1916), field marshal and secretary of state for war, was lost when the cruiser HMS Hampshire, which was carrying him to Russia for meetings with Russian commanders, struck a German mine off the Orkney Islands on the

evening of 5 June 1916. Although popular with the *hoi polloi*, Kitchener had many enemies in the Establishment and the conspiracy theories that surround his death may have some substance.

183. Sir John Tomlinson Brunner, the 1ˢᵗ Baronet, held the Northwich seat in 1885–86 and again from 1887 to 1910, when his son Sir John Fowler Brunner, became MP for the Northwich Division, holding the seat until 1918.

184. It seems likely that the goat was a Toggenburg from the Toggenburg Valley in Switzerland. This is the oldest known breed of dairy goat.

185. A reference to the fact that Charles II hid in an oak tree at Boscobel, Shropshire. He was on the run with a thousand-pound price on his head, after seeing Cromwell destroy his army at Worcester on 3 September 1651.

186. According to the school log book, she was on the staff of Calveley School from 3 August 1897 to 28 February 1922.

187. He was the first headmaster of Calveley School, serving from 1874 to 1919. Elsewhere, GWWG estimates his pension at £4.

188. Elsewhere, Sam Williams dies in the 1918–19 influenza pandemic, while the Gores were still at The Kennels.

189. Gloucestershire.

190. A village seven miles southeast of Shrewsbury. The name Cressage appears to be a corruption of Christ's oak. An oak tree grows from the hollow trunk of an even older tree in the field between the road and the river about half a mile from the village. It is marked on Ordnance Survey maps as the Lady Oak, and a number of ley lines meet at this point which was an ancient crossing point on the River Severn. Tradition has it that at the end of the sixth century, Saint Augustine's missionaries preached Christianity under the oak to worshipers of an older religion that had always held it sacred.

191. Salop is an alternative name for Shropshire and was, in fact, the official name of the county from 1974 to 1980. Salopsberia is an old name for Shrewsbury, so Salop sometimes refers to the town rather than the county.

192. About five miles away on the other side of the River Severn.

193. GWWG married Margaret Wilson at Hartford on 5 June 1937 and, after their honeymoon, took up a teaching job at Hucknall, Notts. Margaret was still at The Heysoms when William Gore died 30 July 1937.

194. Founded by Thomas Aldersey in 1594. George F. Dutton was an assistant master there in 1896, so *Button* may be an error.

195. Admiral of the Fleet David Beatty, 1st Earl Beatty (1871–1936), the Royal Navy's most distinguished commander in the First World War period, but his subsequent rivalry with Trenchard did not put either the navy or the air force on a sound basis for renewed war with Germany in 1939.

196. Land that has remained untilled for some time.

197. A prominent hill, 1,334 feet high, about seven miles east of Shrewsbury.

198. Partridges were classified as game, not to be slain without appropriate licenses.

199. Ovine foot rot is a bacterial disease.

200. Other references indicate that the move to Queensgate took place in 1921, although Constance taught at Calveley until February 1922.

201. Erysipelas is a skin infection typically caused by group A beta-hemolytic streptococci, although other streptococcal groups are occasionally causative agents.

202. Annie and Levi Newman are buried there with their daughters Rosie and Connie and their grandson, Geoffrey, and his wife Margaret. William Gore is buried at Bunbury with his first wife, Annie, and daughter Dodie.

203. Possibly Alzheimer's disease. Annie would have been in her late seventies at this time.

204. On-demand gas water heaters were widely used in England.

205. Geissler tubes are gas discharge tubes in which light is produced when electricity is passed through the gas in the tube. Named for Heinrich Geissler (1814–79), a German mechanic and inventor.

206. Sir John Gustav Jarmay. His wife, Charlotte, was awarded the O.B.E. in 1920, presumably for her Red Cross services.

207. Sir John Fowler Brunner (1865–1929), the second baronet, married Lucy Marianne Vaughan in 1894.

208. Sir John Tomlinson Brunner (1842–1919) was made a baronet in 1895, and his son John Fowler Brunner succeeded to the title. GWWG was obviously thinking of the mysterious death of Sir John Tomlinson Brunner's third son, Roscoe Brunner, and his authoress wife, Ethel (neé Houston)—the parents of Shelagh Salome, mentioned above. The couple were found dead 3 November 1926, days after Roscoe had played a leading role in the establishment of I.C.I. The police investigation was inept but the file is protected as a state secret by the British "Hundred Years Rule" until 2026. The case is discussed in *Formula for Murder* by R.M. Bevan, 2003, C.C. Publishing, Chester.

209. Castle is that part of Northwich which stands on the heights west of the River Weaver, extending along Chester Road toward Greenbank. Queensgate and The Heysoms are located where Castle and Greenbank meet.

210. Wagons.

211. Leftwich is the area on the right bank of the River Weaver, south of the old town of Northwich.

212. Wife of Harold Driver, senior physics master at Sir John Deane's Grammar School, which was located at the end of The Crescent. He had been a boy bugler during the First World War and had lost a leg. The Drivers lived next door to the Gores on The Crescent. Both houses backed onto the river, but as they were above the 1945 flood level, only their back gardens were flooded.

213. George II honored the 22nd (Cheshires) with the oak leaf badge for saving his bacon at Dettingen. It's a good story, but when the Battle of Dettingen was fought, 27 June 1743, the 22nd were in garrison in Minorca.

214. Auscultation involved listening with a stethoscope to judge by sound the condition of heart or lungs.

215. Robert Nixon may have been born in 1467, or in the reign of James I, or he may have been no more than an 18th century propaganda tool to give legitimacy to the Hanoverian cause. He is reputed to have said: When an eagle shall sit on top of the house (Vale Royal), then an heir shall be born to the Cholmondeley family.

216. The Flashes are a peculiarity of the mid-Cheshire landscape. They are lakes caused by subsidence of the land above beds of salt that have been dissolved in water and pumped out as brine by the chemical industry.

217. The .22 calibre Morris tube allowed cheap and relatively harmless .22 ammunition to be fired from a rifle designed to fire military .303 inch cartridges.

218. The tangent of this new angle would be equal to the range (opposite) divided by the 100-yard (adjacent) side. In other words: tangent x 100 = range (yards)

219. The cavalry had traditionally met this requirement.

220. Bishop Charles Gore (1853–1932) was successively Bishop of Worcester, Birmingham and Oxford. He lectured in Theology at King's from 1919 and was made a Life Governor. From 1924 to 1928 he was Dean of the London University Faculty of Theology. Noted for his socialist leanings.

221. William Ralph Inge (1860–1954), was Dean of St. Paul's from 1911 to 1934. He was known as The Gloomy Dean for his acerbic views on democracy and modern civilization.

222. Somerset House was next door to the principal campus of King's College on the Strand.

223. Since 1215, one of London's biggest spectacles. A newly-elected mayor has to travel from the City to Westminster to pledge allegiance to the Crown.

224. Lyon's Corner House Café in Piccadilly had three floors. Dorothy L. Sayers said two were exactly the same except that one had a male orchestra in evening dress playing *My Canary Has Circles Under his Eyes,* the other a female orchestra in blue playing excerpts from *The Gondoliers* (*Have his Carcase*, Gollancz, 1932).

225. TOC H was army telephone jargon for TH. The original Talbot House was opened by a young army chaplain, the Rev. Tubby Clayton, in Poperinge, Belgium, during the First World War as a rest center for soldiers. After the war, men who had experienced something out of the ordinary there, tried to recreate the TOC H experience, and over the next eighty-five years the organization prospered as a service organization *trying to get behind the labels that divide people,* as the organization puts it.

226. St. Ethelfreda's is a church school near the London Docks in an area where grave social problems persist.

227. Dr. Hawley Harvey Crippen (1861–1910) lived at 39 Hilldrop Crescent, Holloway, North London. He is remembered as the first criminal to be arrested through use of wireless. He was arrested on board ship while attempting to escape to the United States with his mistress. He was hanged in 1910; his house was destroyed by German bombs during the Blitz.

228. Nathaniel Bentley was an ironmonger of Leadenhall Street. The death of his bride-to-be on the eve of their wedding unbalanced him. He never again washed or changed his clothes; when his cats died he didn't dispose of their bodies. When he retired in 1804, the landlord of the Old Port Wine Shop in Bishopsgate bought him out, lock, stock and dead cats. He put his purchases on display at his pub and renamed it Dirty Dick's. In 1870 the pub was, in fact, rebuilt but the dirty contents were retained. The place wasn't cleaned up until the 1980s.

229. Despite the evacuations, more British women and children than British soldiers were killed in the first half of the war. About 60,000 civilians died in the Blitz.

230. Actually the Fairey Swordfish had a top speed of 139 m.p.h. Despite this, the little torpedo-bombers from *Illustrious* scored the first carrier victory of the war at Taranto in November 1940, crippling three Italian battle-ships. It was a Swordfish from *Ark Royal* that torpedoed the steering gear of the *Bismarck*, setting the stage for her destruction 27 May 1941.

231. The Allies revived old invasion plans on 28 March 1940, but the Germans invaded Norway 2–9 April before they could be implemented.

232. A widely-used and reliable anti-aircraft gun of Swedish origin. It came in 20mm and 40mm versions. GWWG's battery was eventually equipped with the 20mm Bofors.

233. Commanding 28th LAA Regiment RA (TA). The regiment had three gun batteries: 53rd Battery at Derby, GWWG's 112th Battery, and 113th Battery at Warwick. At the beginning of the war, 28 LAA was under Northern Command with headquarters in Nottingham. In October 1939 it became part of 50 AA Bde (Derby). In March 1942, as the Japanese occu-

pied Rangoon, the regiment arrived in India. It served in Assam and later in Burma.

234. Captain L.E.G.(Titus) Oates, 6th (Inniskilling) Dragoons, was one of Captain R.F. Scott's companions in 1911–12. When it became clear that his frostbitten feet were a liability to his comrades, Oates chose to walk out of the party's tent to his death in a blizzard.

235. The original Titus Oates (1649–1705) was an English Protestant, who fabricated and testified to the reality of the Popish Plot of 1678. He was imprisoned for perjury in 1685 and pardoned in 1688.

236. The 28th LAA Regiment RA (TA) is not listed among the artillery units in the Tobruk garrison, which was besieged by Rommel from 11 April to 10 December 1941. Asked to hold out for sixty days, the Rats of Tobruk, as Lord Haw-Haw called them, resisted the *Deutsches Afrika-korps* for 242 days before they were relieved, fighting off 593 air raids.

237. Many British companies had brass bands, including Ransome and Marles of Newark, which was one of the better-known.

238. In his *Battle of Britain*, Len Deighton notes that the Rolls-Royce works at Derby were defended by twenty-two guns, while ninety-six of the army's scarce anti-aircraft guns were deployed to protect the Royal Navy at Rosyth in Scotland, although, in theory, warships had anti-aircraft capability. Unfortunately the army was not able to protect *Prince of Wales, Repulse* and *Hood* when they strayed out to sea.

239. Barrage balloons designed to make life difficult for attacking aircraft.

240. Defaulters undergoing punishment.

241. GWWG twice refers to Oates' *cold eye*. W.B. Yeats' epitaph at Drumcliff reads:
> *Cast a cold eye*
> *On life, on death.*
> *Horseman, pass by!*

242. Spillers Pet Food, controlling one-fifth of Europe's pet food market, was sold to Nestlé in 1998 for more than US $1 billion.

243. The drum-fed Lewis gun could be made for about one-fifth of the cost of a Vickers gun, and was also light and portable.

244. A lieutenant, usually OC/2IC of a troop of four guns in the light/medium artillery.

245. At the beginning of the war there was an acute shortage of the Kerrison Predictors that enabled gunners to fire their shells into the path of a plane with some hope of bringing it down.

246. Staff officers.

247. These may have been 40mm Bofors L/60s, which fired a two-pound high explosive shell. They could be towed on a four-wheeled field mounting.

248. Battledress or BD was the functional two-piece suit of woollen blouse and pants, that replaced the First World War-style service dress with its brass buttons and belted tunic.

249. 14 May 1940.

250. The Vickers, a .303 modified Maxim medium machine gun, was used by the British army from 1912 until 1968. It was water-cooled and belt-fed. On one occasion, in August 1916, a Vickers of 100 Company, Machine Gun Corps, reportedly fired 120,000 rounds in action without pause. When a motor cycle-mounted Vickers was used in an anti-aircraft role, the gunner would indeed lie on the ground.

251. Churchill delivered this particular speech in the House of Commons on 4 June 1940.

252. The 7th Bn. Sherwood Foresters, Territorial Army.

253. A widely used antiseptic and disinfectant.

254. The 'witch and broomstick' was the insignia of the 2nd Anti-Aircraft Division (Territorial Army) which swept the skies over the East Midlands and northern East Anglia. The badge was originally red on khaki but this was soon replaced with Royal Artillery colours, red on dark blue.

978-0-595-46666-
0-595-46666-4

Lightning Source UK Ltd.
Milton Keynes UK
01 June 2010

154946UK00002B/344/A